THE
CALLING

CATHERINE MARTIN

THE
CALLING

QuietTime
MINISTRIES
PALM DESERT, CALIFORNIA

Cover by Quiet Time Ministries.
Cover photo by Catherine Martin—myPhotoWalk.com

Interior photos by Catherine Martin available at MYPHOTOWALK.COM—CATHERINEMARTIN.SMUGMUG.COM

The Calling—The Story Of Who You Are And Why You Are Here
Copyright © 2019 by Catherine Martin
Published by Quiet Time Ministries
Palm Desert, California 92255
www.quiettime.org

ISBN-13: 978-0-9979327-7-5

Printed in the United States of America
19 20 21 22 23 24 25 26 27/ LSI / 10 9 8 7 6 5 4 3 2 1

Dedicated to …
the One who has called me day after day in His Word,
the Lord Jesus Christ.

Dedicated to my husband
David G. Martin, M.D.,
who has been my beloved companion
for thirty-seven years
on this journey of the calling.

Dedicated to my precious family
Robert, Kayla, Linda, Andy, Keegan and James.

Dedicated to
all my beloved friends who have partnered
with me in Quiet Time Ministries.
Thank you for sharing in this powerful calling
to teach devotion to God and His Word
to men and women throughout the world.

May we open the pages of God's Word,
draw near to God and listen to His voice,
and experience the story He is telling through our lives…
the life of the calling.

⁓⁓

I pray that the eyes of your heart may be enlightened,
so that you will know what is the hope of His calling,
what are the riches of the glory of His inheritance in the saints.

EPHESIANS 1:18

⁓⁓

Therefore I, the prisoner of the Lord, implore you to walk in a manner worthy
of the calling with which you have been called.

EPHESIANS 4:1

⁓⁓

Jesus answered, "It is written: 'Man shall not live on bread alone,
but on every word that comes from the mouth of God."

MATTHEW 4:4

⁓⁓

For we are God's masterpiece. He has created us anew in Christ Jesus,
so we can do the good things he planned for us long ago.

EPHESIANS 2:10 NLT

⁓⁓

Contents

❧ FOREWORD ❧

When our little daughter Beth, known now by her big girl name Elizabeth, was around five years old, she encountered me in the kitchen by asking, "What am I doin' here?" I wasn't sure what prompted the question, so I suggested that maybe she was looking for the Mystic Mint cookies and had momentarily lost sight of her mission. "No Mama, I know where the cookies are but I don't know what I'm doin' here." It took a bit more questioning for me to realize she was asking why she was on the earth. She was always a deep thinking little person but that question was huge and I wondered what had prompted it. I never did learn what prompted the question other than her typically probing self needed an answer. When I told her the God who created all people decided he wanted a darling little girl Beth Meberg to live on the earth and specifically to live with a mommy named Marilyn and a daddy named Ken. She thought about that answer for a good five minutes and responded by simply saying, "Good for Him." She then went outside to play.

I have giggled over that incident for years. Elizabeth, now working as a psychologist in Marion, Ohio, has not only been called upon to explain life to her clients but may soon need to explain "what am I doin' here" to her little twin granddaughters. The twins are only two as of this writing but if they have inherited their grandma's curiosity about life's origins, it won't be long before Elizabeth will need some insightful words to share with those two little darlings.

The reality is, all of us thinking persons on this planet, have questions about what we're doing here and why. The why questions have initiated numerous space explorations in an effort to know if others, like us or not, are out there somewhere. We simply want to know more about life here or even on another planet.

The Bible, God's Word, addresses our many "why" questions about our life here. My dear friend, Catherine Martin, has written a book I would call a masterpiece. It is entitled *The Calling*. It deals with the many questions we have about why we are on the earth, what we need to do about being here, and how to recognize the enormous privilege of our personal calling to be ambassadors of God's truth. Jesus the Son was called to be the Savior for all of God's children who have been lovingly created to live on this planet. There is a divine meaning to our existence, which, once we more fully understand it, is exhilarating as well as satisfying.

When I describe this book as a masterpiece, it deserves that designation because *The Calling* is indeed a work of outstanding skill and workmanship. Catherine Martin is a summa cum laude graduate of Bethel Theological Seminary with a Master of Arts in Theological Studies. She is not only well trained, her loving heart and deep caring for every single person God puts in her path is overwhelmingly obvious. You feel her caring intensity as she writes "God has an amazing plan and purpose for your life…His call to you is specific, pointed, and personal. He has custom-designed your course of spiritual growth…and planned the specific journey He has in mind for you."

I find that truth enormously comforting. That God is so specific in His call on my life I don't have to cast about worrying whether I am on the right path or not. Bumbling about is not God's calling. His word says "We are called according to His purpose" (Romans 8:28). So there you have it. Open your Bible, start a regular reading schedule, and be reminded God's walking your walk and leading the way. While you're walking, take luxurious sits and read Catherine's brilliant encouragements in her book *The Calling*. I guarantee, it will enrich your ideas about what it means to be called by the God of all creation.

MARILYN MEBERG
Speaker and Writer for Women of Faith
Former English Teacher at Biola University
Former Marriage and Family Counselor

*The calling is the voice of God in His Word claiming you
as His treasured possession. It is the communication of God's choice
entreating you to an intimate vibrant relationship. He has set His love
and affection on you. He makes His home in you. He designs divine
appointments for you. He entrusts responsibilities to be lived out
by Christ in and through you in the power of the Holy Spirit.
This is a beautiful story that declares and displays His glory forever.*

Two little lines I heard one day, traveling along life's busy way;

Bringing conviction to my heart, and from my mind would not depart;

Only one life 'twill soon be past, only what's done for Christ will last.

Only one life, yes only one, soon will its fleeting hours be done;

Then, in 'that day' my Lord to meet, and stand before His Judgment seat;

Only one life 'twill soon be past, only what's done for Christ will last.

Only one life, the still small voice, gently pleads for a better choice

Bidding me selfish aims to leave, and to God's holy will to cleave;

Only one life 'twill soon be past, only what's done for Christ will last.

Only one life, a few brief years, each with its burdens, hopes, and fears;

Each with its clays I must fulfill, living for self or in His will

Only one life 'twill soon be past, only what's done for Christ will last.

When this bright world would tempt me sore, when Satan would a victory score;

When self would seek to have its way, then help me, Lord, with joy to say;

Only one life 'twill soon be past, only what's done for Christ will last.

Give me Father, a purpose deep, in joy or sorrow Thy Word to keep;

Faithful and true, what e'er the strife, pleasing Thee in my daily life;

Only one life 'twill soon be past, only what's done for Christ will last.

Oh let my love with fervor burn, and from the world now let me turn;

Living for Thee, and Thee alone, bringing Thee pleasure on Thy throne;

Only one life 'twill soon be past, only what's done for Christ will last.

Only one life, yes only one, now let me say "Thy will be done";

And when at last I'll hear the call, I know I'll say "twas worth it all";

Only one life 'twill soon be past, only what's done for Christ will last.

Only one life 'twill soon be past, only what's done for Christ will last.

And when I'm dying, how happy I'll be,

If the lamp of my life has been burned out for Thee.

C.T. Studd (1860-1931) — Only One Life

～ MY STORY ～

I walked down the sidewalk at Arizona State University with a newfound joy in my heart. I had just made the most important commitment imaginable; I had given my life to Jesus Christ. And I just could not wait to see what He was going to do. So many things were new to me. Carrying a Bible and actually reading it shocked my college roommates. I think it shocked me, too, because I surely never thought of myself as someone who would be religious. However, this journey felt quite unlike religion. It felt real and authentic, as though I was on a new path, headed toward a new destination. My roommates had never seen me show the slightest interest in God and now I was reading the Bible. Now, surprisingly, I was attending Bible studies hosted by Campus Crusade for Christ International at Arizona State University. It was a brave new world for me that included new friends and significant influences.

More than anything, I wanted to grow in my relationship with Christ. I barely knew Him. And yet, His influence was unmistakable. I sensed Him leading me each day and opening doors all along the way. Near the end of my senior year in college, I applied for a Campus Crusade summer project in San Diego. A short while later, I received a letter in the mail informing me that the project was full and I wouldn't be able to go. I was devastated. The Lord had said no, and I didn't like it one bit. This was one of my first experiences of the promise from God in Proverbs 16:9, "We can make our plans, but the Lord determines our steps." I did not yet understand that when God says no to one thing, it's usually because He has something higher and greater in mind for us.

A few days later I received a phone call from a man who said, "Catherine, my name is Paul McKean. I understand that you applied to a summer project in San Diego but you can't go because it's full. I would like to invite you to attend the summer project in Hawaii."

Was this a dream? I exclaimed with wonder, "You mean Hawaii as in Honolulu, Hawaii?"

"Yes, we would love to have you be a part of our summer project."

I was so taken aback that I told him I would need to pray about it — and then I hung up the phone. I was just blown away. I couldn't believe such a remarkable turn of events. Five minutes later I called back and said, "Yes!"

Oh, how that one event altered the course of my life. Just when you think life is over or things aren't happening the way you'd like, God surprises you with something from another direction. I learned that I would have to trust God for the travel expenses of $500, and then I would need a job once I got to Hawaii.

You see, the whole idea behind the summer projects was that students would work during the day integrating with the community. Then, in the evenings and weekends those students would learn how to share their faith and grow in their relationship with the Lord. I had never traveled anywhere as exotic as Hawaii and certainly never anywhere significant without my family. I was scared and excited both at the same time.

The Lord brought in that $500 in record time. My mother got into the whole spirit of the thing by putting a map in the kitchen. Every time someone would give money, we recorded it on the map. Soon we could see how the Lord was opening up the path for me to go to Hawaii for the summer. This new adventure of going to Hawaii suddenly seemed personal and powerful from the Lord.

So the big day finally arrived. My mother and brother went with me to the airport where I met all the other students traveling from Arizona. We flew from Phoenix to Los Angeles, then on to Honolulu. I will never forget my first moment walking off the plane in Hawaii and feeling the tropical warmth of one of the most beautiful places in the world. It was a God-ordained holy moment orchestrated by the Lord. I said, "Thank You Lord, for bringing me here. I can't wait to see what You are going to do."

We stayed at La Pietra Hawaii School for Girls, a beautiful coral Tuscan-inspired campus on the slopes of Diamond Head in Honolulu, Hawaii. The campus was lush with tropical flowers and greenery everywhere. My favorite place was a walled-in field on the perimeter of the property. The first night after our group meeting, I sensed a calling, a great desire in my heart, to walk out to that field to be alone with the Lord. I stood there in the field in the dark of the night, just still and quiet. Then, I looked up and what I saw took my breath away. A blanket of millions of stars and planets sparkled like diamonds in the sky. That first view of the night sky in Hawaii just stole my heart. I said, "Oh Lord, I've never seen anything so beautiful." After I exclaimed my joy to Him, a shooting star soared from one end of the sky to the other. I felt like the Lord did that just for me. "So Lord, here we are together in this place. This is what it's all about. Knowing You. Communing with You. You are taking me on quite an adventure, aren't You!"

The intimacy with the Lord I experienced that night in Hawaii was only the beginning of what I now call the great adventure of knowing God. Oh, what an adventure He took me on there in Hawaii. I was one of the last to get a job that summer. I walked to the bus stop one morning, frustrated at my inability to find any work. Everyone else had gotten a job, but not me. What was God doing? Well, He surely knew. And I surely did not. I noticed a young man walking to the bus stop, so I stopped him and asked if he had any idea where I could get a job. Surprisingly, he said that he had just gotten hired and maybe they would hire me as well. I went to the Hawaiian Marketplace pineapple stand he had told me about. An Hawaiian woman was standing behind the counter. I walked up and said, "I'd like to apply for a job." She smiled and said, "Okay, let me get an application." While she was in the back, I noticed music playing and the song was one of my favorites—"My Tribute" by Andrae Crouch. As the chorus of "To God be the glory" played in the background, tears came to my eyes. I knew this was God's job for me. When the woman came back, I asked her, "What is your name?" She replied, "Emma." I said, "Emma, why do you have such a big smile?" She immediately smiled again and replied, "Because I have Jesus Christ in my life." Needless to say, I got the job.

My job there in Hawaii was working in a hotel lobby selling pineapples, papayas, and coconuts to tourists from all over the world. So there I stood each day behind the counter of a pineapple stand. And people would come up and ask me, "What's a young girl like you doing in a place like this?" I would then ask, "Do you really want to know?" They would say, "Yes." And I would say, "I'm here to tell you how you can have a relationship with God. Would you like to hear more?" Most of the time they would say, "Yes, I want to hear." Then, I would share the gospel of Jesus Christ with them. And I would ask if they wanted to pray to receive Christ and establish a relationship with God. And almost all whom I shared with would respond, "Yes!" So I put up my "Be Right Back" sign, we went to a quiet place in the hotel lobby, and we prayed together. This happened many, many times that summer. I was watching the Lord do something only He could do. And I was beginning to understand that Jesus was taking me on the journey that He had in mind.

Every night I would run out to that lone field at the base of Diamond Head and share all the adventures of the day with Jesus. Sometimes tears would just run freely down my face out of love and adoration for Him. It was such a close and intimate time with Him. He was there and I knew it. Sometimes stars would shoot across the sky, and I sensed over and over that they flew through the blanket of stars just for me. Knowing Him and walking with Him meant an intimate, personal relationship—a radical intimacy.

One day, Paul McKean, the director of the summer project, received a phone call from a Christian television show that aired locally there in the Hawaiian Islands. They said, "We have heard stories about a pineapple girl who is part of your summer project. We are wondering if you and she would be interviewed on our television show?" And so it was, that little me who could have never imagined being on television, or even being in beautiful Hawaii, was able to share stories of how the Lord had worked to draw people to Himself in such a powerful way. The show aired in all the Hawaiian Islands. I was humbled and amazed at the same time.

My experience in Hawaii did not end there. I met some girls there on the island who told me how much they wanted to grow in their relationship with the Lord. Then they asked, "Will you lead us in a Bible study?" So the first time we met, there were eight to ten girls who gathered with me for Bible study. We had such amazing, intimate times in the Word of God, praying together, and sharing in all it meant to walk with the Lord. Those times of discipleship were so unexpected. No one else on the project was doing anything like leading a Bible study. I became dimly aware that the Lord Jesus was calling me on a certain and unique journey with Him. He was leading me and training me for a purpose He had in mind. I knew whatever it was, it was a high purpose; not because it made me rich or famous or anything else the world can offer, but because of the One who was calling me.

So the time came to leave Hawaii. I was sad. I didn't want to go. I loved the girls who were in my Bible study. And I was transformed because of the fellowship I experienced with the Lord. I sat in the airport terminal waiting for our plane and thinking about the summer. Then I noticed the movement of people coming towards me. All the girls from my Hawaiian Bible study had come to say good-bye. They were carrying multi-color leis with tropical flowers of plumeria and orchids. It was a tradition that when you said good-bye to someone in Hawaii, you presented the one you loved with a lei. One by one, they hugged me and put their lei around my neck. Soon we were all crying and hugging one another. So there I was with a multitude of leis around my neck surrounded by beautiful girls who were in my heart because of the time we spent together.

I've never forgotten those defining moments in Hawaii. They changed me forever and were a fitting beginning to forty years of walking with the Lord. I learned that Jesus has a story He wants to tell in and through each of our lives. He calls out to us day-by-day and moment-by-moment, drawing us into a deeper and more intimate relationship, and leading in the direction He has in mind. I have rarely known in advance what God was going to do. He mostly surprises me with things that never even entered my mind. And I have learned that He is more interested in who I am with Him than what I do for Him. He is writing a unique story with our lives. My story has included Quiet Time Ministries, writing nearly thirty books, speaking at retreats and conferences, leading women's ministries at churches, and teaching on the adjunct faculty for Biola University. And now, I want to talk about your story, the story that God is telling with your life as He calls you to Himself moment by moment and day after day, with a unique and specific calling.

❧ INTRODUCTION ❧

Who are you? Why are you here? What is the story of your life? Francis Schaeffer, a 20th Century theologian, philosopher, and pastor, wrote a book about God with a title I have never forgotten—*He Is There and He Is Not Silent.* Just the title alone declares the existence of God and His desire to communicate with those who live on planet earth. If God does indeed exist and He does indeed have something to say to us, then His words would certainly speak to the heart of the meaning and purpose of our lives.

I am not talking about religion. In fact, I am not the least bit interested in religion. Religion has never done anything for me and has, in fact, hurt me deeply at times. I began with my own story because my own experience shows there is more to life and knowing God than doing a bunch of religious things. I have witnessed something in recent years that has filled me with sorrow and a passion to share the nuggets of truth contained in this book. I have seen the church I have grown to love over the years become more like a social club than a Spirit-led ministry where Jesus Christ is in action doing His work. I have watched power and profession take the place of passion for Christ. And more than that, I have seen religion with a dry, barren set of motions replace the thriving Spirit-filled relationship with Christ present in the first century Church. People no longer talk about what God is teaching them. And very few notice how the Lord is working in and through their lives.

Jesus is calling out to us in His Word. He summons, commands, cries out, claims us as His treasure, and invites us to higher ground and something deeper, more intimate, and transformational. He says, "Are you tired? Worn out? Burned out on religion? Come to me. Get away with me and you'll recover your life. I'll show you how to take a real rest. Walk with me and work with me—watch how I do it. Learn the unforced rhythms of grace. I won't lay anything heavy or ill-fitting on you. Keep company with me and you'll learn to live freely and lightly" (Matthew 11:28-30 The Message).

Do you hear Him calling out to you even now? Do you need to shed the things that are blinding you to life, real life? Have you been going through the motions yet have no sense of the reality of Jesus with you? Are you tired of all the trappings of religion and long for a real, firsthand experience with the Lord Jesus Christ? Do you long for the kind of journey where you are aware of the Lord telling His story in and through you?

Then, I invite you to step into the world of *The Calling.* The calling is more than a principle and more than just a word; the calling is a life to be lived as you travel on your journey home.

The calling of Jesus to salvation is only the beginning of this adventure with the Lord. But there is more, so much more. He is calling you deeper into life with Him than you have ever even dreamed is possible. I have had times in the course of forty years of walking and talking with Him where I have become so overwhelmed with the things He is showing me that I have held up my hand and said, "Lord, I think You need to stop a moment. This is so glorious; I can't comprehend it. I need a moment just to drink in Your beauty."

We are on a journey home and Jesus wants to walk with us, pour out His love on us, commune with us, and lead us every step of the way. I remember standing with my brother at the cemetery for my mother's burial service. My brother looked across the cemetery grounds at all the gravestones and remarked, "All these people have lived on earth, had a life, now they're buried, and for the most part, forgotten." The unspoken part of what my brother said at the time is that we too, are on that journey home. Here's the question, as we go on our way: *will we live life with Jesus and invest in the things that last forever, or will we only live for the things of this world that are passing away?*

I believe the awareness of the audience of One, living in the presence of God, and walking and talking with Him is something to cultivate for all seasons. There is a horizontal way to live life where we focus mainly on people and circumstances each day. But there is also a vertical way to live life, where we are looking up to God and heaven, we see the glory of God, and we become more aware of our journey heavenward to our eternal home with the Lord. How are we going to live our lives? Will we have a life filled with purpose where we live vertically for things eternal, or will we have a life that seems to fade away where we live horizontally only for temporal things?

How are you going to live your life? I long so very much for you to know the Lord in a new and deeper way; in the way He has in mind for you. To know Him and love Him is a radical intimacy because it's a walk and talk with the King of Kings and Lord of Lords. Oh, how He longs for this journey with you. Sometimes it simply means you stop, turn to Him, and then walk with Him in a new direction with more depth, meaning and purpose. He is calling out to you even now with these words, "Stop at the crossroads and look around. Ask for the old, godly way, and walk in it. Travel its path, and you will find rest for your souls" (Jeremiah 6:16 NLT).

I believe many in the world today simply miss *the calling*. So many Bibles are literally sitting on shelves instead of being embraced, lived in, and pored over. I have had times where I was so broken and crushed that I couldn't hear Him calling. The Word of God at times felt like words on a page rather than living and active in my life.

Over the last five years I have experienced the deaths of my father and mother and a change in ministry—all of it left me devastated beyond words. And then, out of the dark valley of the shadow, the voice of Jesus called me into a deeper fellowship with Him—a sharing of His sufferings as we walked together. He spoke to me from verses I had never before seen or noticed in His Word.

Out of that journey came two books sharing all that I have been learning from the Lord: *One Holy Passion* and *The Calling*.

Through all God has been teaching me, He has picked me up and put me back together in a new and stronger way. I am still growing in the grace and knowledge of the Lord Jesus Christ (2 Peter 3:18). And that is my desire for you. I believe knowing, understanding, and living out the calling is absolutely essential for you to become the person God wants you to be. Two of the most important questions we can ever ask are: *Who am I?* and *Why am I here?* As you listen to God calling to you in His Word, day-by-day, you will discover the answers to those questions. You and I both need the calling wherever we happen to be in our lives right now — whether we are new Christians or years into our walk with the Lord — He is calling to us in every season of our life.

I remember walking with a group of photographers across the parking lot of Logan's Pass in Glacier National Park, Montana. Surrounded by majestic mountains, green trees, cascading flowers in bloom everywhere, I couldn't help but stand in awe of God's greatness. One mountain in particular stood out to me, Heavy Runner Mountain. With my Nikon D7000 camera in hand and my Gitzo tripod, I climbed down the hill to get a clean view of the path with the flowers in the foreground, the landscape dominated by the curve and height of the mountain, and the view of the sky filled with clouds at the top. That was the image composition I saw and captured, and it always reminds me of the majesty of God. The photographic image on the cover of *The Calling* is what I saw that day. And to me, it is the perfect depiction of all I desire for you in this book. I want you to hear the calling of God to go with Him on the journey heavenward. I want you to see the path and know the way He is leading you to go. I want you to realize that He is calling you to come up on the mountain so you can hear Him speak to you. Then you will grow closer to Him, catch glimpses of His majestic glory, understand who you are and why you are here, and receive from Him all you need to live out the story He has in mind for you. Oh, how I long for this in your life and mine.

When I look at the myPhotoWalk majestic mountain cover image of *The Calling*, I can't help but think of Moses. Moses, the man of God, heard the voice of the Lord many times. He could have ignored it. He could have walked away from it. But he didn't. The first time he heard God call his name, Moses "turned aside to look" (Exodus 3:4). He learned who he was to God and what God wanted to do in and through him. Thus, began the adventures of Moses and God and a beautiful relationship where "the Lord used to speak to Moses face to face, just as a man speaks to his friend" (Exodus 33:11). As the conversation continued between the Lord and Moses, their relationship grew more intimate. More than anything, Moses wanted to know God. He expressed his desire when he asked God to show Him His ways that Moses might know Him (Exodus 33:13). And then, he prayed a great prayer, "Show me Your glory" (Exodus 33:18). God responded by saying to Moses, "So be ready by morning, and come up in the morning to Mount Sinai, and present yourself there to Me on the top of the mountain" (Exodus 34:2). When Moses finally reached the top of the mountain, for a brief moment, God pulled down the shades and allowed Moses to catch a glimpse of His glory.

I believe God calls us again and again to the top of that mountain to catch glimpses of His glory, grow in a radical intimacy with Him, and experience personal spiritual revival where we receive from Him all that we need to live out His plan and purpose in our lives. Then, He tells the story He has written on the pages of your heart, a story that touches a lost and hurting world with His message. Those are the eternal things that never fade away but lead to a future and a hope designed for you by God.

It takes a lifetime to appreciate this truth of the calling. I could never have written this book forty years ago. Quite honestly, *The Calling* almost didn't see the light of day. It has been one of the most challenging books I have ever written, because sometimes I found it nearly impossible to articulate the deep truths found in God's Word that I wanted to convey. Writing it now gives you a benefit of learned lessons and insights from walking with the Lord a long time, writing many books, and enduring deep suffering. Contained in these pages are different truths I have shared over the years in messages I've given, and in the quiet time studies and other books I've written. I am still learning, growing, and thinking about these things. I know these truths, but I need to know them in even more depth. I have walked with the Lord, but I want and I need to walk more closely with Him. And I want you to experience such a radical intimacy with the Lord. The wealth of shared experiences you have with your Lord grows your intimacy with Him.

So, dear friend, will you take the path to climb the mountain to hear God calling to you? Together, let's apply these words by J.I. Packer from *Knowing God*, "We are in the position of travelers who, after surveying a great mountain from afar, traveling round it, and observing how it dominates the landscape and determines the features of the surrounding countryside, now approach it directly, with the intention of climbing it."[1]

God has an amazing plan and purpose for your life. How can you live it out? Pick up your Bible and begin to listen for His voice. He is calling you even now. Oh, His voice is beautiful. The more tuned your ears are to hear Him speak, the more you will learn to see, and the greater your understanding will be of all He is saying to you. His call to you is specific, pointed, and personal. He has custom-designed your course of spiritual growth, ordered the verses in His Word that He has in mind to illumine for you through the power of the Holy Spirit, and planned the specific journey He has in mind for you. He does want you to respond to everything He says to you. Sometimes the things He says are so deep and incomprehensible, they require meditation – the ability to stay long with the thought. The more you think about His words, the more profound you realize they are. This is God, the Creator of the Universe, awesome and mighty, speaking with you, dear friend. Oh, the fellowship you are going to have with your Lord. There is nothing in the world that compares with knowing Him. It is, as Paul says, a priceless privilege (Philippians 3:8).

In *The Calling*, we will touch on significant verses outlining specific aspects of God's calling in your life. We will cover the deeper life with Christ where you experience Him living in and through you. We will talk about how to hear the Lord, spend time with him, and follow Him where He leads. You will learn how to see with the eternal perspective, share God's heart, and influence others with your faith. *The Calling* includes the fellowship of His sufferings, spiritual warfare, believing God in impossible situations, and living victoriously when you forget your calling and wrestle with failure, regret, and imperfection. Finally, your journey in *The Calling* will include the kingdom of God, making the most of your time, experiencing God's sovereign plan where He tells a unique story with your life, saying yes to Him, and your intimate journey home. Throughout *The Calling* are examples of simple men and women of God, heroes of the faith, who said yes to God when they heard Him call. Their stories are personal and powerful. And your story will touch a lost and hurting world, just like theirs did, as you live the life of the calling.

I encourage you to get *The Quiet Time Journal* (Journal Pages and Prayer Pages adapted from *The Quiet Time Notebook*) where you can write your thoughts as you engage and interact with the thoughts, insights, and teaching in *The Calling*. I have created a simple devotional guide in the Appendix with questions and journal prompts with guidance to help you think, write, and create. I have provided encouragement to include art and photography along the way to drink in these truths more deeply than perhaps you ever have before. You might be thinking, "Catherine, I'm not a writer, photographer, or an artist. I've never done any of that before." I totally understand what you're thinking, but I'd like you to set those thoughts aside, and launch out into this new journey. You are going to think as you have never thought before, and see new and beautiful sights that you never viewed until now. This devotional guide in the Appendix is optional, but I do encourage you to use it to go deeper with your Lord.

I would also like to invite you to the private *The Calling* Facebook Community where we will share all we are learning. We will also share what we are writing and our photography and artwork inspired by *The Calling*. You can join at https://www.facebook.com/groups/thecallingcommunity/.

I have filmed six companion multimedia messages that can be used for added encouragement to help you go deeper into *The Calling* with your Lord. With these audio and video messages and the organization of chapters into five journeys, you can also experience *The Calling* with a group or an entire church in a 5-week study. Viewer Guides are included in the Appendix to accompany the *The Calling* DVDs, downloadable Digital M4V Video, downloadable Digital MP3 Audio, as well as HD 1080p Digital M4V of the HD Leader's Kits for a professional large group experience. Search the Quiet Time Ministries Online Store at www.quiettime.org or call Quiet Time Ministries at 1-800-925-6458.

So, dear friend, I now invite you to walk with the Lord on a new path into this adventure of *The Calling*. As you experience the priceless privilege of knowing Christ, your fellowship with Him will tune your ears to hear His calling every day. He will tell the unique story of your life, and change the world in and through you. The calling is more than a principle and much more than a word, it is an abundant life. So, get ready, dear friend, for the deeper life of the calling.

CALLED TO A LIFE

Ephesians 1:18

The calling is really a life where you walk and talk with the Lord Jesus who has taken up residence in your heart. You are never alone again. You have a moment-by-moment intimacy with Him that feeds your soul, gives you meaning and purpose, and carries you into the stream of His will for something much greater than yourself.

A VOICE FROM A DISTANT LAND

Do not fear, for I have redeemed you; I have called you by name; you are Mine!
ISAIAH 43:1

In college, my goal in life was to have fun. I was searching for the answer to the question: *What is life all about?* A couple had come to my dormitory room and shared a verse from the Bible with me — some words of Jesus — "I am the way, and the truth, and the life; no one comes to the Father but through Me" (John 14:6). I could not get those words out of my mind. It was as though they were spoken to me again and again. I tried to ignore the words. But still they came in moments when I least expected to hear them. I might be out on a date and the words would come into my mind. Or I would lie in bed trying to drift off to sleep and again, the words would come. What I didn't realize at the time was that Jesus was calling me to Himself. And He would not let me go.

Finally, at the end of my third year in college, I decided to confront Jesus' statement, deal with it, and make a decision. I knew that eventually I would have to deal with this statement because it was relevant to my life. Jesus was basically saying He is the only way to God. He was making an exclusive claim. He was saying He is the truth. This meant following any other way of life is to live for a lie. Jesus was saying that He is the life — not money, not success, not even enjoyment — only He is the life. Jesus' claims pierced my heart. I realized that God exists, and He desires a relationship with me. Through Jesus I could know God, and through that relationship I might have life itself. I realized that to have life includes the experience of meaning, purpose and fulfillment in life.

That morning, at the end of my third year in college, it was as though the Lord met me face to face. The most significant thought was realizing that if Jesus is *the* truth, then to live for anything or anyone else is to live for a lie. I reasoned through the life of Christ, His claims, and His resurrection from the dead. It would have taken more faith for me to reject the words of Christ than to accept them. And so, right then and there, I handed over the control of my life to Jesus. I got on my knees at the side of my bed, bowed my head, asked for forgiveness of my sins, and expressed my desire for Jesus to take over my life. I prayed a simple prayer asking Jesus to come into my life and received the gift—the free gift—that God was offering me as He called out to me.

I brushed up against the beginnings of my understanding of the calling. I realized the calling was more than just a simple invitation. The calling is like a summons to hear, a command to obey, and a door to walk through leading to a new world and a grand adventure with God. When I prayed to the Lord, at that very moment, I entered into a love relationship with God. This was the love relationship I had been created for, and had longed for, all along. At that very moment, the Triune God — Father, Son, and Holy Spirit — made His home in my heart. My life moved from a journey to an adventure – the great adventure of knowing God.

I share my story so you can think about your story. The irresistible voice of God is calling out your name. I wonder if you can hear Him. His is a voice from a distant land — far away and wholly other — and yet, so close to your heart because the One calling out to you knows you intimately. He is personal when He speaks. The calling is the very voice of God. He knows you better than you will ever know yourself. He made you. He loves you. He has His eye on you. And He wants you for His very own in an intimate, ongoing, vibrant relationship. And He just will not give up.

You need to know that God speaks and is speaking in His Word, the "living and active" Word of God (Hebrews 4:12). *The Amplified Bible* helps us understand how God is fully present when He speaks His Word and thus, His Word has immeasurable power: "For the Word that God speaks is alive and full of power [making it active, operative, energizing, and effective]; it is sharper than any two-edged sword, penetrating to the dividing line of the breath of life (soul) and [the immortal] spirit, and of joints and marrow [of the deepest parts of our nature], exposing and sifting and analyzing and judging the very thoughts and purposes of the heart" (Hebrews 4:12 AMP).

In the Word, God expresses what is on His heart and mind. For example, the Bible begins with God saying four words, "Let there be light" (Genesis 1:3), expressing His desire for light, and with those words He spoke light into existence. When God speaks, the words are creative and powerful, bringing about change and transformation. Pastor and author, Mark Batterson, writes, "There is nothing God's voice cannot say, cannot do. And, frankly, He can do it however He pleases! He can speak through burning bushes, Balaam's donkey, or Bethlehem's star. His voice can write on palace walls or shut the mouths of lions. It can quench the flames of a fiery furnace or stop a storm on the Sea of Galilee."[1]

God describes in detail how He called out to His people in the Old Testament. He says, "I revealed myself to those who did not ask for me; I was found by those who did not seek me. To a nation that did not call on my name, I said, 'Here am I, here am I'" (Isaiah 65:1 NIV). In the New Testament, Jesus speaks of His call as the Shepherd calling His sheep. He says, "My sheep listen to my voice; I know them, and they follow me. I give them eternal life, and they shall never perish; no one will snatch them out of my hand" (John 10:27-28). What an amazing truth that the God of the universe calls out to each one of us with a voice that can be heard by us in His Word and motivated by the good intention of loving and leading us in life.

One of the first and most important books I read after I entered into a personal relationship with Christ was *The Pursuit of God* by pastor and author, A.W. Tozer. In my favorite chapter, entitled "The Speaking Voice," Tozer writes about God's voice and the Bible, His Word. It was these words by Tozer that helped me begin to truly understand God's calling in His Word. Tozer says, "He [God] spoke a Book and lives in His spoken words, constantly speaking His words and causing the power of them to persist across the years...It is the nature of God to speak. The second Person of the Holy Trinity is called the Word. The Bible is the inevitable outcome of God's continuous speech. It is the infallible declaration of His mind for us put into our familiar human words. I think a new world will arise out of the religious mists when we approach our Bible with the idea that it is not only a book which was once spoken, but a book which is *now speaking*...If you would follow on to know the Lord, come at once to the open Bible expecting it to speak to you. Do not come with the notion that it is a thing which you may push around at your convenience. It is more than a thing; it is a voice, a word, the very Word of the living God."[2]

The importance of God's calling at every stage and season of our lives cannot be over-emphasized. One of Paul's greatest prayers for the church was that they would know "the hope of His calling" (Ephesians 1:18). God's Word does indeed bring us hope and is, therefore imperative in our lives (Romans 15:4).

Again and again, God's voice speaks from every verse in the Bible just for us with perfect timing in a unique order custom-designed just for us. He speaks with purpose and intention to accomplish His desires and His will. He says, "It is the same with my word. I send it out, and it always produces fruit. It will accomplish all I want it to, and it will prosper everywhere I send it" (Isaiah 55:11 NLT). Everything we hear forms the critical mass of our calling in life. Author and theologian Dallas Willard describes the calling this way: "In the gloom a light glimmers and glows. We have received an invitation. We are invited to make a pilgrimage—into the heart and life of God."[3]

The calling helps us understand God and ourselves. Os Guinness, an English author born to medical missionaries, graduate of Oxford University, and former leader at L'Abri in Switzerland, writes, "My discovery of my calling enabled me to find what I was. Having wrestled with the stirring saga of calling in history and having taken up the challenge of God's individual call to me, I have been mastered by this truth. God's call has become a sure beacon ahead of me and a blazing fire within me as I have tried to figure out my way and negotiate the challenges of the extraordinary times in which we live."[4] Through the calling you will discover who you are, whose you are, and why you're here. Peter encourages each one of us to hear the calling when he writes for us to "Be all the more diligent to make certain about His calling and choosing you; for as long as you practice these things, you will never stumble" (2 Peter 1:10).

Ethel Waters was the child of a teenage rape victim and grew up in the slums of Philadelphia. She was on her own at a very young age with no one to love or care for her. One thing set her apart from most people. She had a big voice and she could sing. She became a well-known American entertainer, singing such great songs as ""Stormy Weather" at the famous Cotton Club and an Irving Berlin song written just for her, "Supper Time," on Broadway. In the late 1950s, something happened that altered the course of her life. She attended a Billy Graham crusade and discovered God loved her and had His eye on her. She turned from aimless pursuits in the world to a life of purpose with God. She was a regular performer at Billy Graham Crusades, recorded religious albums, and became best known for her very favorite song, "His Eye Is On The Sparrow." Those words became the title of her autobiography. But more than that, they described the wonderful result of God's calling to Ethel Waters as He brought meaning and purpose in spite of her difficult beginnings in life and a successful career in life.

His eye is on you, my friend. And no matter where you've been or what you've done, He is calling out to you. The calling in its simplest form is God speaking to you in His Word through the power of the Holy Spirit. He speaks with direct invitations, commands, encouragements, and promises. Where can you hear His calling? In a general way, known as general revelation, God speaks continually in His creation, sending forth a message to us about Himself. You learn about His craftsmanship and limitless all-powerful ability just by looking at what He has made. As you gaze on all He has created, you hear and see the wondrous declarations of His glory (Psalm 19:1). Job observed the beauty of the heavens as "a whisper of His power" calling out to him about the kinds of things that God can do (Job 26:14). Paul describes the witness of creation when he writes, "For since the creation of the world His invisible attributes, His eternal power and divine nature, have been clearly seen, being understood through what has been made" (Romans 1:20). God's creation is His multimedia enhancing your understanding of who He is, what He does, and what He says.

But the calling is heard clearly and succinctly in the Bible. The Bible is literally God calling you. Paul explains, "All Scripture is inspired by God and is useful to teach us what is true and to make us realize what is wrong in our lives. It corrects us when we are wrong and teaches us to do what is right. God uses it to prepare and equip his people to do every good work" (2 Timothy 3:16-17 NLT).

The writer of Hebrews reveals that God has spoken: "God, after He spoke long ago to the fathers in the prophets in many portions and in many ways, in these last days has spoken to us in His Son" (Hebrews 1:1-2). In the Bible, we are able to hear what God says, from Genesis to Revelation, through the prophets, and in His Son, as we discover Christ — His Person, works, and words.

So let me ask you, dear friend, have you opened your Bible lately with the conscious expectation that God has something to say to you? Do you realize that God is calling out to you personally from every verse in His Word? Dallas Willard, a 20th century American philosopher known for his writings on spiritual formation, explains in his book, *Hearing God*, how the very Person of God is behind all He says in His Word. He writes, "The *word of God*, when no further qualification is added, is his speaking, his communicating. When God speaks, he expresses his mind, his character, and his purposes. Thus God is always present with his word."[5] When you read the Bible, you are never alone. God is right there with you, speaking, calling out to you with the very truths on His mind for you, with the revelation of who He is, and with all you need to know to live in the world. His calling is essential for you to know and live out every day of your life.

Jesus modeled the calling for us and demonstrated His own reliance on the Word when He was tempted in the wilderness: "It is written, 'Man shall not live on bread alone, but on every word that proceeds out of the mouth of God'" (Matthew 4:4). Jesus confirms that God's Word is vital, alive, and coming from God Himself.

From Genesis to Revelation, God is calling you to Himself, inviting you to an intimate, vibrant eternal relationship through Christ, giving you a new identity in Christ, determining to make His home in you and have you for His own treasure and inheritance, and preparing you as an instrument for His use, transforming you as Christ lives His life in and through you until the day you step into heaven and live in your eternal home with Him.

Richard Foster, author of *Life With God*, explains that "there is a vast difference between reading the surface of the biblical text and encountering the God who divinely superintended its delivery into our hands—the God who proclaims to you and to me, 'I am with you…will you be with Me?'"[6]

David, the man after God's own heart, experienced the calling of God and said, "The voice of the Lord is upon the waters; the God of glory thunders, the Lord is over many waters. The voice of the Lord is powerful, the voice of the Lord is majestic" (Psalm 29:3-4 NLT).

The calling is the voice of God in His Word claiming you as His treasured possession. It is the communication of God's choice entreating you to an intimate vibrant relationship. He has set His love and affection on you. He makes His home in you. He designs divine appointments for you. He entrusts responsibilities to be lived out by Christ in and through you in the power of the Holy Spirit. The calling is a beautiful story that declares and displays His glory forever.

Many have thought of God's calling in their lives as a vocation. One person has said that our vocation is what we are paid for and our calling is what we are made for. I would maintain that God's calling in your life will most certainly lead to jobs and vocations. But when you read all that the Bible says about God's calling, you discover His calling will also lead to so much more.

Every truth in God's Word is God's continuous calling to you again and again. In Ephesians 4:1, Paul speaks of walking in a manner worthy of the calling to which we have been called. Here we see two Greek words working together to help us understand that God is calling to us (*kaleo*), and everything He calls us to is a calling (*klesis*) where He is literally inviting us to something higher and greater than ourselves. As He speaks in His Word, and you hear Him speak, you learn more about who you are and why you are here.

God longs for you to know His purpose and plan for you. And so, when He calls, He takes the initiative with you and communicates all that is on His heart for you. He calls you to something He wants for you, has chosen for you, and has designed for you. First and foremost, He wants you to experience salvation and all that goes with it including forgiveness of sins, justification, sanctification, spiritual growth, grace, filling of the Holy Spirit, eternal life, glorification, and more. His calling includes character qualities like holiness or humility. His calling in your life can also include a position or role such as a teacher or mother and a place to live in a particular area of a country (it will be the place where He touches lives in and through you). Even your experiences of suffering are a calling, peculiar as that may seem. We share in His sufferings, as you will see in more detail later in this book. You are so united with Christ that He calls *your* sufferings *His* sufferings, He gives you an eternal relationship with Him, and He makes you His inheritance. You share His glory, become God's son or daughter, and a royal member of the kingdom of God. You are royalty. You are made to live the way He has planned (by faith not by sight), to be a branch with Jesus as the vine (John 15), to be filled with the Holy Spirit (Ephesians 5:18), and united with Christ (Romans 6:5, Galatians 2:20). All the ways you experience the calling from God, day by day, become the sum total of your calling in life. So you see, your calling is truly a unique and personal, custom-designed experience just for you.

As you read verses in the Bible, God reveals His heart and desires to you so that your calling from Him is crystal clear. God says, "For you are a holy people, who belong to the Lord your God. Of all the people on earth, the Lord your God has chosen you to be his own special treasure" (Deuteronomy 7:6 NLT). As a result, you hear God's calling you to be holy, realizing that you belong to Him, you are chosen, and you are His special treasure. God says, "I have loved you, my people, with an everlasting love. With unfailing love I have drawn you to myself" (Jeremiah 31:3 NLT).

For the rest of your life, you can know that God has called you to be the recipient of His everlasting love. As you enter into the life of the calling, you become a light in the world, shining with the love of the Lord (Matthew 5:14, Philippians 2:15). He has called you to be a beacon of light as He shines in you.

Calling is a biblical word and it's various forms (call, called, calling) are used more than 700 times in the Bible.[7] The calling is a divine initiative meaning it is God's message and He is directing it to us. His divine initiative and message are found throughout God's Word. Paul confirmed our calling many times when he referred to the things we are called to. We are "called according to His purpose" (Romans 8:28), "called into fellowship with His Son" (1 Corinthians 1:9), "called us to peace" (1 Corinthians 7:15), and "called to freedom" (Galatians 5:13).

God speaks and His voice is powerful and personal. God says, "Do not fear, for I have redeemed you; I have called you by name; you are Mine!" (Isaiah 43:1). Jesus confirmed the personal nature of His calling as the shepherd of the sheep, "…the sheep recognize his voice and come to him. He calls his own sheep by name and leads them out" (John 10:3 NLT). And we see just how personal the Lord in the lives of men and women throughout the Bible. God called to Moses with His voice from the burning bush by saying, "Moses! Moses" (Exodus 3:4), and to Samuel by name in the temple, "Samuel! Samuel!" (1 Samuel 3:10). Jesus called more than once to others in the crowd. "And Jesus stopped and said, "Call him here." So they called the blind man, saying to him, "Take courage, stand up! He is calling for you" (Mark 10:49). Martha secretly went to Mary and said, "The Teacher is here and is calling for you" (John 11:28). When Jesus met Mary in the garden following His resurrection, He called to her by name, "Mary" (John 20:16). Just as the Lord knew their names, so He knows your name.

You see, this calling from the Lord is personal, practical, and powerful as He speaks to you. I am not talking about voices in the physical realm. Hearing God's voice in His Word occurs very simply, spiritually, and powerfully when you slow down and read what He says. The Holy Spirit takes the Word of God and speaks it into your heart, directing it to you, with your name in mind. "But the Helper, the Holy Spirit, whom the Father will send in My name, He will teach you all things, and bring to your remembrance all that I said to you" (John 14:26). So as you read, you hear God calling those words to you and you gain understanding about His message for you from His Word. I have had times where it seemed as though the words were leaping off the page because they were so significant to me. This is the illumination of the Holy Spirit, where He is enlightening your spiritual sight and bringing light to God's Word.

All of this requires a shift in thinking where you begin to realize that God is here and He is not silent. Every moment of your life is important and every detail is significant because God is always calling you and at work carrying out His plan and purpose. To find out what God has in mind for you, simply open the pages of His Word. That is where you hear the calling day after day as He communicates and sets forth and initiates His unique and special purpose and plan and design and desire — all that is on His heart — for you on whom He has set His affection by grace. In the Bible it is as though God is saying in one verse after another, *I am calling you to this and this and this. It's what is on My heart for you.* Every day His voice is calling out to you. Do you hear Him speaking? The only way is to open the Word and listen. The Holy Spirit is faithful to teach you and to issue forth the calling (John 14:26). So every day when you open the pages of His Word, you want to ask the Lord what His call is for you today. "Lord, what do you want me to know, learn, and what do You have in mind today in and through me? What is Your calling for me today? Speak Lord, Your servant is listening."

It is not as though He is asking us, *is it okay, will you do it?* It's more as though He is saying, *This is what I choose for you and have designed for you or have done for you — now I am extending the invitation to you — it's from Me to you — will you receive it, will you accept it, will you believe it, and will you enter in to this with Me?*

One of my favorite examples of the calling is a man named Saul who lived in the first century. He was a Pharisee and he believed that this new group of people who followed someone named Jesus Christ were blasphemers and dangerous. So he set out to have them arrested. While he was on his way to persecute some more of these so-called Christians, a light flashed all around him, and he heard a voice calling out to him, "Saul, Saul, why are you persecuting me" (Acts 9:4). He fell to the ground and cried out, "Who are you, Lord?" Then he heard words he would never forget. "I am Jesus, the one you are persecuting! Now get up and go into the city, and you will be told what you must do." That was the beginning of the adventure of Jesus Christ at work in and through the apostle Paul to bring many to Him and to write most of what we now know as the New Testament.

Paul was so burdened with the desire that you would experience and know the life the calling that he wrote: "I pray that the eyes of your heart may be enlightened, so that you will know what is the hope of His calling, what are the riches of the glory of His inheritance in the saints" (Ephesians 1:18). He also wrote these words from prison about the calling: "As a prisoner for the Lord, then, I urge you to live a life worthy of the calling you have received" (Ephesians 4:1 NIV).

One day a man was out on the backside of the desert near Mt. Sinai tending to his father-in-law's flock. In the midst of the mundane, a miraculous calling came to Moses. A bush began to burn, and a voice came from that bush calling out his name. That was the beginning of a relationship between Moses and God where God would speak with Moses the way a man speaks with his friend (Exodus 33:11).

It all began and continued for Moses with a calling from God. And so it is for you, dear friend. Everything begins and continues with God calling to you. The bush is burning even now as the

Holy Spirit illumines truth in God's Word. The question is, will you turn aside like Moses did, to look at the Lord, and hear God's voice?

The calling is really a life where you walk and talk with the Lord Jesus who has taken up residence in your heart. You are never alone again. You have a moment-by-moment intimacy with Him that feeds your soul, gives you meaning and purpose, and carries you into the stream of His will for something much greater than yourself.

The apostle Paul describes how he lived out his calling from the Lord: "I count everything as loss compared to the possession of the priceless privilege (the overwhelming preciousness, the surpassing worth, and supreme advantage) of knowing Christ Jesus my Lord *and* of progressively becoming more deeply *and* intimately acquainted with Him [of perceiving and recognizing and understanding Him more fully and clearly]…forgetting what lies behind and straining forward to what lies ahead, I press on toward the goal to win the [supreme and heavenly] prize to which God in Christ Jesus is calling us upward" (Philippians 3:8, 13-14 AMP). Paul was brilliant and passionate, and clearly understood that he was called to know Christ. He was determined to live out that calling and was, as a result, captured and captivated by Christ.

So I ask you now, are you experiencing the life of the calling? So many today are missing the calling in their lives because they simply have not drawn near to God. Many rarely open their Bible. According to the Barna Group, a visionary research and resource company located in Ventura, California, 87% in America own a Bible. However, a recent study by Nashville-based Lifeway Research revealed that 53% of Americans have read relatively little in the Bible. In fact, many Christians never open a Bible in church or outside of church. They talk about the Bible, but rarely read it. Statistics from Barna Group show that of those who attend church only 34% ever open a Bible outside of their time in church. This means there are many Christians who don't know the calling and all the blessings of it for themselves. They hear about it, but they don't know it as a firsthand experience. So many are spectators, not participants. God intends for each one of us to be a participant and live out His plan and purpose for our lives.

Jesus, in speaking to the church of Laodicea, gives the picture of the calling where He is standing at the door and knocking, and waiting for us to open the door. He says, "Look! I stand at the door and knock. If you hear my voice and open the door, I will come in, and we will share a meal together as friends" (Revelation 3:20 NLT). He is asking, yes calling, for such intimacy and fellowship that it is as though you will share a meal together with Him as a friend.

When we open the door, and the Lord Jesus Christ moves in and makes His home in our hearts, everything about our lives is transformed. Maybe, just maybe, you are sensing the need for a deeper transformation and a greater experience of intimacy with the Lord and moment-by-moment fellowship with Him. Maybe you made a decision like I did to give your life to Him, but that decision happened a long time ago. And maybe you have gotten caught up in the demands of life and have ignored the Person and presence of God. Or maybe you've just adopted the culture of church and religion but have lost the sense of your relationship with God where you walk and talk with Him moment by moment. Have you gone through a traumatic and devastating loss that has left you numb and you no longer have any sense of meaning or purpose in your life? You feel the need for a new touch from the Lord and connection with Him. Maybe you have never given your life to the Lord but you would like to enter in and make room in your heart to have Him live there. If that is the case, you can pray a simple prayer like I did and invite Him in. He's offering you the adventure of knowing Him in an intimate relationship as a gift. But you have to receive that gift. If that is the case, I invite you to pray: *Lord Jesus, I need You. Thank You for dying on the cross for my sins. I ask You to come into my life, forgive my sins, and make me the person You want me to be. Amen.*

Dear friend, God has set His affection on you. No matter where you are in your relationship with Him right now, you can know that He is calling out to you. He knows where you are, who you are, and how you are. He has something to say to you even now. Will you hear Him? Now is the time to go in a new direction dear friend. Make this the defining moment of the calling where you stop everything to hear from God. There is always more of Him to know, more of His love to experience, and more of His calling to hear in your life. Will you walk outside, gaze at His creation, and realize His magnificent design? Will you pour out your heart to Him? Grab your Bible, open its pages, and live in some of the words. What is God saying to you? Wouldn't you like to know? What have you been thinking about lately? Where in the Bible do you seem to be drawn these days? If a verse from the Bible comes to your mind, then pay attention to it, think about it, and write thoughts and insights in *The Quiet Time Journal*. Dear friend, you are brushing up against His calling in your life. Oh yes, His calling is all around you. Jesus is ever present and you can realize His presence every day. Open the Bible and realize God is speaking and He is speaking to you. Listen to God in His Word, and you will hear His voice and realize in a new and deeper way His choice of you and how great His love is for you. You are His treasure.

Why should I feel discouraged, why should the shadows come,
Why should my heart be lonely, and long for heav'n and home,
When Jesus is my portion? My constant Friend is He:
His eye is on the sparrow, and I know He watches me;
His eye is on the sparrow, and I know He watches me.

Refrain:
I sing because I'm happy, I sing because I'm free,
For His eye is on the sparrow, and I know He watches me.

CIVILLA D. MARTIN, HIS EYE IS ON THE SPARROW, 1905

WHEN FAIRY TALES BECOME REAL

*For this is how God loved the world: He gave his one and only Son, so that
everyone who believes in him will not perish but have eternal life.*

JOHN 3:16 NLT

She never heard her name spoken with kindness in the house where she lived. Her stepsisters and stepmother treated her with disdain and made her their servant. Her days were filled with cleaning, cooking, and meeting the whims of her selfish stepsisters. One day the King in the land decided to hold a ball for his son, the Prince. All girls in the surrounding area were invited with the hopes of being chosen by the Prince to be his wife. The two stepsisters aspired to be the chosen one. Oh, how the servant girl wished to go even though she was not permitted to attend. Now things sound ominous in this story and hopeless for the girl. But this is a fairy tale. And in those kinds of stories, magical things can happen.

For Cinderella, she was met by a fairy godmother that dressed her in the most beautiful gown, styled her hair, gave her glass slippers, and a horse-drawn carriage to take her to the ball. The only thing she needed to remember was returning home before midnight because everything would disappear in that moment. She would return to who she was before all the magic happened.

When she attended the ball, the Prince fell in love with her in an instant. He knew she was the one for him and he wanted to marry her. Cinderella forgot about the time until it was almost midnight. She ran out of the room and made it to the carriage just in time to disappear into the night. But in her escape, she left one thing behind — a glass slipper. The Prince found that glass slipper and knew it would help him find his true love. So he went throughout the land searching for his bride. He finally came to the home of the stepsisters. He asked if there was anyone else there. They brought out Cinderella. He put the glass slipper on her foot and when he saw that it fit, he recognized her as the one he had been seeking. He pulled her into his arms vowing to never let her go. They married, and as all fairy tales end, they lived happily ever after.

Now that's the fairy tale. And when you read the story, you may think, "Well, a beautiful turn of events working out for the one in distress only happens in fairy tales." And maybe you have imagined that the fairy tale dream of love and grace with wonderful long-lasting results is just an illusion. Everyone would love it, but very few ever think it's even possible. Those who hope for it are usually called dreamers, not living in the real world.

What if all the critics and cynics are wrong? And what if those who dare to imagine something beautiful, dream of those things because they are made for something more?

There is only one you. You are unique and special. Created by God, you were literally woven by Him in your mother's womb (Psalm 139:15). He thought of you before you were ever born. He has always had His eye on you. And He watches you and thinks of you even now. He imagined and laid out exactly what He had in mind for you — your gifts, talents, looks — everything. But more than that, His great desire and passion has always been to live with you forever. He loves you more than life itself. Literally, He sacrificed everything to make you His. And so, He calls to you. Here's where the fairy tale becomes real.

Haven't you often wondered what life is all about? Who are you and why are you here? And where are you going? The answers to those questions are wrapped up in something that happened before you were born.

Josephus, a Jewish historian, devoted considerable space in his massive history of Israel to bring to light a fact of history: two thousand years ago an extraordinary person lived in the area of Jerusalem. His name was Jesus. He performed miracles and amazed all who came into contact with Him. He would touch someone who was paralyzed and that person would walk. He would look into the eyes of a prostitute, and as tears came to her eyes, she would be filled with a desire to be good, holy and righteous. He would walk over to a blind man, put His hands on the man's face, and that man would see. He made an amazing claim — He claimed to be God! While people from all over Galilee flocked to be with Him, the religious leaders plotted to kill Him, not because of what Jesus did, but because of who He claimed to be!

Larry King, the famous talk show host, was once asked who he would choose if he could interview one person throughout all of history. He replied that he would like to interview Jesus Christ and that he would ask him one question: "Are you indeed virgin born? The answer to that question," said King, "would explain history to me."

Could it be that, indeed, God has visited us on earth — that Jesus is indeed God? If so, why? Here is where the story of your life begins. And here is where His story is linked to your story. But it's only the beginning of the calling and the story that is meant for you. You will soon see that there is so much more than we realize; a deeper life with Christ is possible and there are far too few who even know the reality of it or have dared to draw near to Him.

Let's step back. Let's place *The Calling* in perspective. The story of your life is the greatest love story imaginable. John tells the story best in just a small paragraph: "For this is how God loved the world: He gave his one and only Son, so that everyone who believes in him will not perish but have eternal life. God sent his Son into the world not to judge the world, but to save the world through him" (John 3:16 NLT).

So why did God purpose this plan of redemption? Sending His Son to come to earth and die on a cross is not without a grand and glorious purpose. He did it for one reason. You. If you had been the only one ever born, He still would have carried out His plan. Why? He loves you and He wants you with Him forever. I cannot say it any more simply than that. Peter, one of Jesus' disciples, said the same thing to a crowd of three thousand: "The promise is for you and for your children and for all who are far off, everyone whom the Lord our God calls to himself" (Acts 2:39 ESV). God has always wanted you with Him forever. He wants to be our God and desires us to be His people, His treasured possession. God is calling you, dear friend, to be His forever. And that calling is only the first of many callings. He is calling, always calling. He wants to walk and talk with you and calls out to you with His Word to strengthen, comfort, and empower you to live the life He has designed for you. It's never too late. God has the ability to weave every thread of your life together into a beautiful story He has in mind.

You are created with a heart that is designed to be a home for God. Jesus said, "All who love me will do what I say. My Father will love them, and we will come and make our home with each of them." (John 14:23 NLT). Paul spoke of the importance of this truth when he said, "This is the secret: Christ lives in you. This gives you assurance of sharing his glory" (Colossians 1:27 NLT). You are meant to be a temple of the Holy Spirit and the place where God Himself lives (1 Corinthians 6:19).

Only God is big enough to fill a human heart. And until God comes to live within you, you will experience a restlessness and dissatisfaction. Augustine, a 4th century Christian theologian and philosopher, has said, "You have made us for yourself, O Lord, and our heart is restless until it rests in you." Blaise Pascal, a French mathematician, physicist, and theologian from the 1600s, wrote, "…this infinite abyss can be filled only with an infinite and immutable object; in other words by God himself." In Ecclesiastes 3:11 we learn that God has set eternity in our hearts. Indeed, we are made to know God and live with Him forever.

The apostle John speaks of Jesus and the way we come to know Him and have Him make His home in us. He writes, "The one who is the true light, who gives light to everyone, was coming into the world. He came into the very world he created, but the world didn't recognize him. He came to his own people, and even they rejected him. But to all who believed him and accepted him, he gave the right to become children of God. They are reborn—not with a physical birth resulting from human passion or plan, but a birth that comes from God" (John 1:9-13 NLT). We are called to become something completely new, indwelt by God Himself, and experiencing new life with Him. Paul explains this initial calling, "This means that anyone who belongs to Christ has become a new person. The old life is gone; a new life has begun! And all of this is a gift from God, who brought us back to himself through Christ (2 Corinthians 5:17-18).

Before I really knew the Lord, I sat on top of a mountain in Sedona, Arizona and wrote a prayer, pouring out my heart to the Lord in response to reading the sermon on the mount in Matthew 5-7. More than anything, I wanted to experience the kind of life Jesus described to His first century audience. I buried that piece of paper on the top of that mountain. I believe God honored my prayer for He created me to know Him. He was preparing me for the new life in Christ that I would soon experience firsthand for myself. Since that time, Sedona has become a very special place for me where I go to spend time alone with God.

You, dear friend, are called to a new life in Christ. Is it really possible for people to become new and different? Imagine with me the true story of a slave trader turning into a hymn writer? His empty heart became the home for God. God came to live with him and changed everything about him. John Newton, a slave trader found himself on a ship caught in a terrible storm off the coast of Ireland. He prayed to God and miraculously the ship drifted to safety instead of sinking. Newton turned his life over to God. He eventually renounced the slave trade, became an Anglican priest, and wrote more than 200 songs to accompany his services. The words of one of those songs has become probably the most beloved hymn ever written—*Amazing Grace*. Just think about the profound ramifications when God fills a human heart—something as beautiful as *Amazing Grace* makes its way into the lives of millions worldwide.

I wonder what God intends for you? How can you discover who you are and why you are here? Imagine that God has made a way to live with you and in you—in your heart. And imagine that once He has made His home in you, He so changes you that your life will never be the same again. And now, He is going to make you who you are designed to be, and lead you into His plans and purposes for your life. When He lives in you, He will lead you and help you step into the stream of His will and desires. He has designed you for something that only He knows until you come into a relationship with Him. It's the story He wants to tell through your life. And then begins the great adventure of knowing Him where you literally walk and talk with Him every day of your time on earth. And once He has made His home in you, He will never leave or forsake you. You have a future with Him—eternal life—in heaven once you step from time into eternity.

Now the question is, what does this mean for you and how can you experience God's plan and purpose for your life? Once you experience salvation through Christ, a beautiful love story between you and God begins. Then, we have to ask the question, I wonder what God has in mind as He comes to live with you and in you? The answers come through the calling, where the Lord calls to you again and again and again, with one verse after another in His Word. He calls out to you in Psalm 46:10 "Be still and know that I am God," calling you to know Him. He calls to you in Matthew 11:28 "Come to Me, all you who are weary, and I will give you rest," calling you to come to Him. He calls out to you in John 7:37 "If anyone is thirsty, let him come to Me and drink," calling you to refreshment and the filling of the Holy Spirit. Oh yes, He is calling out to you even now. And His calling is more than an invitation or even a command. It is the expression of God's great love in His words and actions. And beyond the calling is a world of all the best gifts—blessings from knowing God—that are waiting to be unwrapped. The calling will change your life forever. It is the deeper life in Christ.

Amazing grace, how sweet the sound
That saved a wretch like me.
I once was lost, but now am found
Was blind but now I see.

'Twas grace that taught my heart to fear,
And grace my fears relieved;
How precious did that grace appear
The hour I first believed.

When we've been there ten thousand years,
Bright shining as the sun,
We've no less days to sing God's praise
Than when we'd first begun.

JOHN NEWTON, AMAZING GRACE, 1779

ANSWERING THE CALLING

*Look! I stand at the door and knock. If you hear my voice and open the
door, I will come in, and we will share a meal together as friends.*

REVELATION 3:20 NLT

At the age of seventeen in the mid-1800s, Dwight Lyman Moody traveled from the New
England farming community of Northfield, Massachusetts where he grew up, to Boston,
seeking employment. His uncle hired him as a shoe clerk in his business, Holton's shoe store. One
of the requirements of the job was attending a local church—Mount Vernon Congregational
Church. Moody was totally bored with church. But the Sunday school teacher, Edward Kimball,
did not give up on him.

One day Kimball visited Moody at the shoe store. Moody was wrapping shoes. Mr. Kimball
walked up to him and said, "I want to tell you how much Christ loves you." Those words pierced
Moody's heart. The Lord was calling him with the absolute truth of His love. Moody could not
resist, and surrendered his life to Christ in response, answering the call of the Lord.

He describes the moment like this: "I was in a new world. The birds sang sweeter, the sun
shone brighter. I'd never known such peace." Moody knew his life was changed forever. And he
was right. That was the beginning of an amazing life of a great evangelist who spoke to millions
and saw literally thousands of men and women come to Christ.

D. L. Moody became practiced in answering the calling of the Lord in his life. Two years after
he gave his life to Christ, he moved to Chicago and worked in the shoe store of another uncle. But
burning in his heart was a desire to teach the Bible to young people and lead them to the Lord.
God had designed him for speaking and teaching and gave him a deep desire to read and study
the Bible. He spent hours in God's Word learning about those things that were on the heart of
God. God placed a heavy burden for people and their salvation on Moody's heart. Moody wanted
to teach the Bible to them and help them know and love God. There were so many young people
in Moody's Sunday school group that he had to teach them on the shores of Lake Michigan. A
conviction for winning souls for Christ grew so strong in Moody that in June, 1860, he left his
shoe store job to teach the Bible and tell more people about Christ. God was calling him in a
definite direction and Moody was answering that call.

Moody was led to a deeper commitment and experience of God's calling through two different people. His friend Henry Varley said, "The world has yet to see what God can do with and for and through and in a man who is fully and wholly consecrated to Him." Moody was deeply moved by those words. Some time later he attended a meeting where the great preacher, Charles Haddon Spurgeon, was speaking. As he listened to Spurgeon, the words of his friend, Henry Varley, came to his mind.

"Varley meant any man! Varley didn't say he had to be educated, or brilliant, or anything else. Just a man! Well, by the Holy Spirit in him, he'd be one of those men… It was not Mr. Spurgeon, after all, who was doing that work; it was God. And if God could use Mr. Spurgeon, why should He not use the rest of us, and why should we not all just lay ourselves at the Master's feet and say to Him, 'Send me! Use me!'?"

With a deep commitment, Moody responded to Varley's statement about what God can accomplish through any of us by saying, "I aim to be that man." God was calling Moody with the biblical truth that He is looking for those who will give themselves to Him and rely on His power to do a great and mighty work in and through them. "The eyes of the Lord search the whole earth in order to strengthen those whose hearts are fully committed to him" (2 Chronicles 16:9 NLT). And God surely did a mighty work in and through D.L. Moody, founder of Moody Bible Institute. He became a great evangelist impacting millions for Christ.

Think about the life of D.L. Moody for a moment. How important were those defining moments when Moody answered God's calling in his life? How significant was his time in God's Word? And how life-changing were the times when Moody talked with God, thought about all He was saying, and then answered Him with decisions and actions?

I'd like you to think about what would have been lost had Moody not answered the calling. I had the opportunity to visit Moody Bible Institute in Chicago during a speaking engagement at a nearby church. I visited the D.L. Moody museum and saw some samples of his messages. He would handwrite his messages on sheets of paper the same size as his Bible. Then, he would keep each message in little blue envelopes where he would record the dates and places for each of the messages. I made my way to the basement of Moody Bible Institute to view the Moody archives. The man in charge gave me a tour where I saw such treasures as the Bibles of R.A. Torrey and Kenneth Wuest, two great men of God from the past who were now with the Lord.

As we were walking around in the basement, I was thinking about one thing: those sermons and the blue envelopes.

"Is there anything in particular that you would like to see?"

I immediately exclaimed, "Is there any way for me to see Moody's sermons in the blue envelopes!"

He responded with a smile, "Sure, no problem." He walked over to a file cabinet, pulled out a folder, and led me to a conference room and invited me to look through as many blue envelopes as I wanted. So there I sat, reading through one sermon after another, and literally handling the very pages written by Moody himself. I felt as though Moody was actually there with me, instructing me about the dedication and response to God necessary as we walk with Him. His words in each sermon moved me to tears. I sat for many hours in that quiet room—thinking with Moody, communing with Jesus, and embracing the defining moment of another calling from my Lord.

I left the archives and went upstairs to eat lunch in the Moody Bible Institute cafeteria. I looked around at all the students. They were walking to class, studying, talking and laughing together. But God was doing something powerful inside me. It was as though God was saying to me, *Look at all these students. They are in training, studying God's Word. This is the result, the ripple effect, of what I have done through a simple man wholeheartedly yielded to me — D.L. Moody.* I realized none of this would have even existed if D.L. Moody hadn't answered God as He spoke to him. It seemed as though the Lord was showing me that He will do powerful things in and through any of us if we will give ourselves to Him. We might not become D.L. Moody. But we will be who He has designed us to be. And then God turned His attention completely to me. It was as though He was saying, *Cath, do you see what can happen if you will yield yourself wholeheartedly to Me?*

Yes Lord, I see. It became a defining moment as I realized how absolutely imperative it is that we live in His power and answer His call to live His life in and through us as He makes His home in our hearts. I knew in my heart of hearts that my Lord was asking for a commitment of my will to Him. *Lord, here I am, send me, use me in any way You please.* I gave myself to God again in that moment, in a new and deeper way, desiring His will more than anything else in my life. I left that place so excited about the life before me. I couldn't wait to see all that God would do in the years ahead.

As I think through my life, many defining moments of God's calling me come to mind. They were times where I heard Him speak in His Word in my quiet time, through preachers and teachers of the Word, and in books where I read insights on His Word. I think about the time early on when I first gave my life to the Lord there in college. I was filled with a great desire to disciple women. I imagined great and mighty things like speaking to thousands. Writing books. I dreamed of a certain life where I would see hundreds of thousands impacted. I remember sitting in the chapel at Arrowhead Springs during a Campus Crusade Christmas conference and praying a simple prayer of commitment to go wherever the Lord led me in life.

Of course, I had a certain picture in my mind of how my life would go. However, my life didn't unfold for me the way I imagined. A verse in the Bible that has been very important to me over the years is Proverbs 16:9— "We can make our plans, but the Lord determines our steps." Yes, He has had me write many books and speak to many different groups of people. I have had the privilege of leading hundreds of women in ministry and I'm currently leading and teaching women at a church in Palm Desert, California, in addition to speaking and writing through Quiet Time Ministries.

But I have also suffered many, many hardships. In the midst of a busy and productive ministry, my precious mother who is my very best friend, entered into advanced stages of multiple sclerosis. She fell and broke her neck. And my life took a turn as I focused much of my attention on her care for many years. Then, when my books were coming out two a year, the publishing industry took a downturn as many Christian bookstores closed. And, yet later, I have walked through great loss in the last five years with both my father and mother going home to be with the Lord. I lived in what I call "the valley of the shadow" for at least two years, with a broken heart and a crushed spirit. I have discovered life is just not easy and sometimes seemingly impossible. But I am never alone for I have the best companion a person could ever have—the Lord Jesus Christ. And He is with me, calling to me, comforting me, strengthening me, and encouraging me to follow Him.

I'm inspired by D.L. Moody and I have learned the power of responding to God's call from him. However, I am not called to be D.L. Moody. I am called to be Catherine Martin and live a life vastly different from the one Moody led. And *you* are called to be *you* as the Lord works in and through you. *Who are you? Why are you here?* I ask these questions because I think they are very important for all seasons and stages of our journey. Every life tells a story. And the Lord is the One writing the story of our lives. And sometimes there are chapters that absolutely don't make sense to us. However, they fit together in the picture that God is painting in and through our lives to show off His greatness and glory.

God has led me through many dark times where I have learned to draw near to Him, hear His voice in His Word, and then respond to what He is saying to me. Those are the most important parts of the calling for me. And they are for you, too. It's where the Lord has made my heart into a more comfortable place where He lives. I can walk and talk more easily together with my Lord. And He makes me into an instrument for His use wherever He chooses to work in and through me each day. I don't think any of us will ever know all the ways He has used us. Sometimes He will roll down the shade a bit and give us a glimpse of how He is working. And then we can sit in awe remembering it is His work and we just need to answer His call every day.

I will never forget an email I received from a girl who attended a church in Gilbert, Arizona. I had spoken there a number of years earlier. She wrote to tell me how she had been sitting in the front row, wounded and broken. Upon hearing the message, she surrendered her life to Christ. And now God was using her in the lives of many as a leader in that church. She just wrote to say "thank you." I was overwhelmed that God had done such a miraculous work. I had no idea it had happened until she contacted me. The "thank you" was truly mine to both God and her. God had used me and I could hardly believe it. But there was an incredible joy and excitement in me at the thought of being a vessel God could use to accomplish His work.

There is a moment, an imperceptible moment, when you become aware that God has designs on you, He has targeted you for His love, set His affection on you and will absolutely have you for His own. His desire for you is from the foundation of the world—marked in eternity. You become aware of it at some point in your life, and that becomes one of your defining moments in the calling. When those defining moments happen, you must respond.

When Jesus walked on earth more than two thousands years ago, He spent three years in public ministry. You can open your Bible to the gospels—Matthew, Mark, Luke, and John—and walk with Jesus through all the different events in His ministry. There is one thing you will notice again and again. Whenever He spoke, Jesus always asked for a response. Everything He said was important and expressed with purpose and intention. And sometimes the responses are included to emphasize the point. For example, when Jesus taught about the seed and different soils in the ground, He asked those listening to truly hear and understand the Word of God (Matthew 13:23). When He taught that parable He was calling those who listened to give priority to His Word over any other thing including the world, possessions, and money.

You can see another example of Jesus asking for a response in Matthew 4:19. He walked by some fisherman and said, "Come follow me, and I will show you how to fish for people." Just in those words alone, Jesus was calling them to high service where they would be used by Him to touch people in the world." How did they respond? "They left their nets at once, and followed him" (Matthew 4:20 NLT).

What response is the Lord asking of you today? Are you experiencing life-changing times when you talk with God, think about all He was saying, and then answer Him with decisions and actions? Every time the Lord calls out to you, He will ask for a response. He has a definite plan for your life. In Psalm 139:16 we see the intricacy of detail that God has created for your life. "You saw me before I was born. Every day of my life was recorded in your book. Every moment was laid out before a single day had passed." Because this is true, then the question becomes, "How are you going to live your life?" Will you live according to the calling placed on your life as He leads you and allow Jesus who lives in you to do all He has on His heart to accomplish through you in the power of the Holy Spirit? Or will you ignore the calling and live for yourself, experiencing a wasted life? What a waste to live with no sense of destiny, purpose or plan where one day goes into another, and you fritter away all your days until you pass on from this earth. Oh the life experience of the calling is a high calling indeed.

I love how Paul describes the mighty work accomplished in and through us. He says, "But thanks be to God, who always puts us on display in Christ and through us spreads the aroma of the knowledge of Him in every place. For to God we are the fragrance of Christ among those who are being saved and among those who are perishing" (2 Corinthians 2:14-15 HCSB).

I was studying late into the night, outlining the book of Romans for one of my New Testament seminary classes. And when I finished living in the book of Romans for literally hours, my eyes were drawn back to Romans 12:1 where I heard the call from God to "present your bodies a living and holy sacrifice, acceptable to God, which is your spiritual service of worship." I knew I had to respond to the Lord in that moment. I slipped out of the chair and got on my face before God. *Lord, here is all of me for You to use for Your glory - my hands, my feet, my eyes, my smile, all of me.* It was a holy moment with God and I've never forgotten it. And it was after that time alone with God that I received the idea from Him for Quiet Time Ministries where I have been serving Him for more than thirty years now.

When you answer the call, you will have the amazing joy when you step into heaven, of seeing the face of Jesus and hearing His words "Well done, good and faithful servant." Hearing praise from God is something worth so much more than any earthly adulation. It is as though we are in the audience of One—God Himself.

There was one servant of God who basically got a standing ovation from the Lord. His name was David, the shepherd boy who became king of Israel. You can read much of what David wrote in many of the Psalms in the Old Testament. Here's what God said about David. "I have found David son of Jesse, a man after my own heart. He will do everything I want him to do" (Acts 13:22).

What set David apart from all the others? He always asked God what He wanted. And when God called out to him, David always said *yes*. He didn't argue with God. He loved God. He understood the need for a response to God's call. In fact, he delighted in God so much that he often walked and talked with Him. He knew God loved him, wanted him for His own treasure, and had set His affection on him.

When God calls out to you, He is tenacious and persistent in what He desires for you. C.S. Lewis had a friend, Sheldon VanAuken, who had many doubts and questions about God. They began a correspondence of letters back and forth talking about the deep things of God. At one point in the correspondence, C.S. Lewis ended his letter by writing, "I think you are already in the meshes of the net! The Holy Spirit is after you. I doubt if you'll get away!"[1] And C.S. Lewis was right. He knew the ways of God. When God calls, it's almost impossible not to respond to Him. He will not stop calling. And eventually you do have to answer. You can run, but you cannot hide. Sheldon VanAuken did eventually give his life to Christ. C.S. Lewis wrote these words to him following his decision: "Blessings on you and a hundred thousand welcomes. Make use of me in any way you please: and let us pray for each other always."

Imagine again the picture that Jesus gives the church of Laodicea in Revelation 3:20. He says, "Look! I stand at the door and knock. If you hear my voice and open the door, I will come in, and we will share a meal together as friends." Where in your life do you need to answer the Lord's calling? How will you respond to Him? Will you open the door and invite Him in? Will you enjoy a meal with Him as your Lord and friend? Your responses to God make or break the course of your life as you lean in to God and trust Him to carry out His work in and through you. And you are never too young or too old to walk and talk with the Lord. As long as He has you here on earth, He has a plan for you and a work to accomplish in and through you. And if your life is seemingly hopeless and impossible, then you can know that God is calling you to draw even nearer to Him so you can hear all He has for you and wants you to know. Oh yes, He is calling you even now. At all points in your life, God is working in you (Philippians 2:13) and will "continue his work until it is finally finished on the day when Christ Jesus returns" (Philippians 1:6 NLT).

Annie Johnson Flint, a young woman living in New York in the mid-1800s, suffered from crippling arthritis and had to abandon her dreams of being a concert pianist. When the arthritis advanced in her body, she was shut in to only one mode of expression—poetry. In the beginning she regarded it as an insignificant, small thing. She wrote, "Verse-making was so easy and so pleasant to do that it never seem a work or a duty. It appeared so small a thing that I held it of no importance. I was like a Syrian general who would not have shrunk from doing some great or difficult task, but despised the seven dippings in the Jordan."[2] Since it was all she could do, it became all she did, in response to the calling of God. With time in the daily walking and talking with Jesus and hearing His daily calling in her life, she came to realize it as an occupation for the Lord and a comfort and delight. These words, written by Annie Johnson Flint, show her response to God's calling. May we all, in both the peaks and the valleys of life, respond to God by answering His calling, whatever it may be.

"The cross awaits me"? Yes I know. "The night is dark"? But He is near.
"The path is rough"? His arm upholds. "I cannot see"? But I can hear,
And where He leads I follow on; He calls me, and I may not stay;
His strength is mine through all the days; His light is sown along the way.
O loved Redeemer, loving Lord! I hear Thy voice; it calleth me
Through joy and grief, through toil and pain, to rest beyond the stormy sea;
O're mount and valley, plain and stream, unto the place where I would be,
Unto the heaven where Thou hast gone, I follow Thee—I follow Thee.
ANNIE JOHNSON FLINT, AND HE SAITH, "FOLLOW ME"

THE LIFE OF CHRIST IN YOU

I have been crucified with Christ; and it is no longer I who live, but
Christ lives in me; and the life which I now live in the flesh I live by faith
in the Son of God, who loved me and gave Himself up for me.
GALATIANS 2:20

I have loved reading books since I was a little girl. And my favorite type of book is a biography. Biographies are about real people with real lives and they give me the opportunity to learn from their example. One of my favorite biographies is *Hudson Taylor's Spiritual Secret*. In that book, I did learn Hudson Taylor's spiritual secret and it became a powerful truth for me related to the kind of life God is calling me to live—the crucified life where it's no longer I who live, but Christ lives in me.

J. Hudson Taylor was a British Protestant missionary in the mid-1800s, founder of the China Inland Mission, an organization that brought more than 800 missionaries to China, began 125 schools, and was directly responsible for at least 18,000 conversions to Christ. Things weren't easy spiritually for Taylor. He speaks of a time when he was extremely frustrated and defeated in his ministry: "I knew that if only I could abide in Christ all would be well, but I could not. I would begin the day with prayer, determined not to take my eye off Him for a moment, but pressure of duties, sometimes very trying, and constant interruptions apt to be so wearing, caused me to forget Him…Instead of growing stronger, I seemed to be getting weaker and to have less power against sin; and no wonder, for faith and even hope were getting low. I hated myself, I hated my sin, yet gained no strength against it…All the time I felt assured that there was in Christ all I needed, but the practical question was—how to get it out. He was rich truly, but I was poor; He was strong, but I weak. I knew full well that there was in the root, the stem, abundant fatness, but how to get it into my puny little branch was the question. As gradually light dawned, I saw that faith was the only requisite—was the hand to lay hold on His fullness and make it mine. But I had not this faith."[1]

In the height of his agony of soul, one sentence in a letter from his dear missionary friend, John McCarthy, set him free. "But how to get faith strengthened? Not by striving after faith, but by resting on the Faithful One."[2]

"As I read, I saw it all!" Taylor goes on to describe the light of his discovery revealed to him by the Lord. "I saw not only that Jesus will never leave me, but that I am a member of His body, of His flesh and of His bones. The vine is not the root merely, but all—root, stem, branches, twigs, leaves, flowers, fruit. And Jesus is not that alone—He is soil and sunshine, air and showers, and ten thousand times more than we have ever dreamed, wished for or needed. Oh, the joy of seeing this truth!"[3]

What Hudson Taylor realized in that moment when he read that letter was that he had been relying on his own resources to live his life. He had been completely unaware that the affairs of his life were Christ's concern and that Christ and His resources were present in him and ready to handle everything that came his way. He experienced a new awareness of his union with Christ; Christ lived in him and worked through him every moment of the day. He realized his responsibility was to trust and rest. It was the Lord's work, not his work. The realization of these truths made a radical difference in the life and ministry of Hudson Taylor. He accomplished more in Christ than he ever would have on his own. This is what happens when you realize that you are united with Christ and it's no longer your life. He is your life. It's a beautiful, wondrous exchange—you are in Christ and He is in you.

Some truths are not easily discovered or comprehended. They cannot even be told, but instead must be revealed by God in His time and way. Our union with Christ, the ramifications of His life in us, and living with Christ each day in the real world are those kinds of truths. And they are learned through a lifetime of walking with the Lord. I did not even realize Christ was living in me and that I was united with Him when I first surrendered my life to Christ. However, I definitely remember the first time I became dimly aware of His presence in me, and that truth literally blew me away! I opened the pages of this little book, *Principles of Spiritual Growth* by Miles J. Stanford (also known as *The Green Letters*). I thought, *How can there be much in a book this small?* However, it had been recommended by one of my favorite people, Ney Bailey, a staff member with Campus Crusade for Christ, who is a dear friend. So I immediately began living in it, chapter by chapter. After the second chapter, I said to myself, *These are profound truths, but I'm not even sure what they mean.* Then, I came to the third chapter, entitled "Acceptance." I came to this sentence about a believer's life in Christ by William Newell who wrote the book, *Romans Verse by Verse*, that opened my eyes to something new and amazing. "As to his life past, *it does not exist* before God: he died at the cross, and *Christ is his Life.*" Those words just knocked me down. I realized that something very powerful happened at the cross that impacts me now because I am united with Christ in every way.

Then, Newell wrote about our attitude under grace and our discoveries about grace. He said, "To believe, and to consent to be *loved while unworthy*, is the great secret…To 'hope to be better' (hence acceptable) is to fail to see yourself *in Christ only*. To be *disappointed* with yourself, is to have *believed* in yourself."

When I read that chapter, I closed the book, and said out loud, "Whoa, wait a minute. Am I truly united with Christ? Is He actually living in me? And He is my life? And I belong to Him? Really?" This was not something I had ever heard before. *I am in Christ and He is in me. I am to believe in Him every moment and never to look to myself to live life.* Stanford wrote, "As the Lord Jesus is allowed to express Himself through our personality, this poor, sin-sick world will see 'Christ in you, the hope of glory' (Colossians 1:27)."

So how is it possible for Christ to live in me? That was my new question after realizing these truths. I came to the chapter entitled "Identification." I read all these quotes about being crucified with Christ and united with Christ in death, burial, and resurrection. Andrew Murray wrote: "Like Christ, the believer too has died to sin." Watchman Nee pointed out that "Our sins are dealt with by the Blood, but we ourselves are dealt with by the Cross." The quote by L.E. Maxwell in his book *Christian Victory*, was profound: "Believers in Christ were joined to Him at the cross, united to Him in death and resurrection. We died with Christ. He died for us, and we died with Him. This is a great fact, true of all believers." *What did all of this mean?*

Then I discovered Galatians 2:20 while I was reading all these truths in Stanford's book, and the Lord opened my eyes to understand what has been called *the crucified life* or *the exchanged life*. "I have been crucified with Christ; and it is no longer I who live, but Christ lives in me; and the life which I now live in the flesh I live by faith in the Son of God, who loved me and gave Himself up for me" (Galatians 2:20). I memorized that verse and thought through it every day. I still think about the truths contained in it.

Here is what I came to understand about this deeper life in Christ. I am so inextricably united with Christ that when He died, I died. When He was buried, so was I. And when He rose from the dead, I rose to new life also—His life in me. He lives in me. As Stanford writes: "There cannot be two masters in our lives. If the old 'I' is in active possession of us, then Christ cannot be. But if we gladly take hold of the great fact of redemption—'I have been crucified with Christ'—then Christ by His Spirit takes up the exercise of the function of life within us, and leads us as His bond-slaves (disciples), in the train of His triumph."[4]

After I read all these words, I exclaimed, "I am not alone. I am never alone! The Lord Jesus Christ is with me forever." I'll be the first to say that being dead to self and alive to Christ at the same time is a challenge to understand and then actually live out in life. Paul the apostle thought so too and you can see his struggle in his letter to the Romans. He speaks in Romans 6:5-8 about how we are united with Christ, have died with Him, are freed from sin, and now live with Him. Then, in Romans 7, with real authenticity, he writes about his conflict and struggle between two natures—the old and the new. And then, in Romans 8 we see the glorious victory because Christ now lives in us through the power of the Holy Spirit. "There is therefore now no condemnation for those who are in Christ Jesus. For the law of the spirit of life in Christ Jesus has set you free from the law of sin and death...If Christ is in you, though the body is dead because of sin, yet the spirit is alive because of righteousness" (Romans 8:1-2, 10). Your position before God is that you are *in Christ*. God sees you *in Christ*. Your sins are forgiven and you are a child of God. It is a complete mystery and it will take a lifetime to uncover all the truths and ramifications of the fact that Christ is in you and you are in Christ. But Paul encourages us to make room in our lives for the mystery of it all and allow God to reveal these truths to us in His time. He says, "God willed to make known what is the riches of the glory of this mystery among the Gentiles, which is Christ in you, the hope of glory" (Colossians 1:27).

So what is His calling in these truths about your union with Christ in His death, burial and resurrection? You are called to be a home for Christ, a place where He can live while you are on this earth. William O. Carver was a Professor of Missions in the earlier 20th Century and wrote a commentary on Ephesians. He believes that the entire book of Ephesians is a description of the calling of a Christian. And when you read through Ephesians, you will arrive at one main truth. Christ lives in you. Carver notes that Paul gives us the most fully developed concept of Christ continuing His presence and work in history in and through the Church and those who are part of the Church. Paul prays in Ephesians 3:16-17 "That He would grant you, according to the riches of His glory, to be strengthened with power through His Spirit in the inner man, so that Christ may dwell in your hearts through faith." In Ephesians 4:12-16 Paul speaks of us as the body of Christ and the need to "grow up in all aspects into Him who is the head, even Christ, from whom the whole body, being fitted and held together by what every joint supplies, according to the proper working of each individual part, causes the growth of the body for the building up of itself in love." William Carver writes: "You are to be made so strong by His Spirit coming into and working within you that the Christ may have in you—the Church—a place to dwell, a sphere to work in, and instrument of action."[5] Carver made a daring declaration in the classes he taught: "The calling of the Christian and the church is to be the continuation of the incarnation of Jesus Christ!" In that one statement, he was pointing out that Christ was continuing His life and work on earth in and through those who are spiritually born again and have entered into a relationship with Him. Jesus Christ living in and through us is our calling. No wonder Jesus said, "Truly, truly, I say to you, he who believes in Me, the works that I do, he will do also; and greater works than these he will do; because I go to the Father. Whatever you ask in My name, that will I do, so that the Father may be glorified in the Son. If you ask Me anything in My name, I will do it" (John 14:12-14).

Jesus is calling to you to a deep and rich life with Him—to know and understand that He is living His life with you, in you, and through you. Behind this truth is the passionate heart of God who has always wanted to live with His people. He walked and talked with Adam and Eve in the garden of Eden. And then, He told the children of Israel that He would dwell among them and they would be His people and He would be their God (Exodus 25:8, 29:45). John tells us "the Word became human and made his home among us. He was full of unfailing love and faithfulness. And we have seen his glory, the glory of the Father's one and only Son" (John 1:14 NLT). Once again, we see just how much God wants to be with His people. Jesus rose from the dead and ascended into heaven, making it possible that once people are born again, the Holy Spirit lives in them. In this way Christ is able to make His home in all those who belong to Him. "Don't you realize that your body is the temple of the Holy Spirit, who lives in you and was given to you by God" (1 Corinthians 6:19 NLT). The ultimate fulfillment of all God's desire is seen in Revelation 21:3 following the creation of a new heaven and a new earth in eternity. "And I heard a loud voice from the throne, saying, "Behold, the tabernacle of God is among men, and He will dwell among them, and they shall be His people, and God Himself will be among them."

The fact that Christ lives in us and makes His home in us now is such good news. The Christian life is not just difficult. It's nearly impossible. But the Lord never intended you to live it alone. He intends to live it in and through you. His strength and power is more than enough to handle anything that comes your way. You can exclaim with Paul, "I can do all things through Him who strengthens me" (Philippians 4:13).

I love how C.S. Lewis, a British writer, theologian, and Oxford University scholar in the early 1900s, describes our relationship with Christ in his book, *Mere Christianity*. He borrows a parable from George MacDonald: "Imagine yourself as a living house. God comes in to rebuild that house. At first, perhaps, you can understand what He is doing. He is getting the drains right and stopping the leaks in the roof and so on; you knew that those jobs needed doing and so you are not surprised. But presently He starts knocking the house about in a way that hurts abominably and does not seem to make any sense. What on earth is He up to? The explanation is that He is building quite a different house from the one you thought of—throwing out a new wing here, putting on an extra floor there, running up towers, making courtyards. You thought you were being made into a decent little cottage: but He is building a palace. He intends to come and live in it Himself."[6] You, dear friend, are called to be a palace where Jesus Christ, the King of Kings now resides. Just take a moment to drink in this magnificent truth. You are a palace for the Lord Himself!

In John 15, Jesus gives us a picture to help us understand our union with Him using the metaphor of vine and branches in a vineyard. He said, "I am the vine; you are the branches. Those who remain in me, and I in them, will produce much fruit. For apart from me you can do nothing" (John 15:5 NLT). The life of the branch is not in itself, but is in the Vine. Everything the branch is and needs is found in the Vine. This picture helps us understand our need for Christ every day. In this day and age, the church is becoming so much like the world that there is an enticement for us to become stronger and stronger. The real truth is that the Lord accomplishes His most powerful work in and through Christians who are weak, but depend on the power of Christ in them through the Holy Spirit. This should be an encouragement to any who feel as though everything is against them and they have no more resources. That is just the time when the Lord comes alongside you as He did with Paul, and says, "My grace is all you need. My power works best in weakness" (2 Corinthians 12:9 NLT). God can do the most with those who have the least. The weaker you are the better it is for the Lord to do His work. Paul points out the great provision for those in Christ in 1 Corinthians 1:30, "But by His doing you are in Christ Jesus, who became to us wisdom from God, and righteousness and sanctification, and redemption." You have everything you need in Christ.

Again and again, the apostle Paul taught those in the first-century church the truth that Christ was living in them. He approached this truth from a number of angles. He told the Galatians that he labored in ministry until Christ was "formed" in them (Galatians 4:19). That word "formed" implies that the very image of Christ would be literally impressed on their heart. To the Ephesians, he wanted to see the fullness and completeness of Christ in them (Ephesians 4:13). And to the Romans, Paul taught that they were destined to be molded into Christ's image and share His likeness (Romans 8:29). To the Corinthians, Paul taught that the Holy Spirit would make them more and more like Christ (2 Corinthians 3:18), and that the light of Christ was literally shining in their hearts revealing the glory of God in the face of Christ (2 Corinthians 4:6). Christ is living His life in us through the power of the Holy Spirit and we will become like Him in every way as we grow in our relationship with Him. G.D. Watson, who lived in England in the early 1900s, explains in his book, *Soul Food,* that "our earlier views of Him [Christ] are eclipsed by deeper and sweeter visions of His person and character."[7] This beautiful intimacy with Christ is personal, passionate, and powerful.

A.B. Simpson, founder of the Christian and Missionary Alliance, said that when Christ lives in us, we "have the very person of Christ possessing our being; the thoughts of Christ, the desires of Christ, the will of Christ, the faith of Christ, the purity of Christ, the love of Christ, the unselfishness of Christ, the single aim of Christ, the obedience of Christ, the humility of Christ, the submission of Christ, the meekness of Christ, the patience of Christ, the gentleness of Christ, the zeal of Christ, the works of Christ, manifest in our mortal flesh."[8] Christ transforms our life.

If Christ lives in you and is making His home in your heart, then whose life is it—His life or your life? This is a question we must come to eventually and answer wholeheartedly if we would go deeper in our relationship with Christ. I remember a time when I was just overwhelmed with all my responsibilities. And I was discouraged. I decided to go to a favorite local bakery and have what I call breakfast with the Lord. Once inside the bakery, I spotted one of my pastor friends sipping on his coffee and reading his Bible. I hadn't seen him in months, so I walked over and greeted him with a smile and a warm hello.

He said, "Catherine, how are you? It's good to see you."

I said, "I'm doing okay. I've been kind of overwhelmed with all my responsibilities. And I've just been wondering what God is doing in my life."

He smiled, "Let me tell you a story."

I said, "Okay," knowing this was going to be good.

"My daughter called me the other day. She said, 'Dad, I'm just not sure what I'm going to do in my life.' Do you know what I said to her?"

"What?" I asked, sensing that I was about to experience an eye-opening truth in this God-ordained appointment.

"I said to my daughter, 'Well, that's your problem. It's not your life. It's His life.' She asked me, 'What do you mean?' I said, 'Well, you've been twice given. And I was there to witness both times. First, when you were born, your mother and I gave you to the Lord. And I was there the day you gave your life to Christ. It's not your life; it's His life."

I looked at my pastor friend, smiled knowingly, and walked to my table, silently talking with God. *Lord, You got me today! My life is not my own, but Yours—such a simple truth, but deep and profound. Thank You for bringing that pastor to a bakery he never frequents just to remind a simple girl wallowing in self-pity that I belong to You and that my life is Yours. A metamorphosis has truly taken place. You now live in and through me, and You have the freedom to take me wherever you desire me to go. I am Yours.*

Do you realize Christ lives in you? Are you aware that you are not alone? He is with you, moment by moment, throughout the day. You can walk and talk with Him at any time. And you will discover that the more time you spend with Him, the more you will become like Him. Do you see that it is no longer your life? It's His life. The life of Christ in you is your calling as you live by faith in the Son of God who loves you (Galatians 2:20). He is your life. He is the One who leads and guides you, taking you where He wants to go. He has a very specific goal and purpose in mind for you, as He tells His story in and through you. He is calling you to trust Him as your very life. He wants you to allow Him to live His life in and through you. He wants you to depend on Him instead of yourself. He will provide for you even in the most adverse circumstances. You won't always see how He is going to do it. Then is the time to remember again it is His life. And then, because it's His life, He is going to tell a particular story in and through you to the world. So don't be surprised if there are bends in the road you didn't expect, times when there is no visible means of support, or circumstances that don't go your way. His ways are higher and bends in the road need not thwart His good work in your life (Isaiah 55:8-9, Romans 8:28). Your faith and trust in Him gives such honor and glory to Christ and He delights in your dependence on Him for everything.

A.W. Tozer, pastor, author, and *Alliance Weekly* magazine editor in the early 1900s encourages us with his words in his book, *The Crucified Life*. "You must set your heart on Jesus Christ. Wherever He takes you, go with Him. Whatever He takes you away from, listen to Him and follow what He says. Whomever you must ignore, move away from. If you want to be all that God wants you to be, set your face like flint and go straight to Jesus."[9] He speaks about the importance of hearing God's voice as He calls out to you as He lives His life in you. "Maybe God is calling you to do something extraordinary, something that does not appear on your calendar or agenda, something to revive your own soul. Maybe God is calling you to do something radical and extreme for your soul. I hope and pray that the world and the 'pleasures' of it are not so great that you are unable to hear Him. The biggest thing in the world is not whether you live to be 100 years old; the biggest thing in the world is whether you can hear God speaking to you now. That is what counts."[10]

I truly believe that God wants a personal revival for you. Sometimes you come across a truth that stirs your soul and takes you to a deeper more meaningful place in life where you walk a profound road with your Lord. It becomes a defining moment where you will never be the same again. I believe the calling can do that for you as you realize the meaning of the cross and the crucified life for yourself. You realize that God has a claim on you—He will have you for His own. He has set His affection on you—He loves you—He has died in your place and paid the price for you that you might be forgiven and live with Him forever—and now He wants an intimate relationship with you where He walks and talks with you forever about everything. Nothing is off the table—everything is in the sphere of His interest in you. You are His. You belong to Him. Will you be His? Will you say *yes* every moment? Will you find joy in the fact that you belong to Him? He delights in every detail of your life. And here's the big truth that changes your whole perspective of His calling. It's not your life. It's His life. The picture of the vine and the branch is real to you where you see that He truly is the source of every single thing in you. It's not just a trivial thing—it's a calling from God—it's what life is all about. You are called and chosen. It's no longer you who live but Christ lives in you and the life you live is by faith in Him who died for you. It's you in Him and Him in you. Your real life is hidden with Christ (Colossians 3:1-4).

So then, you begin to dream God's dreams and share the things that are on His heart. Yes, He has dreams and desires for you that will bring glory to His name. He is at work in you to will and to work for His good pleasure. You make it your ambition to please the Lord. God who begins this good work in you continues His work until it is finally finished.

So what is God working in you? Through the Holy Spirit, the Lord Jesus Christ lives in you and is working in and through you with great plan and purpose. He wants to touch lives in and through you in the place where He has you living for the time that He has you on earth until He takes you home to heaven. This means no matter what age you are, young or old, you live those days with great purpose and intention, for He has something in mind to accomplish in and through you in every season of your life. Oh, this is so incredibly powerful when you begin to grasp it. It means life is never over. Never. You have stepped into the stream of eternal life where you live real life with Jesus from now on into forever in heaven.

I have many uncertainties that are an undercurrent in my life. But the hope and encouragement is that none of it is uncertain to the Lord Jesus. He knows my every need and promises to provide. He is not worried. If He is not worried, then there is no place for worry or anxiety in my life. I can know with certainty that He is going to lead me and take me where I need to go. I am learning to roll every burden onto the Lord for Him to carry instead of me (1 Peter 5:7). After all, it is His life. He surely knows how to handle it all.

The most important thing we can do every day is to draw near to God and spend quiet time alone with Him. In this time, we open His Word to learn from Him, hear Him speak, and then think about what He is saying. We pour out our heart to Him. We're still, knowing He is God, and allowing Him to wash His love through our heart. We must be responsible for the depth of our ministry and life going deep with God and allow Him to be responsible for the breadth of our ministry and life. Our lives will then become a demonstration of what Christ can do in and through those whose hearts are wholly yielded to Him.

With age Thou growest more divine,
More glorious than before,
I fear Thee with a deeper fear,
Because I love Thee more.

With gentle swiftness lead me on,
Dear God! To see Thy face;
And meanwhile in my narrow heart,
Oh make Thyself more space.[11]

FREDERICK FABER

CHRIST IS YOUR LIFE

When Christ, who is your life, is revealed to the whole world,
you will share in all his glory.

COLOSSIANS 3:4 NLT

Charles Thomas Studd, known as C.T. Studd, was born in 1860 in England and grew up in a very wealthy family that had made its fortune as jute and indigo planters in India. He had the very best in education attending Eton college along with his two brothers. While in college, his father was invited by a friend to attend a D.L. Moody revival. He gave his life to Christ and made notable changes including the ending of his involvement in horse racing. One day he invited his sons to spend the day with him. The sons thought they were going to the theater and were quite surprised when the carriage stopped the carriage in front of a hall with the sign, "Moody and Sankey Revival."

It was then that he broke the news to all three boys. "Boys, I might as well tell you now. I've been converted by Mr. Moody. No more racing and gambling. I've found the real thing." Though surprised, none of the boys made the slightest move towards Christ. In fact, C.T. tried to avoid his father as much as possible because salvation was always the subject of the conversation. Many preachers would stay for weekends at the family home. One weekend, a visiting preacher caught C.T. on his way to play cricket and asked him if he was a Christian. The preacher was not convinced with his answer and persisted with presenting Christ and salvation. Finally, C.T. could no longer resist, fell to his knees, and surrendered his life to Christ. He was instantly filled with a joy and peace he had not known. All three brothers came to know Christ that very day.

During this time, C.T. Studd was becoming known as one of the most outstanding cricket players in England. Upon completion of his studies at Eton, he attended Cambridge University. Within two years, he became one of the best cricket players in the world. He was the most well known athlete in England. He was lackluster in his dedication to Christ until he attended Moody-Sankey meetings at Cambridge. Those meetings changed everything for him. The Lord burdened his heart for the salvation of souls and called him to go to China as a missionary. He explained his zeal for missions with these words: "Some want to live within the sound of church or chapel bell; I want to run a rescue shop within a yard of hell."

Six other students joined him in this mission and they became known as the Cambridge Seven. They sailed to Shanghai in 1885, began studying the language, and learning the Chinese culture. Some months later, C.T. inherited $145,000 from his father. He had already decided to give the money to ministries. So he wrote checks totaling the entire amount to D.L. Moody, George Mueller, George Holland, the Salvation Army, and China Inland Mission. D.L. Moody used Studd's donation to start Moody Bible Institute.

Soon after his arrival in Shanghai, he met Priscilla Steward, who later became his wife. They had six children—four girls and two boys. After ten years of service in China, they returned to England for health reasons. C.T. had an asthmatic condition requiring treatment.

Studd became burdened for Africa and ministered there, establishing the Heart Of Africa Mission that later became the Worldwide Evangelization Crusade. Some thought he was wasting his time in a place where missions was such a challenge. He said, "If Jesus Christ be God and died for me, then no sacrifice can be too great for me to make for Him." He continued reaching out in missions to China, India, Africa and the entire unevangelized world. Following his death in Africa in 1931, his son-in-law, Norman Grubb, carried on the leadership of Worldwide Evangelization Crusade, which continues today with 1500 missionaries serving in 51 countries throughout the world.

C.T. Studd possessed an undying commitment to serve Christ and his love for Christ is best expressed in a poem he wrote entitled "Only One Life." The most well known stanza is "Only one life 'twill' soon be past; only what's done for Christ will last." When Christ is your life, those words become your deep conviction as you live each day. Christ orders your priorities and with Christ at the helm of your life, your perspective becomes eternal.

There are certain ramifications of the fact that Christ lives in you. Christ becomes your life. Paul lays it out for us in his letter to the Colossians when he writes: "Since you have been raised to new life with Christ, set your sights on the realities of heaven, where Christ sits in the place of honor at God's right hand. Think about the things of heaven, not the things of earth. For you died to this life, and your real life is hidden with Christ in God. And when Christ, who is your life, is revealed to the whole world, you will share in all his glory. So put to death the sinful, earthly things lurking within you…You used to do these things when your life was still part of this world…Put on your new nature, and be renewed as you learn to know your Creator and become like him" (Colossians 3:1-5, 7,10).

In these verses in Colossians, God is calling us to a new reality, truth, and perspective. The Lord Jesus is calling us to a particular life that is literally out of this world. Our real life is now Christ. He is calling us to live for Him in such a way that when we think about our life only one thing comes to our mind—Christ and the things of heaven. The truth is that your real life is hidden with Christ in God. You are "in Christ." You are safe, my friend, in Him. And in Him, you possess an eternal inheritance that no one can take from you.

Ruth Paxson, Bible teacher, missionary, and author of *Life on the Highest Plane*, writes, "To be in Christ is to share what Christ has. All that Christ possesses, we possess. Every spiritual blessing in Him—joy, peace, victory, power, holiness—is ours here and now." Yes, you are still on earth for a brief moment compared to eternity. But heaven is your reality instead of earth. The things we think are so important here on earth are less meaningful because of the reality of so much more in heaven. Literally, Jesus is calling you to fill your mind with the things of heaven, not the things of the earth. And so, you no longer think primarily of the things of the earth, but instead, you think more about the things of heaven because that's where your real life is. Now I am going to be the first to say that this does not come easily. It takes practice and discipline. The Lord makes it possible through His power within. People have said that you can be so heavenly-minded that you're no earthly good. I believe being heavenly-minded is the only way to be any earthly good.

How can we live with Christ as our life when we have jobs, family, and countless responsibilities? How can we live out the calling to Christ as our life? Christ as our life transcends every other thing. The Lord Jesus Christ is pre-eminent. He is supreme. He is the light for your life even when things are dark. He is the intelligence and provision in your job, the love for your family, and the wisdom and strength in every responsibility. There is a deep realization as you go about your day that *He is here*. He is walking with you and living in you. You walk and talk with Him in everything, no matter what you face in the day. His Word becomes your treasure as you awaken to hear Him calling to you with guidance, encouragement, wisdom, and comfort. All decisions count on His desires and direction. He is the source of everything you need because His resources are yours. You become filled with those things that burden His heart. You pray, "Every day my steps are ordered by You, dear Lord." S.D. Gordon, prolific author and lay minister in the latter part of the 19th century and early part of the 20th century, wrote in his book, *Quiet Talks On John's Gospel*, "Figure Him in big, as big as He is, in all sorts of circumstances and planning and meeting of difficulties." Instead of your weakness, you have His strength. Instead of your own lack of understanding, you may have His wisdom. Instead of your sin, you have His holiness. Instead of your own selfishness, you have His love and compassion. What an amazing exchange takes place when Christ is your life.

Dallas Willard writes, "Christian spirituality as practiced through the ages takes the form of this companionship with Jesus. Spiritual people are not those who engage in certain spiritual practices; they are those who *draw their life from a conversational relationship with God*. They do not live their lives merely in terms of the human order in the visible world; they have 'a life beyond.'"[1] And that life is the heavenly life—Christ Himself.

Do you realize Jesus is present with you right now? Are you walking and talking with Him? Jesus promised, "And be sure of this; I am with you always…" (Matthew 28:20). Dallas Willard explains, "He is with us now, and he speaks with us and we with him. He speaks with us in our heart, which burns from the characteristic impact of His word (see Luke 24:32). His presence with us is, of course, much greater than his words to us. But it is turned into *companionship* only by the actual *communications* we have between us and him, communications that are frequently confirmed by external events as life moves along."[2] So then, this life in Christ is not only possible; it's essential.

This calling from Christ to be our very life as seen in Colossians 3:1-5 takes us deeper with Him than we may have ever gone before. In his book, *The Sufficiency of Christ*, an unknown Christian writes, "Christ must become everything to us not merely in a doctrinal way; He is every aspect of our life. Christ is our completion, our rest, our new beginning, our enjoyment, our joy, our food, our drink, and our satisfaction. Although Christ is universally vast, He is also all the detailed aspects of our practical daily living. Day by day, Jesus is our breath, our life, our everything."

As you read through the gospels and watch Christ in action, those events take on a whole new meaning when you realize this same Lord is in action in and through you. The way He is in those gospels is *the way He is*. He is the explanation of God (John 1:18), the radiance of God's glory, a way He has spoken in these last days, and the exact representation of His nature (Hebrews 1:2-3). This same Lord is now your life. Alan Redpath, 20th century British evangelist, pastor, and author, writes in his book, *Victorious Christian Faith*: "The way Jesus lives among men will necessarily be the way He lives in you and me. He is our life, not just the Patron of our theological system, but our life; not just Lord of our devotions, while we continue to live as religious pagans, but our LIFE."[3]

Jesus, the one and only Son, who is himself God (John 1:18 NIV), will turn your life upside down and work in such a ways as to do great and mighty things in and through you. He will not always be who you want Him to be. Brennan Manning, author, speaker, and Franciscan priest, writes in his book, *The Signature of Jesus*, "There is a tendency in every Christian mind to remake the Man of Galilee, to concoct the kind of Jesus we can live with, to project a Christ who confirms our preferences and prejudices."[4] The truth is that Jesus who lives in you is the real Jesus who walked on this earth over 2000 years ago and who is revealed to us in great depth in the Bible.

Oh, it is an exciting adventure when Jesus is your life. He has things He'd like to do, people He'd like to touch, and places He'd like to go—in and through you and you alone. It's personal for Him as He works in and through your life. I am constantly astonished by certain encounters I would have never chosen. And yet, I am aware the Lord wanted to encourage or challenge or comfort a person in need in and through me. Walking down a hallway where I teach Bible study, an older man asked me what I was doing. "I'm leading a Bible study." He replied, "I'm not interested. I lost my wife a year ago and now I have nothing." I replied, "Sir, God loves you. He wants a relationship with you." I saw tears well up in his eyes. He walked away. The powerful thing about that conversation is that the Lord has great love for that man and wanted to touch his life that day. Every day, the Lord is living His life in and through us, and touching a lost and hurting world.

There is only one you. Unique and special, you are His design for something very special. Just like He made C.T. Studd to motivate others to missions and to take the gospel to the world and burdened his heart for those things, so He has made you for a specific purpose. With Christ as your life, as you live for Christ, you will be filled with very specific burdens and desires to serve. Those burdens and desires are not happenstance, but come from Him, as He intends to live in and through you.

With Christ as your life, you become the recipient of His amazing love. Oh how He loves you. You see His love in His sacrifice for you on the cross. You witness His love in his interactions with His disciples. In John 15:12, Jesus said, "Love one another, just as I have loved you." Those disciples knew He loved them.

The Song of Solomon is thought by more than one commentator to represent the love Jesus has for us. The words in Song of Solomon 2:10-13 give us a whole new view of His passion for us. "My beloved spoke, and said to me: 'Rise up, my love, my fair one, And come away. For lo, the winter is past, the rain is over *and* gone. The flowers appear on the earth; The time of singing has come, And the voice of the turtledove is heard in our land. The fig tree puts forth her green figs, And the vines *with* the tender grapes Give a good smell. Rise up, my love, my fair one, And come away!'" Can you hear His heart for you in these words? I love the response of the beloved in Song of Solomon 2:3-4—"I sat down in his shade with great delight, and his fruit was sweet to my taste. He brought me to the banqueting house, and his banner over me was love." There is such intimacy in these words—a radical intimacy with the Lord Jesus that you are privileged to enjoy all the days of your life on earth and then forever in heaven.

I truly want you to imagine the love of Christ for you as something passionate and all consuming that lasts forever. He cannot wait to spend eternity with you. He is preparing a place for you even now where you will live forever with Him. The temporal things of this world will fade as the permanent nature of your eternal home with Him becomes your own experience. Nothing can separate you from His love according to Romans 8:38-39 and we are "more than conquerors through Him who loved us" (Romans 8:37). Think of His love everyday and you will realize more and more that He is your life.

How can you think more about the things of heaven than the things of earth? We are in the world, but not of the world. Living in the world is a challenge and we need the constant reminder of the eternal perspective where we clearly see the things of heaven. Living in the Word of God is imperative to help us think of the things of heaven. And the Holy Spirit is faithful to bring to your remembrance all that Christ says (John 14:26).

When you step back and look at the lives of great men and women of God down through the centuries, you realize that their decisions in defining moments had a ripple effect often involving hundreds of thousands of lives. C.T. Studd's son-in-law was Norman Grubb who went on to leads hundreds of thousands and write many books. Just think about how God used C.T. Studd to give a large sum of money to D.L. Moody, enabling him to begin Moody Bible Institute. Our decisions right now impact many more than we realize.

Who are you living for—yourself or Christ? Is Christ your life? Or is your life wrapped up in something else? These are important questions because they determine the outcome and influence you will have during your time on earth and for hundreds of years beyond your life. Now is the moment to sit with the Lord and give your life to Him anew, determined to live with Him as your life.

One of my heroes of the faith is Charles Haddon Spurgeon, the great 19th century English pastor, who has been called the Prince of Preachers. Christ was his life and he was used mightily during his time on earth and is still influencing thousands today, including me. Near the end of his life, he said to his wife, "Oh wifey, I have had such a blessed time with my Lord." I think about those words often. They truly describe one whose life is consumed with Christ and passionate for Christ. For Spurgeon, his life was all Christ. Everyday, it's all about living each moment of the day *with* the Lord—thinking about Him, talking with Him, loving Him, learning from Him, listening to Him. It's your calling. Christ is your life.

CALLED TO A PERSON

Philippians 3:8

Let us never lose this vision of our calling to be filled with the Holy Spirit and rely on His power for Christ to live in and through us. I believe we need a revival of just such a life—a Spirit-filled life. We tend to look at people around us to show us how to live. There is very little of the Spirit-filled life occurring on a large scale. So we need to stop looking at people and look to the Lord. Oh, we need to think the thoughts of Christ and hear His words as we open our Bibles to get our perspective and calling from Him.

A PASSION TO KNOW JESUS

Everything else is worthless when compared with the infinite value of knowing Christ Jesus my Lord.

PHILIPPIANS 3:8 NLT

As a young girl, Gladys Aylward, 20th century missionary to China, was consumed with a passion to be an actress. She had very little interest in religious things. However, God had something in mind for her and He was about to give her the first touch of His calling in her life. For an unexplainable reason, she decided to go to a religious meeting. She describes the impact of that one meeting: "There, for the first time, I realized that God had a claim on my life, and I accepted Jesus Christ as my Saviour. I joined the Young Life Campaign, and in one of their magazines I read an article about China that made a terrific impression on me. To realize that millions of Chinese had never heard of Jesus Christ was to me a staggering thought, and I felt we ought to do something about it."[1]

Planted in her heart was a burden for China that remained throughout her life. She worked for a year earning enough money to travel to China with the dream of serving the Lord there for the rest of her life. She joined an older woman in ministry in China, and spent her first years there learning the language, and becoming as much like the Chinese as possible. She had dark hair and was 4 feet 10 inches tall, and wore the same quilted trousers and jacket that the Chinese country women wore. She looked at every circumstance as a door opened by Christ and made the most of those opportunities. The Mandarin, a scholarly bureaucrat in charge of the area where she lived, appointed her as the representative to go from house to house as a foot inspector, ensuring that all women and children in the house were no longer wrapping their feet in the foot-binding tradition of the past.

Gladys Aylward knew that if she could go to all the villages, she would be able to take the good news of Jesus Christ with her into those homes. She told the Mandarin she was going to preach the gospel. He agreed to let her do it, believing if they became Christians they would no longer bind feet. Reflecting on this amazing door of ministry, Gladys writes, "As I look back, I am amazed at the way God opened up the opportunities for service. I had longed to go to China, but never in my wildest dreams had I imagined that God would overrule in such a way that I would be given entrance into every village home [not just every village]; have authority to banish a cruel, horrible custom; have government protection; and be paid to preach the gospel of Jesus Christ as I inspected feet."[2]

Through the years, she thoroughly assimilated with the Chinese, walking and talking just as those around her, so that they listened to everything she had to say. One missionary described how much like the Chinese Gladys had become. "She could spit with the best of them, and when she bit on a piece of gristle at a feast, it shot out of her mouth with utmost precision to where the dog under the table was waiting to snap it up." She gained the respect of everyone around her, including the Mandarin.

One day she came to the Mandarin to talk with him about the child-dealers, criminals who were selling children for money. He told her to turn the other cheek and ignore the practice. She turned to him as she was leaving and said, "I have to inform you, Mandarin, that I did not come to China only to observe your laws. I came for the love of Jesus Christ, and I shall act upon the principles of his teaching, no matter what you say." Some time later, the Mandarin told her how much those words earned his respect and friendship. The Mandarin eventually came to Christ as a result of Gladys Aylward. During that time, she saw a young child for sale at the side of the road. She bought the child with all the money she had. One child led to more until she finally was taking care of more than 100 children.

In 1937 war became a real threat. But Gladys Aylward was firm in her commitment to Christ and living for Him where He had led her. She said, "These are my people, God has given them to me, and I will live or die with them for him and his glory."[3] When war came, Gladys Aylward was forced to flee the area where she lived. And she did not leave alone. She took more than a hundred children with her, trusting Christ every step of the way. She truly did not know how they would survive and only had enough food for two days. However, she knew her Lord. She had spent years learning from Him as He revealed Himself to her, and then living by faith, trusting Him. And when she went on the run with all those children, she relied on Him to care and provide for them. And He did. Once the children were safe and secure, she spent some time in England, then traveled to Taiwan where she served in a ministry with orphans until she stepped from earth to heaven with her Lord. Her story was made famous when it was portrayed in the film, *The Inn of the Sixth Happiness*, starring Ingrid Bergman.

When I first read about Gladys Aylward, I was truly overwhelmed with her single-minded focus on Christ, following Him to the far side of the world. I thought, *How in the world, can someone do what she did? I can't even imagine doing all those things.* Her life challenged me because she only had eyes for the Lord, and wanted only what He wanted. She was bold and courageous because she intimately knew the Lord and knew He reigned supreme. Even when she had nothing, she trusted Him to take care of her in every way. Behind her life of adventure was another life—an interior life of devotion to Christ where she spent time alone with Him each day. Two important books, almost her only possessions, were her Bible and *Daily Light on the Daily Path*. Those two books gave her unlimited time with the Lord in His Word where she could hear Him calling and see Him as He really is.

Her life inspires me even now to a deeper commitment to serve the Lord and a greater passion to know the Lord. *What is your passion in life? What is it that consumes your thoughts and motivates you day by day? Where is your focus?* No time is wasted in drawing near to God. And the result will be a life focused on Christ, filled with His presence, and a passion to serve Him.

I think about Paul's words as he served the Lord Jesus in ministry. He said, "For to me, to live is Christ and to die is gain. But if I am to live on in the flesh, this will mean fruitful labor for me" (Philippians 1:21-22). In those words of Paul I sense a deep passion for Christ, almost an obsession. Paul continued on to say, "Everything else is worthless when compared with the infinite value of knowing Christ Jesus my Lord" (Philippians 3:8 NLT). In those words we see that his passion led to an overall pursuit in life—*knowing Christ*. Even Peter engaged in this pursuit and encouraged others to "grow in the grace and knowledge of our Lord and Savior Jesus Christ" (2 Peter 3:19).

In Paul's words and in the example of Gladys Aylward, we hear another calling from the Lord. He wants us to make knowing Him a lifelong pursuit. I want to ask you: *do you know Him?* Do you realize who Jesus is, what He does, and what He says? He is, as John Flavel, a Puritan pastor in the 1600s wrote, "altogether lovely." Oh yes, He is beautiful. And we have only begun to see His beauty.

I remember when I first came to know the Lord, I was reading in the Psalms. And I came to Psalm 27:4 and was pierced to the heart with David's words. They literally leaped off the page. He wrote, "One thing I have asked from the Lord, that I shall seek: That I may dwell in the house of the Lord all the days of my life, to behold the beauty of the Lord and to meditate in His temple" (Psalm 27:4). David didn't want to just talk about the Lord. He wanted to know Him for himself in a firsthand experience. Psalm 27:4 became my life verse, calling out to me to go deeper with my Lord and pursue a lifelong intimacy with Him. I said to the Lord when I read those words, *Lord, this is what I want for my life. I want to spend the rest of my days knowing You and beholding Your beauty.* And so, the Lord Jesus Christ became the passion of my life. I began to set aside many other things to pursue the one thing: *knowing Him and living for Him.*

The Bible is filled with truth about Christ to help you know Him better. Author and pastor Alistair Begg writes: "We find Christ in all the Scriptures. In the Old Testament he is predicted, in the Gospels he is revealed, in Acts he is preached, in the Epistles he is explained, and in Revelation he is expected."[4] Always remember that if you want to know what God is like, then look at Jesus (Hebrews 1:1-3). Here is just a glimpse of who Jesus is as He has revealed Himself in the Bible. He is…Your Sufficiency (2 Corinthians 12:9), Shepherd (John 10:11), Redeemer (Luke 1:68), Savior (Luke 2:11), Companion (Matthew 28:20), Liberator (John 8:36), Friend (John 15:14), Helper (Philippians 4:13), Peace (John 14:27), Forgiver (1 John 1:9), Purifier (Isaiah 43:25), Intercessor (Romans 8:34), Mediator (1 Timothy 2:5), Sanctifier (Hebrews 10:10), Finisher of Faith (Hebrews 12:2), Lord (Revelation 17:14), King (Revelation 17:14), Life (1 John 5:12), Truth (John 14:6), Hope (1 Timothy 1:1), Light of the World (John 9:5), Master (Matthew 12:8), Hiding Place (Psalm 32:7), Protector (Psalm 32:7), Wonderful Counselor, Mighty God, Eternal Father, Prince of Peace (Isaiah 9:6), Shield (Psalm 3:3) Victory (Exodus 15:2), Comforter (Revelation 21:4), Joy (Psalm 43:4), Abiding Place (Acts 17:28), Lover of your soul (Jeremiah 31:3), Your Bridegroom (Isaiah 62:5), Your All in All (Colossians 3:11), and Your Everything (Colossians 2:10).

Again I ask: *do you know Jesus?* Every time you learn one of these truths about Jesus, that truth implies something about you, and requires something of you. For example, when you learn that He is your Shepherd, the truth implies that you are a sheep, and that He will care for you as one of His flock. When you learn He is your Helper, it implies you need help, and that He will help you in every circumstance. You cannot trust what you don't know. And so, the more you know Christ, the more you will trust Him. He is truly everything you need for every circumstance of life.

Jesus is a real Person—the Person of God—who can be known. He has personality, heart, sensitivity, compassion, and a tender touch to the soul. I imagine Him walking with the Father outside in the beautiful surrounding countryside near Bethany where his friends Mary, Martha and Lazarus lived. I think about Him sitting somewhere alone, with the wildlife and everything else He created—listening to the birds sing their songs and watching the animals in their habitat. I wonder if they ventured near, instinctively knowing they were safe in the presence of their Creator. The Lord's beauty is all around us and is within us where He lives as He makes His home in our hearts. And when we take time with Him, He shows us wondrous glimpses of His glory, giving us a window into a beauty that sometimes only He knows and sees. He loves to share those surprises and reveal Himself to us. And in all these moments, our love relationship with Him grows deep and we are moved to say along with Paul, "For me to live is Christ."

He is winsome, joyful, and so much more than the images we often see of Him in art and film. Bruce Marchiano was given the privilege to play the role of Jesus in *The Gospel According to Matthew*, a movie with the complete text of the first gospel in the New Testament. He remarked about his journey in discovering Jesus, that he was "quite simply blown away with the unique and extraordinary experience of portraying Jesus." As he walked where Jesus walked through the events of His life, he found Jesus to be more than he ever dreamed or hoped He could be, and in the process, he fell in love with Jesus. He says Jesus was a "Man among men."[5]

Jesus wants to be our first love. He is calling us to a great love. He holds the pre-eminent place in our heart. In fact, in His letter to the church at Ephesus in Revelation, Jesus wrote about how impressed He was with their perseverance. But He continued on to say that He had one thing against them: "you have left your first love" (Revelation 2:4). These words loom large on the horizon for all believers, especially in this day where our hours can be wasted away on things that have nothing to do with the Lord. The Lord knows where we are with Him. There is no act or masquerade with Him. He sees past it all the way to our hearts. Could His words to Ephesus be said to us also? May it not be so! May we resolve, with Paul, to "count everything as loss compared with the priceless privilege of knowing Christ" (Philippians 3:8 wms).

Basilea Schlink was a 20th century German religious leader and writer and a nun with the Evangelical Sisterhood of Mary. I first learned of her when I was in seminary. There was a very special retreat organized by one of the professors and part of the recommended reading included *My All For Him* by Basilea Schlink. I had never heard of this book or the author and was intrigued. I got the book and began living in the words. What I found in the pages of this book was a rare passion for Christ. I thought as I read her words, *I love this woman's heart for the Lord. I want that kind of heart.* She believes the love between Christ and us is "bridal"—He loves us as our Bridegroom and we love Him as His bride (see Mark 2:18-20, John 3:29-30, 2 Corinthians 11:2). Think about that for a moment. *Does your heart beat for Christ in that way?* He is calling you to that depth of love and intimate relationship. He looks at you as His bride. *Do you look at Him as your Bridegroom?*

Schlink writes, "He yearns for us to love Him. But it is a special kind of love He seeks. It is the love that is reflected in the relationship between an earthly bride and her bridegroom. An exclusive love. A love that tolerates no rivals. A love that gives the beloved, the bridegroom, first place. As the heavenly Bridegroom, Jesus lays claim to such first love. Because He loves us so dearly, He longs to have the whole of us. Jesus gave Himself unreservedly for us. Now He yearns for us to give ourselves completely to Him, with all that we are and have, so that He can truly be our first love."[6]

Do you sense the calling of Jesus to passionately love Him? Dwight Hervey Small, 20th century pastor, speaker, and author, in his book, *No Rival Love*, describes the call of Jesus to love Him, "Jesus doesn't ask that we love Him only, but that we love Him supremely—with a love that has no rival. Our love for Him must be our highest love, that which informs and controls every other love."[7] The more you know Jesus, the more you will love Him. You will be more sensitive to rival loves, lay them aside, and draw ever nearer to Christ. He will become, more and more, your supreme love.

Ray Vander Laan, founder of That The World May Know Ministries, has taken over 10,000 people to Israel on his study tours. These tours became the foundation of the different educational films of the *That The World May Know* series produced and released by Focus on the Family. I remember watching one of the films and learning something that changed my whole view of Christ. Ray Vander Laan explained that in the Jewish culture when a man wanted to marry a woman, he would go to the father for permission. Once he gained permission he would make his offer to the woman. If she said yes, then he would go back to his family's home to prepare the place where they would live together. She would have to wait patiently, not knowing when he would arrive to take her to their home together. He loved her. He was preparing the place for them. And she was getting herself ready to be with him as his bride to live with him forever. This is the picture behind the words of Jesus in John 14:2 when He told His disciples, "Don't let your hearts be troubled. Trust in God, and trust also in me. There is more than enough room in my Father's home. If this were not so, would I have told you that I am going to prepare a place for you? When everything is ready, I will come and get you, so that you will always be with me where I am" (John 14:1-3 NLT).

Just think, dear friend, about what this implies for you and the Lord. *Do you realize that the Lord looks at you as His beloved bride? Do you know that your Lord is preparing the home you will share together?* He is really that personal and interested in you. And He is with you even now through the Holy Spirit, empowering you and leading you safely home. He will not leave you alone, for you are His beloved and belong to Him. He loves and cherishes you. It is an incomprehensible mystery how He is in us now and we are in Him; yet it is true. He longs for your love as you walk with Him, day by day. He wants you to know Him and will reveal Himself to you more and more as you spend time together. He is calling you nearer, always nearer. So draw near to Him even now expressing this prayer, *Lord, I want to know You. I live for You.*

Frances Ridley Havergal, an English poet and hymn-writer in the 1800s, went for a visit one day to a home filled with mostly non-Christians. And those who knew Christ did not seem to be very committed to Him. She was so burdened for the people that she prayed a simple prayer: *Lord, give me all in this house.* She saw the Lord move in every one of their lives. His work was so profound to her that it became a defining moment in her own life. She renewed her commitment to Christ with the words of a hymn that has become one of the most beloved of all time. As you think about your own desire to know and love Christ, may these words become your life prayer.

Take my life and let it be
Consecrated, Lord, to Thee.
Take my moments and my days,
Let them flow in endless praise.

Take my hands and let them move
At the impulse of Thy love.
Take my feet and let them be
Swift and beautiful for Thee.

Take my voice and let me sing,
Always, only for my King.
Take my lips and let them be
Filled with messages from Thee.

Take my silver and my gold,
Not a mite would I withhold.
Take my intellect and use
Every pow'r as Thou shalt choose.

Take my will and make it Thine,
It shall be no longer mine.
Take my heart, it is Thine own,
It shall be Thy royal throne.

Take my love, my Lord, I pour
At Thy feet its treasure store.
Take myself and I will be
Ever, only, all for Thee.

FRANCES RIDLEY HAVERGAL, TAKE MY LIFE AND LET IT BE, 1874

THE WIND IN YOUR SAILS

Be filled with the Holy Spirit.
EPHESIANS 5:18 NLT

My husband and I were sitting in the stern of a beautiful sailboat with the sun just setting to the west off Lahaina, Hawaii. I felt this queasiness begin to take over within and knew I was starting to get seasick. We had not even left the dock. I told my husband, "David, I am feeling really sick." He looked at me with concern, then suggested, "Try looking at the horizon," thinking it would go away.

Well, I tried the idea of looking at the horizon. After five minutes, I decided to look for another answer to my problem. I went below to the place where the crew was getting everything ready for our wonderful sunset sailboat excursion.

I said, "I'm starting to feel seasick. Do you have anything that can help me."

"Lady, we haven't even left the dock!"

"I know—what can I do?"

"Dramamine cocktails. Drink one." He pointed over to the bar area where there was a group of little cups of Dramamine on a tray.

I walked over, drank one, and within about twenty minutes I began to feel better.

So then we launched out on our wonderful sailing adventure. We just cruised along on the coast beyond Lahaina harbor for about a half an hour. Then, all of a sudden, the sails caught the wind, and with great force, the sailboat lurched forward, and it was as though we were flying across the waves. These are the moments those captains live for, and ours was very excited. He exclaimed, "Yee Hah!" and sounded like a cowboy in some western movie.

I have never forgotten the power of the wind in the sails of our boat and the strong movement across the water. There is a nautical term, "bearaway," that means "to change the course of a ship so that she can run before the wind." For that to happen, it is imperative that the sails are set to catch the wind, harnessing the power so that the boat can move with the wind.

Just before Jesus ascended into heaven following the crucifixion and resurrection, He gave some final instructions to His disciples. First, He said, "And now I will send the Holy Spirit, just as my Father promised. But stay here in the city until the Holy Spirit comes and fills you with power from heaven" (Luke 24:49 NLT). Jesus was telling those disciples to wait for His power. And then, His last words reminded them of this power and His assignment for them as they lived in the world. "But you will receive power when the Holy Spirit has come upon you; and you shall be My witnesses both in Jerusalem, and in all Judea and Samaria, and even to the remotest part of the earth" (Acts 1:8). He also promised in John 14:12-14, "I tell you the truth, anyone who believes in me will do the same works I have done, and even greater works, because I am going to be with the Father. You can ask for anything in my name, and I will do it, so that the Son can bring glory to the Father. Yes, ask me for anything in my name, and I will do it!" Jesus was promising a life of power that would come from Him in us through the work of the Holy Spirit.

This Holy Spirit power is part of the calling in our lives. However, many seem to miss this calling. In fact, I would go so far to say that these words from Jesus seem to be fading into the background more and more in many churches. Some churches are more focused on "lights, camera, and action" than Father, Son, and Holy Spirit. It is amazing how many people try to do God's work in their own power without the Holy Spirit.

Jesus is calling us to live in His power, the power of the Holy Spirit, moment by moment every day of our lives. He is calling us to live a Spirit-filled life. This is how He lives His life in and through you. He does it through the power of the Holy Spirit. He calls out to us with these words, "Don't be drunk with wine, because that will ruin your life. Instead, be filled with the Holy Spirit" (Ephesians 5:18 NLT). To be filled with the Spirit is to be controlled and empowered by Christ Himself. The Holy Spirit is, as R.A. Torrey, the great 19th-20th century evangelist and pastor, aptly described, like a fire in our souls.[1] And that fire in our souls will spread the love of Christ everywhere. When you are filled with His Spirit, you have yielded control of your life to the Lord Jesus, and you have surrendered the throne of your life to Him. He rules and reigns in your life, leading and guiding you. You are literally setting the sail of your life to catch the Holy Spirit's power and *run before the wind.*[2]

Many years ago when I was working at a church as Director of Women's Ministries, I had to learn how to turn on the sound system. It was a complicated set of switches and buttons. I followed every step in my notes, and then turned the switch for the whole system to "On." Nothing happened. *Now what am I going to do?* I went back through all my notes, making sure I had done everything right. I tried again and still, nothing happened. Frustrated, I went to one of the tech guys, "Jeff, I can't get the sound system to work. I did everything I was supposed to do and it's just not working. Can you help me?" He checked out everything on the system. Then, he looked behind the sound system, and turned to me with a huge grin on his face. He held up the power cord and said, "Catherine, you do have to plug in to the power." I started laughing. But there was a profound lesson in that experience and I have never forgotten it. How many times do we try something in our own strength without turning to the Lord for His power and His performance? Andrew Murray writes, "We want to get possession of the Power and use it. God wants the Power to get possession of us and use us."[3]

The New Testament church in Acts is a living testimony to the power and work of the Holy Spirit in average men and women. We see in beautiful ways how the Lord Jesus continued His work in and through those first disciples and accomplished even more than He did during His three years of ministry prior to the crucifixion. With the Holy Spirit indwelling and filling us, the Lord Jesus is able to live His life in and through hundreds of thousands of Christians worldwide. When you read the book of Acts, you notice that the disciples are no longer so afraid that they are running for their lives as they did when Jesus was arrested. Instead, they are bold and courageous, sacrificing all to tell others the good news about Jesus Christ. There is only one way to account for the change. They were not operating in their own strength, but in the power of the Holy Spirit. There was Someone else living supernaturally in and through their lives. They were transformed. What we witness in their lives is Jesus doing a mighty work in and through them in the power of the Holy Spirit. He wants to make the same kind of transformation in us and do the same kinds of extraordinary works through us.

A defining moment came soon after Pentecost when the disciples were filled with the Holy Spirit. Some in the crowd who witnessed the move of the Holy Spirit in the lives of the disciples ridiculed them, saying "They're just drunk, that's all" (Acts 2:13 NLT). Peter stepped forward and shouted to the crowd, "Listen carefully, all of you…" Peter proceeded to give his first sermon. Here is an uneducated simple fisherman boldly articulating the person and work of Jesus Christ to a crowd of thousands. He shared the good news of forgiveness of sins and the power of the Holy Spirit. He closed his sermon with these words, "So let everyone in Israel know for certain that God has made this Jesus, whom you crucified, to be both Lord and Messiah" (Acts 2:36). Peter must have been surprised by the boldness and eloquence flowing out of him. It wasn't him, but Christ in him through the power of the Holy Spirit. This crowd was pierced to the heart and asked, "What must we do?" Three thousand people came to Christ, believed, and were baptized that day.

Just think about the impact of that one event. Now the followers of Jesus were seeing Christ in action across entire crowds and the numbers multiplied with very little effort on their part. This was clearly the work of Christ in His power. They had seen it before. They had watched Jesus move through crowds of people, touching and changing lives everywhere. And now, Jesus was at work again. They recognized the fruit of His labor in their midst. It was clearly not those disciples doing the work. It was all Jesus.

And this is what will be true in our own life. It will be *all* Jesus. Let us never lose this vision of our calling to be filled with the Holy Spirit and rely on His power for Christ to live in and through us. I believe we need a revival of just such a life—a Spirit-filled life. We tend to look at people around us to show us how to live. There is very little of the Spirit-filled life occurring on a large scale. So we need to stop looking at people and look to the Lord. Oh, we need to think the thoughts of Christ and hear His words as we open our Bibles to get our perspective and calling from Him.

So how can you be filled with the Holy Spirit? You need to set the sail of your life to catch His life-giving wind flowing in and through you. Jesus spoke of way to this life when He said, "Anyone who is thirsty may come to me! Anyone who believes in me may come and drink! For the Scriptures declare, 'Rivers of living water will flow from his heart'" (John 7:37-38). Once you receive Christ and enter into a relationship with Him, you are born again spiritually (John 3:7-8), and are indwelt by the Holy Spirit. If you want His rivers of living water to flow, then go to Jesus and ask Him to fill you with His Spirit. Confess your sins and surrender control of your life to Him, continually and moment by moment (1 John 1:9). He promises to fill you with the Holy Spirit, empowering you in life.

How can you tell if you are filled with the Holy Spirit? The fruit of the Spirit-filled life is "love, joy, peace, patience, kindness, goodness, faithfulness, gentleness, and self-control" and will literally flow from you (Galatians 5:22-23 NLT). You will see the life of Jesus at work in and through you. You will know, more and more, that what you are seeing is not you at work, but Him. You will experience personal, spiritual revival as the Lord works out His plan and purpose in you. You will notice opportunities opening up for you to express love and kindness to someone else. You may even be asked to stand up in front of a group and teach the Bible or tell your story of how you came to Christ. Don't be surprised at how God may choose to use you in life.

One of the great results of the wind of the Holy Spirit on the move is revival. Brian Edwards, an author and minister in the United Kingdom, defines revival as "a going out of God among his people, and an awareness of God laying hold of the community."[4] The history of the church gives evidence of certain times when God has poured out His Spirit and swept through whole groups of people with a mighty wind reviving their hearts, filling them with a new spiritual desire, giving a passion for worship and prayer, a conviction of sin, a longing for Christ, and a hunger for holiness. When God starts a revival, He is the One who makes a mighty move and initiates the work.

In the Welsh Revival of 1904-1905, responding to a preacher's prayer, "Lord, bend us," a young 25-year old man named Evan Roberts, who had been working the coal mines in Wales, walked up to the front of the room and cried out, "Lord, bend me!" He said that at the very moment of his prayer, he was set on fire within to go the length and breadth of Wales to tell of the Savior. His preaching was unorthodox as he would walk up and down the aisles in churches. It has been said that all of Wales was like a prayer meeting and sometimes preaching was out of the question as people only wanted to draw near to God. When the Spirit of God sweeps through your life, He will draw you and others to Christ.

Jonathan Edwards, an American revivalist and one of the key figures in the Great Awakening of 1730-1755, wrote a sermon entitled "Sinners In The Hands of an Angry God" and delivered it at a church in Enfield, Connecticut on July 8, 1741. It is said that he simply stood in front of the people and held the papers up in front of his face, reading what he had written word-for-word. There was no drama in the delivery. But when the Spirit of God is at work, there is no need for a performance. He was unable to finish the sermon because people were moaning, shrieking, and crying out for salvation. It is a happy day when the Spirit of God convicts you of sin, because then you will turn to the Lord.

Perhaps one of the greatest moves of the Holy Spirit occurred on the Island of Lewis during the years of 1949-1953. It is difficult to say exactly when it began, but most likely in the small cottage of two obscure and unknown women, Peggy and Christine Smith, who decided to pray. Peggy was eighty-four and blind, and her sister was eight-two with crippling arthritis. God's Spirit had burdened them for the people who lived in their area and they were determined to pray until God sent revival. A point must be made that you are never too old to be filled with the Holy Spirit and used by Him to impact hundreds of thousands of lives. There are no excuses to sit on the sidelines and no retirement in the kingdom of God. One person has prayed: *I am a disciple of Jesus. I must go till He comes, give till I drop, preach till all know, and work till He stops me. And when He comes for His own, He will have no problem recognizing me—my banner will be clear.*

God answered the prayers of the Smith sisters and brought Duncan Campbell, a Scottish preacher to Lewis to share the gospel of Christ with the people there. Duncan Campbell, in his eyewitness account of this move of God, shares "When I went to the door of the church I saw a congregation of approximately six hundred people. Where had they come from? What had happened? I believe that very night God swept by in Pentecostal power, the power of the Holy Ghost. And what happened in the early days of the Apostles was now happening in the parish of Barvas." Campbell made it clear that there were no special efforts of man. God simply swept across the island by the power of His Spirit. People were falling on the ground repenting to the Lord of their sins, then making their way to church. There were no flyers sent out and no meetings announced. Hundreds of thousands of men and women came to the church, desperate for God. The fruit of that revival was easily seen. Bars closed and those in attendance became members of the church and joined the choir. All businesses are closed on Sundays even to this present day as people attend church to worship God.

Perhaps even now God longs to start a revival in you. Before there is ever widespread revival,

---

there is personal revival in a single heart. And maybe the heart that God is going to revive and set on fire in a new and deeper way through His Spirit is yours. Personal spiritual revival is "a quickening of heart and soul by God, imparting whatever is necessary to sustain one's spiritual life and restore one to his or her original purpose in life as ordained by God."[5] This is the kind of revival we need every day through the work of the Holy Spirit in our lives.

I encourage you to slip out of your chair, get on your knees, pray with an open Bible, and ask God to start a revival in your heart. Pray *Lord set my heart on fire*. Cry out with the words of the psalmist *Revive me, O LORD* (Psalm 119:107). *Fill me with Your Spirit*. Then get ready. It is very possible that the world has yet to see what God can do in and through one whose heart is wholly yielded to Him. May He do a great and mighty work in and through you.

> I stood on the shore beside the sea;
> The wind from the West blew fresh and free,
> While past the rocks at the harbor's mouth
> The ships went North, and the ships went South,
> And some sailed out on an unknown quest,
> And some sailed into the harbor's rest;
> Yet ever the wind blew out from the West.
>
> I said to one who had sailed the sea
> That this was a marvel unto me;
> For how can the ships go safely forth,
> Some to the South and some to the North,
> Far out to sea on the golden quest,
> Or in to the harbor's calm and rest,
> And ever the wind blew out of the West?
>
> The sailor smiled as he answered me,
> "Go where you will when you're on the sea,
> Though head winds baffle and flaws delay,
> You can keep the course by night and day,
> Drive with the breeze or against the gale;
> It will not matter what winds prevail,
> For all depends on the set of the sail."

Voyager soul on the sea of life,
O'er waves of sorrow and sin and strife,
When fogs bewilder and foes betray,
Steer straight on your course from day to day;
Though unseen currents run deep and swift,
Where rocks are hidden and sandbars shift,
All helpless and aimless, you need not drift.

Oh, set your sail to the heavenly gale,
And then, no matter what winds prevail,
No reef shall wreck you, no calm delay,
No mist shall hinder, no storm shall stay;
Though far you wander and long you roam,
Though salt sea-spray and o'er white sea-foam,
No wind that can blow but shall speed you home.[6]

Annie Johnson Flint, The Set of the Sail

THE MAGNIFICENT STORY OF YOU

I have made them for my glory. It was I who created them.
ISAIAH 43:7

John Bunyan, in the 1600s, was a simple tinker in Bedford, Bedfordshire, England, trained to travel from place to place, fixing pans and other metal utensils. He was a rough kind of man and grew up godless and unschooled, seemingly having no interest in spiritual things. He swore so much that people were terrorized in his presence. Had you known him then, you may have wondered, "Can God do anything with John Bunyan?"

One day Bunyan heard some women talking about God, and he drew near to listen in on their conversation—he describes his experience: "But upon a day, the good providence of God did cast me to Bedford, to work on my calling; and in one of the streets of that town, I came where there were three or four poor women sitting at a door in the sun, and talking about the things of God; and being now willing to hear them discourse, I drew near to hear what they said, for I was now a brisk talker also myself in the matters of religion, but now I may say, I heard, but I understood not; for they were far above, out of my reach; for their talk was about a new birth, the work of God on their hearts, also how they were convinced of their miserable state by nature; they talked how God had visited their souls with his love in the Lord Jesus, and with what words and promises they had been refreshed, comforted, and supported against the temptations of the devil."[1]

Bunyan was interested and wanted to know more. God was calling him and would soon have him for His own. After listening to the women talk about God, Bunyan set out to be a better person and gain approval from God. He reformed his speech, cursed less, and people were impressed. He began to read the Bible to try and gain a vast knowledge of the Scriptures, but had no understanding of anything he was reading. No matter how hard he tried, he could not control his emotions or thoughts, and was often given to evil. Finally, he became so discouraged that he told God to go if He wanted. Well, the Lord had no intention of letting Bunyan go, for He had great things in mind for him and loved him.

God used the Bible through the Holy Spirit to finally open Bunyan's eyes and heart. One day, Bunyan realized for the very first time, through 1 Corinthians 1:30, that it was Jesus Christ and His righteousness that set him free. He said, "For by this scripture, I saw that the man Christ Jesus, as he is distinct from us, as touching his bodily presence, so he is our righteousness and sanctification before God."[2] It was not about Bunyan's works, but Christ and His work on Bunyan's behalf. What a life-changing thought for Bunyan. He realized that Christ became for him righteousness, wisdom, and sanctification. His self-image and identity were changed forever as he entered into a relationship with Christ.

Everything had changed for John Bunyan and now he had one obsession: *Christ and only Christ*. His friends and family urged him to preach the Word of God to them. At first he was afraid, but then he became convinced that God was calling him to give others the Word. God used Bunyan as a preacher in such a powerful way, that the great theologian John Owen loved to attend his services just to hear him preach. He remarked to King Charles II of England, "May it please your Majesty, could I possess the tinker's ability for preaching, I would willingly relinquish all my learning." After Bunyan came to Christ, he discovered that he possessed this newfound ability to preach. He was Bible-saturated to the point that Spurgeon noted, after reading Bunyan's work, *The Pilgrim's Progress*, "'Why, this man is a living Bible!' Prick him anywhere—his blood is Bibline, the very essence of the Bible flows from him. He cannot speak without quoting a text, for his very soul is full of the Word of God. I commend his example to you, beloved."

The law of the land forbade Bunyan to preach as an independent of the Anglican Church to the extent that he was imprisoned for more than twelve years. This too, played exactly into the story God had in mind for Bunyan. God was now calling this simple tinker from Bedford to write in prison. During the twelve-year imprisonment, he wrote his spiritual autobiography, *Grace Abounding to the Chief of Sinners*. During another six-month imprisonment, he wrote *The Pilgrim's Progress*, one of the most influential works ever written. Translated into over 200 languages, *The Pilgrim's Progress* is a powerful allegory. Just two years after it was written, it ranked second only to the King James Bible as the most important book in evangelical Protestant households.

Why do I share the story of Bunyan? I believe he is such a great example for us because his story is impossible and magnificent at the same time. Here is an unschooled tinker who was made brand new in Christ and designed to do more than he could imagine through the power of the Holy Spirit. Because of Christ, he became someone new and different than he had been before. He was given new gifts and talents, new spiritual wealth and possessions, an eternal future, and blessed with every spiritual blessing in the heavenly places in Christ. And God told a unique story in and through his life to display His glory.

Dear friend, God has designed you with great purpose. According to Psalm 139:13-14 you are fearfully and wonderfully made as He wove you in your mother's womb. He designed you for His glory. "I have made them for my glory. It was I who created them" (Isaiah 43:7 NLT). Your life is meant to give honor to the Lord. You shine for Him as you live out the life He calls you to live. No wonder Jesus said, "Let your good deeds shine out for all to see, so that everyone will praise your heavenly Father" (Matthew 5:16 NLT). Everything we do is for the glory of the Lord (1 Corinthians 10:31). Paul elaborates on the purpose of our story in his prayer for the Colossian church: "We ask God to give you complete knowledge of his will and to give you spiritual wisdom and understanding. Then the way you live will always honor and please the Lord, and your lives will produce every kind of good fruit. All the while, you will grow as you learn to know God better and better" (Colossians 1:10-12 NLT).

Just like John Bunyan, God has a unique life in mind for you and a story to tell in and through you. He is calling you to the story that He is writing in and through you. Will you say *yes* to the story of your life? That story is designed to bring great glory to God and please Him in every way. He wants to tell a story that you may not even envision at this time in your life. Paul explains, "you are a letter of Christ, cared for by us, written not with ink but with the Spirit of the living God, not on tablets of stone but on tablets of human hearts" (2 Corinthians 3:3). Your story is filled with victories, losses, success, and even failure. Sometimes it seems as though everything is against you. There are many unexplainable bends in the road that come your way. And when the story is not obvious and life becomes almost impossible, then our faith is challenged. These times are not by accident and can be expected during certain seasons of our story (John 16:33 NLT).

So when trials and sorrows become part of our story, we may wonder what God is up to. You can know that whatever has come your way is not a surprise to God. When this happens, make it a point to draw near and know your God in a deeper way. "Those who know your name trust in you, for you, O Lord, do not abandon those who search for you" (Psalm 9:10 NLT). In difficult times, you can know that God is at work in ways well beyond the realm of your knowledge and understanding. "'My thoughts are nothing like your thoughts,' says the Lord. 'And my ways are far beyond anything you could imagine. For just as the heavens are higher than the earth, so my ways are higher than your ways and my thoughts higher than your thoughts'" (Isaiah 55:9-10 NLT). Even when you don't understand, you can know God is at work for your good and for His glory (Romans 8:28). And He will continue to call you through His Word to help you grow and lead you on in His plan for your life. It's a custom-designed course of growth laid out by God and matching the very story He is writing in and through your life.

Now, what am I to do? thought the young woman of twenty-six, holding the hands of her two young children, after watching her husband of five years walk out of their Phoenix house forever. "How will I make it?" she cried out to God. Packing her bags, she took her children and went back to stay with her parents in Pennsylvania for a few weeks, trying to make a decision about her future. Tears flowed easily down her face. "Mother, what's wrong?" cried her little girl, only five years old at the time. She looked into the face of her daughter with great love, completely at a loss. One day, her parents sat her down said, "Elizabeth, if you are not going to step up, be strong and take care of these two children, then we are going to adopt them and raise them right here." "No, you can't," she replied instantly and with determination. "God has given these two children to me, I'm their mother, and I will give them the best life I can." What she did next was only possible by the strength and grace of God. *I can do two things: teach and play the piano*, she thought. The ideas and actions were borne at the same moment. She would apply for a teaching job, go back to school, get a Master's Degree in education, and earn extra money giving piano lessons and playing the organ at local churches in Phoenix, Arizona.

That's the story of how my Mother used all her gifts and earned enough money to give my brother and me many wonderful opportunities in life, including college. Her great bend in the road could have been the end of the road but she surrendered to God in all of the trial. God wove it together into the story of her life. She loved us with an unconditional love, raised us to believe in God, and live for Him. She is a great hero of the faith to me.

Will you receive certain bends in the road from the Lord as part of your own story? I have to ask you that question because sometimes we get caught up in one-dimensional thinking. So many events that you would rather avoid or escape altogether may be the very chapters in your story that the Spirit of God is writing on the tablet of your heart. We sometimes wish away parts of our lives that are actually part of the plot and message that God is writing. We have something in our life that we don't want, and fail to realize that God is weaving it together for something beautiful that will bring Him great glory. This is where, once again, we need to say *yes* to the story of our life that the Lord is writing.

"We're going to move *where*?" I asked my husband many years ago. "We're leaving beautiful San Diego and moving to Palm Desert in the very hot, nowhere, and sandy desert of California?" My mind began to swirl with imaginings. *God, You are making a huge mistake!* I thought to myself. *If I go there, my ministry will totally end forever. I don't know anyone there. I don't want to go, Lord! I don't want to go!*

Some months later, the move accomplished, I sat in the same large leather chair in our new living room in Palm Desert, tears freely flowing, day after day. I was clearly deeply depressed. "I've lost the smile of God," I told my friends in San Diego. "Catherine, we'll pray for you that you get back the smile of God," they would say. No one really knew what to make of my despair. Neither did I.

After a few months, I said to myself, *Enough is enough, Catherine*. And I made a decision. *I've got to open the pages of my Bible and live there. I need to give God an opportunity to speak to me.* The only appealing place in the Bible at that time for me was the Psalms. I began in Psalm 84. The first day of my journey in the Psalms, I came to Psalm 84:5, "Blessed are those whose strength is in you, whose hearts are set on pilgrimage."

Pilgrimage! My heart is to be set on pilgrimage! My life is a pilgrimage! I thought about the ramifications of that one word describing my life. God was calling out to me in that verse, opening my eyes to see that our life is a pilgrimage and that God is writing a story as He leads us to our home in heaven. I realized He didn't want me ever to sink my roots deeply in places or the things of this world. He also showed me that I have to be ready for Him to take me in new directions as He writes the story of my life. Oh, this was an eye-opening lesson for me. He completely changed my attitude and perspective and I went on to discover many amazing adventures in this new place where He had led me. It was actually here in the desert that I began writing books and leading women in full-time ministry. God had these chapters of my life already planned, but it took a bend in the road that became a trial for me to write the next chapters.

There are so many different bends in the road that are moments of trial like loss, illness, and financial devastation. So what will help us in these moments of trial to hear His voice calling us, to help us get His eternal perspective, take the bend in the road, and continue on and trust God in the difficult chapters of our story? Draw near to God, open the pages of His Word where you will hear Him calling, and then allow His promises to give you His eternal perspective.

Here are some encouragements from God's Word to give God time to develop your story as you live in the world. He wants you to do what is right, love mercy, and walk humbly with Him (Micah 6:8). He encourages you to focus your ambitions on leading a quiet life, attending to your own business, and working with your hands (1 Thessalonians 4:11). And then, humble yourself under His mighty hand so that He may lift you up at the proper time (1 Peter 5:6). Always remember that God's timing is much different than ours, so it is very important to wait on the Lord (Psalm 27:14). He is at work in you both to will and to work for His good pleasure (Philippians 2:13). "After you have suffered for a little while, the God of all grace, who called you to His eternal glory in Christ, will Himself perfect, confirm, strengthen and establish you" (1 Peter 5:10).

Certainly Bunyan, who was unschooled, had no idea he would be a preacher, teacher, and writer with works and messages that would minister to theologians and intellectuals worldwide down through the centuries. He never considered being a preacher until people started asking him to give them the Word of God. God used friends in his life to weave preaching into his story. He also most likely never imagined writing one of the greatest books of all time. And Bunyan would never have chosen more than twelve years in prison as part of his own story. And yet, prison became the workroom of God where He guided Bunyan to write *The Pilgrim's Progress*, one of the greatest works of all time. He has planned more than we thought and is "able, through his mighty power at work within us, to accomplish infinitely more than we might ask or think" (Ephesians 3:20 NLT).

We never know all that God has planned for our lives. But He knows. And He is causing everything to work together even now to bring about His plan and purpose. We may never see all the results during our time on earth. But heaven, dear friend, will tell the story of all that God has done in and through you, His precious and beloved child. And the magnificent story will bring great glory to God.

Thank you for making me so wonderfully complex!
Your workmanship is marvelous—How well I know it.
You watched me as I was being formed in utter seclusion,
As I was woven together in the dark of the womb.
You saw me before I was born.
Every day of my life was recorded in your book.
Every moment was laid out before a single day had passed.

Psalm 139:14-16 NLT

Every Christian should be a clearly written and legible tract,
circulating for the glory of God. Men will not read
the evidences for Christianity contain in learned treatises,
but they are keen to read us.[3]
F.B. Meyer

THE BEAUTIFUL MASTERPIECE OF YOU

For we are God's masterpiece. He has created us anew in Christ
Jesus, so we can do the good things he planned for us long ago.
EPHESIANS 2:10 NLT

Lilias Trotter, a missionary with the Algiers Mission Band, was born with a natural artistic gift. She had an eye to see beauty all around her. She grew up in London in the 1800s in a wealthy family. Her father died when she was twelve and she grew deeper in spiritual things, turning often to God in prayer. When she was in her twenties, John Ruskin, the leading figure of the day in the art world, discovered Lilias and took her under his wing. He became her art mentor in watercolor painting. Lilias was passionate about her art and spent hours refining her skill under Ruskin's tutelage. However, she also discovered a passion for going out in the streets of London and sharing the gospel of Christ to those in great need.

Ruskin felt she was distracted and pushed her to make a decision about her art. He laid it all out for her. "If you will devote yourself to art," he said, "you will be the greatest living painter and do things that will be immortal."[1] Lilias realized she could only have one Master and wrote, "I see as clear as daylight now, I cannot give myself to painting in the way he [Ruskin] means and continue still to seek first the Kingdom of God and His Righteousness."[2]

Lilias was just beginning to truly discover who she was. She recognized the importance of "focus." She wrote, "It is easy to find out whether our lives are focused, and if so, where the focus lies. Where do our thoughts settle when consciousness comes back in the morning? Where do they swing back when the pressure is off during the day? . . . Dare to have it out with God . . . and ask Him to show you whether or not all is focused on Christ and His glory. . ."[3] She focused on Jesus and looked to Him to lead and guide her. She still loved her art and practiced it throughout the course of her ministry. But her focus was on Christ without any distraction.

Ultimately the Lord led her to a lifelong ministry in Algiers where she reached out to the Arab world with the love of Christ. Every day in her quiet time with the Lord, she would read from His Word, meditate on the words of Scripture in *Daily Light*, write in her journal, and paint the beauty of God's creation with watercolor. God used her artistic gift in books and pamphlets she wrote to reach others in Algiers with the gospel of Christ. Her watercolors and writing in her journals became a source of intimacy and nearness to her Lord throughout her life and ministry in Algiers.

For years, her art lay buried in three cardboard boxes at a ministry headquarters in England following her death in 1928. Miriam Rockness, a pastor's wife, discovered Lilias Trotter and began to search for her journals, art, and books. Lilias Trotter's watercolors and writing are only now coming to light through three books by Miriam Rockness—*A Blossom in the Desert, A Passion for the Impossible*, and *Images of Faith*.

Lilias Trotter discovered who she really was in Christ and lived out her days serving Him in the way He had designed for her. She went in an unlikely direction becoming a missionary in Algiers, unknown to any but the Audience of One. She lived faithfully, using her gifts and talents for the glory of God.

Have you begun to discover who you really are? Who you are in Christ is *who you are*. Never forget this. I believe one of the greatest challenges to our faith is living according to *who we are* instead of *how we feel*. You are called to live as *who you really are* in Christ.

Know, first and foremost, that you are a new creation. "Anyone who belongs to Christ has become a new person. The old life is gone; a new life has begun" (2 Corinthians 5:17 NLT). So then the question becomes, *Who am I now?*

God has adopted you into His family (Romans 8:14-17). You are His child and a fellow-heir with Christ in possession of an eternal inheritance. This means you are royalty, dear friend, and possess all the wealth and privileges as God's child. According to Paul in Ephesians 1:3-6, you are chosen, adopted, and blessed with every spiritual blessing in Christ. Saying *yes* to this calling as God's child means you step into all of the royal God-given privileges and live them out every day of your life. You can talk with God anytime and run right into the throne room to cry out to God and receive mercy and grace in your time of need (Hebrews 4:16). Living as the royal one you are also means that you disregard the words of those who try to demoralize you or degrade you. You are beloved of God and are His inheritance (Ephesians 1:18, 1 Thessalonians 1:4). He treasures you and loves you with an everlasting love.

One day, I stood talking with someone I had known for many years in the church discussing a ministry idea. We disagreed. Then, suddenly, it came out of nowhere. "You know, your opinions and views mean nothing to me," the person said in a condescending manner. Astonished, my heart sank seemingly to the floor. No one had ever reduced me to less than nothing quite like this before. I walked away quickly so no one could see the tears rimming my eyes. I went to my car and just sat there, shocked. Then, the Lord began bringing His Word to my mind. *Catherine, you are my masterpiece, designed for good works I have prepared beforehand. You are my child. I have enclosed you behind and before.* One verse after another came to my mind—Ephesians 2:10, Psalm

139, and more. Then, by personalizing the verses, I could truly realize what God was saying to me. Ultimately, I just could not accept the words leveled at me by that person in the church, because they were so opposite the truth I knew about me from God's Word. I believe because we are God's children, we must give one another a level of respect. It took me a long time to get past the words leveled at me, especially from someone I had trusted. But the Lord showed me that the reason I had felt offended was a God-related offense, going against what God says in His Word. That helped me walk on past the words and upward to continue living out God's purpose in my life.

I share my own story because my guess is that perhaps you have experienced a time when someone tried to demoralize and degrade you. You need to step back and remember who you are and Whose you are. You are God's child and you belong to Him. You are a child of the King. Never forget it. And woe be to someone who goes against you as God's child and tries to bring you down in order to lift themselves up. God has a way of making things right in His own time and His own way. I have seen it time and time again.

You are "chosen of God, holy, and beloved" (Colossians 3:12). God cherishes you and loves you. In Ephesians 1:7-8 you discover that He has lavished His grace on you. Lavish grace is great wealth in and of itself. To have God's grace at work in such an immeasurable way means that you always have everything you need for every circumstance of life. Paul says it this way, "And God is able to make all grace abound to you, so that always having all sufficiency in everything, you may have an abundance for every good deed" (2 Corinthians 9:8). Count on God's provision and care for you even when you can't see solutions to your need.

Paul tells us "we are God's masterpiece. He has created us anew in Christ Jesus, so we can do the good things he planned for us long ago" (Ephesians 2:10). The Greek word for "masterpiece" is *poiema*, and means, "something made by God Himself."[4] It is how we derive the English words, "poem" and "poetry." Sam Gordon, a Bible teacher for Trans World Radio on the program, Truth For Today, in his book, *The Genius of Grace: The Message of Ephesians*, describes God's handiwork this way: "Each of our lives is the papyrus on which the Master is producing a work of art that will fill the everlasting ages with His praise." Just think of it—you are literally God's poetry and art where the Lord is expressing Himself in and through you doing good things for others in a lost and hurting world.

Pastor, theologian, and apologist Timothy Keller writes: "You're beautiful, you're valuable, and you're an expression of the very inner being of the Artist, the Divine Artist, God Himself."[5]

Charles Haddon Spurgeon, the British preacher helps us understand this extraordinary artistry of God in and through us, "You have seen a painter with his palette on his finger and he has ugly little daubs of paint on the palette. What can he do with those spots? Go in and see the picture. What splendid painting! In an even wiser way does Jesus act toward us. He takes us, poor smudges of paint, and He makes the blessed pictures of His grace out of us. It is neither the brush nor the paint He uses, but it is the skill of His own hand which does it all."

You are truly a monument of God's grace. Henry Morris of Institute of Creation Research says, "God has written two poetic masterpieces, as it were, one in the physical creation, one in the lives of men and women redeemed and saved by His grace."

I believe the calling of Ephesians 2:10 is a call from Jesus, first to realize your beauty as God's poetry and work of art. Then, Jesus is calling you to be open as His creation and masterpiece to do more good things than you have ever before thought you could do. Lilias Trotter could have never imagined she would go to Algiers to reach the Arab world for Christ. She didn't know she would have an ability given to her by God to share the love of Christ with those in another country. She never realized that God would use her gift for art and watercolors in such a powerful way in ministry.

Will you open your mind to the possibilities that lie beyond the current life you live? He has shaped you with particular gifts and talents you may not yet know you possess. We have thoughts and ideas of things we'd love to try, but often chalk them up to dreams that will never come to fruition. What is on your heart that perhaps you have never dared pursue? Perhaps it is on your heart because God is wooing you out of your comfort zone in a whole new direction.

Charles Swindoll, pastor, author, and founder of the popular radio program, Insight for Living, writes in his book, *Saying It Well*, "Each of us has an inimitable 'style' that is ours and ours alone. God has gifted each person like no one else. It is essential that you discover your own 'put together,' as my dad would say. Once you find out what that consists of, you need to cultivate being YOU."[6]

As you read this, you may be wondering how suffering, illness, or disability could be part of God's poetry and art. Joni Eareckson Tada, who became a quadriplegic at the age of eighteen, writes, "God has a plan and a purpose for my time on earth. He is the Master Artist or Sculptor, and He is the One who chooses the tools He will use to perfect His workmanship. What of suffering, then? What of illness? What of disability? Am I to tell Him which tools He can use and which tools He can't use in the lifelong task of perfecting me and molding me into the beautiful image of Jesus…Do I, the poem, the thing being written, know more than the poet?"[7] God has used Joni, through her books, art, and music, to profoundly touch the lives of others throughout the world, including me.

What are your unique circumstances and life situations that become the tools God wants to use to write the story of your life to touch the world? Jesus is living in you and wants to draw others to Himself in and through you. And so, He is able to cause "all things to work together for good to those who love God, to those who are called according to His purpose" (Romans 8:28).

Oh, it gets so exciting when we discover more of who we are, then bravely step outside of the box of our norm and accepted life into the great ocean of God's plans and purposes. Certain events in my own life have helped me specifically come to a deeper understanding of who I am and how I am uniquely made.

I had been married for only a few years when one day, while I was sitting at the kitchen table with my Bible open and pen in hand, my husband walked up and said something that ended up sending me in a whole new direction in life.

"Catherine I have an idea," David said in a serious tone. "I've been thinking about it for awhile now."

"Okay, what's on your mind?" I responded hesitantly.

"I think you should go to seminary. You should get a formal degree for all the time you spend studying God's Word. And who knows how God may use it in the future for a career for you." David didn't blink.

Well, I was just floored. "Really? Are you serious?"

That was the beginning of a true adventure where I discovered more about who God has designed me to be. I sat in my first seminary class, heart beating with excitement. I was the only woman in the midst of a whole class of men there at Bethel Seminary. My Old Testament professor, Dr. Ronald Youngblood, who later became a mentor for me, outlined the requirements of my first Old Testament class. Most of the students groaned just at the thought of all the work. Not me. I couldn't wait to dive in and do the work. I wanted nothing more than to study and research and learn.

I brought that first syllabus home and showed it to my husband. He looked at me and smiled, then said, "I'm glad it's you and not me who is in this class."

But I absolutely loved seminary. I realized I was made to study, research, and write. I did not know this about myself until I stepped out of my own expectations and tried this new direction in life. It was a lot of hard work especially because I also had a full-time job. However, I reveled in every class, devoured each syllabus, mapped out assignments, and wrote each paper as though it was a book to be published. Fellow students who were going through seminary as a means to an end like becoming a pastor couldn't understand my excitement and enthusiasm. And I could hardly understand it myself except that it seemed to come from the Lord at work in me.

One day, I sat at the desk of my favorite professor, Dr. Walt Wessel. He handed me my assignment for an independent study class to earn extra credits. "Catherine, I want you to read through this book, *Interpreting the Parables*, by Craig L. Blomberg, and write a paper on it." In retrospect, I think he was asking for a review of the book, maybe ten to fifteen pages or so. After leaving his office, I drove straight to the public library, and checked out twenty books on the parables, so that I could learn as much as possible on the topic. My philosophy of study was that all of my time in seminary would make a difference in all I did in ministry in the future. I spent hours reading, researching, and writing on the parables of Jesus. The paper ended up as a work of epic proportions—definitely more than what my professor was asking. When I got my grade back, it was an A+, and Dr. Wessel wrote this comment—"Just an excellent piece of work. However, it was a bit long, but we'll forgive you for that." That last part has always made me smile. That one paper, above all the other papers, helped me realize how much I love to write.

In my last year of seminary, during a quiet time one morning, my mind turned to the question people often asked me. "Catherine, I want to have a quiet time, but where do I begin?" I thought, "If only I could give people a tool to help them spend time alone with the Lord." Then I got a big idea. *Why not put together a formal Quiet Time Notebook, just like what I use in my own quiet time? Then, I could teach quiet time at retreats and conferences. I could even have a ministry that is all about quiet time!* This was such a big idea I could hardly wrap my mind around it. When my husband came home from work, I wouldn't let him get past the kitchen door. "Honey, I just got the most incredible idea!" When he heard the idea, he said, "Cath, you could call your ministry, Quiet Time Ministries!" *I could call it Quiet Time Ministries!* And that was the beginning of a ministry that is taking the Word of God throughout the world.

I was burdened for others to experience quiet time with God and His Word firsthand— to become participants with God instead of spectators. One day I was at the local Christian bookstore, perusing the shelves to buy yet another book to live in and enjoy. The thought came to my mind, *Here I am buying more books. Maybe it's time I stop buying books and start writing books.* Oh, that was an epic moment for me. I put the book back on the shelf, walked out of that store, got in my car, and drove home. I immediately walked over and sat down at the computer and started outlining my first book of quiet times, *Pilgrimage of the Heart.* It just became clear in my mind to put together a book of quiet times according to the PRAYER Quiet Time Plan God had given me—Prepare Your Heart, Read and Study God's Word, Adore God in Prayer, Yield Yourself to God, Enjoy His Presence, and Rest in His Love. Little did I know that I would write nearly thirty books! One book led to another and another. The ideas just kept flowing from the Lord. I couldn't believe it. But every time I sat down to write, the Lord just helped me put together books to help others draw near to God. The same held true for the messages I wrote. And so, I figured I would be writing messages and books for the rest of my life. That became how I saw myself in life and ministry with the Lord.

Then one day my husband and I went to an electronics store. David said, "Catherine I want to give you a new digital camera, something that you can use for many years, and I want you to choose the one you like." Oh, that was such a life-changing day for me. God had more in store for me than I imagined. And I discovered I was created to do more than I had in mind for myself. I had been walking through a spiritual valley after my mother-in-law went home to be with the Lord. My heart was in a wilderness, broken from the loss. The first morning after I got my new camera, I drove to a quiet place in the California desert where I live. I grabbed my new Nikon D7000 and walked out towards the mountains. The sun was just beginning to make its way to the horizon. I looked through the viewfinder and saw something new. "Oh, there is such beauty here, Lord. You are a magnificent Creator." I captured image after image during that first sunrise. Once the sun was high in the sky and the pink glow had faded into the white clouds, I literally raised my hands and gave the Lord a standing ovation. Through those first experiences out in the desert with my camera, I found that I absolutely loved photography and spent hours learning and growing in it. It was very reminiscent to my time in seminary when studying and writing became a passion.

When I am walking with God out in His creation capturing images with my camera, I feel as though He is showing me beauty that is special just for the two of us to see. I am usually alone and I will even see wildlife appearing on the landscape, like a bird on a branch of a lone tree or widgeon ducks landing on the surface of a pond, or a great white heron on the branch of a tall pine tree. I love the intimacy with my Lord that I experience with photography.

Then God opened some amazing doors for me in the area of photography to allow me to develop even more in my ability to capture images for His glory. One day I discovered a Christian photographer online who worked for Nikon—his name is Bill Fortney. Bill Fortney is a legend in the photography world and is best friends with Dr. Charles Stanley! I wrote a comment on one of Bill Fortney's blog posts. The next day I was surprised to discover an email from none other than Bill Fortney himself! He wrote, "Could I see some of your work?" I asked my husband, "Do you think he wants to see some of my books?" My husband replied, "No honey, he wants to see some of your photography." "Oh no, I can't show him anything! What will he think? I'm terrified!" I was an author, but I had never thought of myself as a photographer. I bravely sent him some links to images. He wrote back and invited me to one of his workshops. Well, it all worked together that I was able to attend his Grand Circle photographic workshop in Monument Valley Utah, Bryce Canyon National Park, Zion National Park, and the Antelope Slot Canyons of Page, Arizona. Later, I also was privileged to go on one of his spectacular workshops (along with beloved preacher Dr. Charles Stanley) in Glacier National Park, Montana. myPhotoWalk Devotional Photography has now become an integral part of Quiet Time Ministries with book covers, photography books, and devotional prints. I had never imagined this back when I was writing books at the beginning of Quiet Time Ministries. But God knew it all along and He called me to go in that direction in His time and way.

Always be ready for a new direction and discovery when you walk with the Lord. I had experienced several years of losses. I was working two different ministry jobs and putting in more than forty hours a week. In the midst of intense work, I found a growing desire to try my hand at painting with watercolors in an art journal. Why painting? I don't know why. I can't even explain it. I just had this new desire bubbling up within me. And I started noticing art everywhere and I was drawn to certain artists online, both secular and Christian. So one day I decided I would start collecting materials to see just where it might take me. I began reading blogs on many different websites about the best supplies. I went to an art store to look at paints, brushes, and paper. At first I just looked. But then I began buying supplies and I literally went kind of crazy with excitement. So I had all these supplies but no idea even what to do with them. In the meantime, I was writing quiet time books and designing new photography books. But still, burning inside me was this new passion for art, especially watercolor. And I even had all the materials to do it. But I can honestly tell you that I was afraid. I told Karryn, who is a dear friend and my manicurist, about my crazy idea for art. She is an artist herself and said, "Catherine I think there will come a day when the time is right for you to begin."

So one day that day came. I just took two plastic cups and filled them with water. I pulled out one of the art journals and a set of watercolors. And I started painting flowers. And here's the surprise. I could paint! Not as Claude Monet or Vincent Van Gogh, but as Catherine Martin. I posted one of my flowers on Facebook and I got a lot of attention; people were writing things like "I didn't know you could paint." Neither did I!

Now, why do I share all of this? Because of you. You are unique. Special. There is only one you. And what if there is more to you than you realize? Chuck Swindoll makes the important observation in his book, *Saying It Well*: "Truth be told, most folks I meet have never made a study of themselves. Therefore, they do not know themselves—not deeply…Most do not know their giftedness and skills, their unique temperament and personality, their strengths and weaknesses…"[8]

I truly believe that there are gifts in you still to be discovered and a story waiting to be told. What if God has something in mind that is only this small idea right now? Maybe you have the idea to write poetry or fiction. Perhaps you have thoughts of leading a Bible study. Have you been saying, "No way, I could never do that!" Think again, dear friend. Maybe the Lord has put that idea inside you because there is something He wants to do in you that has not yet entered your mind. How can you begin to discover more about *who you really are* and *what you are meant to do?* David says in Psalm 37:4 to "Delight yourself in the LORD, and He will give you the desires of your heart." Pour yourself into knowing the Lord and spending time with Him. He will transform you and make you into the person He has designed you to be. And He will fill your heart with His desires (Psalm 37:4).

Author Selwyn Hughes shares how our creativity flows out of our being created in the image of

God (Genesis 1:27). He writes about how the creativity develops in us as a result of our intimacy with the Lord: "Every day we keep seeing new horizons. In His company we begin to see farther, feel for people on a wider scale, act more decisively, and live on the growing edge of adventure. Why? Because a creative God gives to His creation the same creative impulses."[9] I truly believe that there is an artistic side of all of us that touches the soul in ways that nothing else can. The art in you may be expressed many ways; like writing, painting, journaling, blogging, music, cooking, decorating, hospitality, or entertaining.

Always remember that God has a dream of you and your story in this world. Never say, "there's no room for me; someone else is already doing it better than I ever could." Don't be looking around at everyone else and wishing for something different than you and your unique story. Always be you; don't try to be someone else. My mother used to always encourage me with the words from Hamlet, "To thine own self be true." Enjoy, appreciate, and own your individuality. There is a fine line between learning from the example of others and losing yourself in the mimicking of someone else's ways and life. Ann Kiemel's prayer in her book, *I Love The Word Impossible*, has been such an encouragement to me over the years: "Jesus, I like what I am because it was Your idea. Help me to find adventure in my uniqueness, and not want to be what someone else is. God, if I lose sight of the fun of being me, then Your dreams of what I can be in the world will die. Always help me to remember that this is Your way of being creative."[10] This prayer has been so important for me, especially in the times when I look at someone else with all their gifts and talents and the amazing opportunities they have in their life. If I look at them and wish for their life opportunities, the Lord reminds me that I really need to be me. He didn't create me to be them. He created me to be me. I just need to live out the life He has for me, allowing Him to do His work in and through me. It doesn't mean I'll be well known. It doesn't mean I'll have any earthly success. But it does mean that my life will glorify the Lord in the way He has in mind. And when we all get to heaven, the measure will not be earthly success or money, but faithfulness to walk with the Lord.

Even if your life is busy with more than one job so you can bring in an income for your family, as I have for many years now, you can still lay all your desires in the hands of the Lord. Ask Him to give you an opportunity to pursue the directions that are still in your heart. Then, look for small ways to develop and practice in the areas that relate to new ideas you may have. In the meantime, as you live out your story in the power of the Holy Spirit, always live in the Audience of One, like Lilias Trotter. "Do your work heartily as for the Lord" (Colossians 3:23). You may be unknown as Lilias Trotter was, but you are well known in heaven, beloved friend. No one may see your work but God and God alone. You may be reaping a seemingly small earthly benefit in relative obscurity, but your treasure is great in heaven. And heaven will tell the story of how the Lord has worked in and through beautiful and amazing you!

Lilias Trotter was unknown to almost the entire world during her own lifetime. Her faithfulness in ministry and her watercolor paintings in her journal were mostly seen by God and God alone. I sometimes wonder if God reserves His most special saints to dance with Him alone in His presence in this earthly life. S.D. Gordon, in his little book on quiet time, calls this "the sweet modesty of God" where "the sweetest flowers are not found in the shop window."[11] Lilias Trotter thought about these things and gives us her perspective in the closing lines of her book, *Parables of the Cross*: "The results need not end with our earthly days. Should Jesus tarry our works will follow us…God may use, by reason of the wonderful solidarity of His Church, the things that He has wrought in us, for the blessing of souls unknown to us…God only knows the endless possibilities that lie folded in each one of us! Shall we not let Him have His way? Shall we not go all lengths with Him in His plans for us."[12] The Lord will sometimes entrust the most difficult life work to one He considers of such great faith and strength that they will faithfully serve Him without earthly notice or recognition, trusting in Him and Him alone. The reward in eternity and the ripple effect for that one may be much greater than those who enjoyed visible success in the world.

I sat with my dad one evening near the end of his life, just a few weeks before he went home to be with the Lord. He was looking at some of my photography. He turned and looked into my eyes. He said, "Catherine do you know how special you are? There is only one Catherine Martin. You are one in a million." I have never forgotten those words. And I say them now to you. Do you know how special you are? There is only one you. You are one in a million. You are God's masterpiece.

O Jesus the Crucified
I will follow Thee in thy path.
Inspire me for the next step,
whether it leads
down into the shadow
or up into the light.
Surely in what place
my Lord the King shall be,
whether in death or life,
even there also
will Thy servant be.
Amen.[13]

LILIAS TROTTER

SITTING AT HIS FEET

Come away with Me by yourselves to a quiet place and rest a little while.
MARK 6:31 WMS

When I first became a Christian I was given a remarkable book, *The Shadow of the Almighty – The Life & Testament of Jim Elliot* by Christian author and speaker, Elisabeth Elliot. I read the account of Jim Elliot who had the dream in college of taking the gospel to the Auca Indians, an unreached people group deep in the jungles of Ecuador. I was mesmerized at the story of Jim and Elisabeth Elliot, their romance and marriage, and then their journey as missionaries to Ecuador. And then, I was excited when they finally located a group of Auca Indians and reached out to them with the gospel. But the story did not end the way I had expected. On January 8, 1956, all five of the missionary men were martyred by the Aucas. The date of Jim Elliot's death has always been important to me because just three weeks later I was born. So I have always felt a special link to Jim Elliot because he is such a hero of the faith to me.

Jim Elliot greatly influenced my own personal walk with the Lord. When I read *The Shadow of the Almighty*, the story impressed me and Jim Elliot's heart deeply moved me. The book included many excerpts from his journal. He wrote of his love for the Lord, his response to God's Word, his passion for ministry, and his deep commitment to Christ. When I read his words, I was faced with a new decision in my own life. What kind of Christian did I want to be? Did I want to be sold out for Christ or did I want to go along with the crowd of mediocrity? Did I want to spend the hours alone with the Lord that make a Jim Elliot? Or would I, as Tozer wrote, "skip through the corridors of the Kingdom like children through the marketplace, chattering about everything, but pausing to learn the true value of nothing?"

Jim Elliot wrote: "He is no fool who gives up what he cannot keep to gain what he cannot lose." He also wrote: "Wherever you are, be all there! Live to the hilt every situation you believe to be the will of God." Jim Elliot's journal inspired me to go deeper with my own journal writing and literally demonstrated for me in written form how to do it. But there was a cost, and I knew it. I wanted more than anything to have the kind of heart that beat with passionate love for Christ the way Jim Elliot's did. It was then that I set aside the many things for the one thing: to know and love the Lord Jesus with all my heart, soul, mind and strength. It's what Jesus was calling me to embrace. I will be forever grateful to Jim and Elisabeth Elliot for inspiring me to grow deep with the Lord in quiet time and spend much time and many hours with Him.

The calling from Jesus to draw near and intimately know Him is found throughout Scripture. It is a call to stillness and solitude, taking time with Him, living in His Word, resting in His presence, and listening to Him teach you. The more you know Christ, the better you will know who you are and why you are here. Hear His voice as He invites you and yes, as He calls out to you:

"Be still and know that I am God" (Psalm 46:10 NIV).

"Come away with Me by yourselves to a quiet place and rest a little while" (Mark 6:31 WMS).

"Are you tired? Worn out? Burned out on religion? Come to me. Get away with me and you'll recover your life. I'll show you how to take a real rest. Walk with me and work with me—watch how I do it. Learn the unforced rhythms of grace. I won't lay anything heavy or ill-fitting on you. Keep company with me and you'll learn to live freely and lightly" (Matthew 11:28-30 The Message).

"Let the word of Christ richly dwell within you" (Colossians 3:16).

"Draw near to Him, and He will draw near to you" (James 4:8).

"This book of the law shall not depart from your mouth, but you shall meditate on it day and night, so that you may be careful to do according to all that is written in it; for then you will make your way prosperous, and then you will have success" (Joshua 1:8).

"But those who wish to boast should boast in this alone: that they truly know me and understand that I am the LORD who demonstrates unfailing love and who brings justice and righteousness to the earth, and that I delight in these things" (Jeremiah 9:24 NLT).

"Call to Me and I will answer you, and I will tell you great and mighty things, which you do not know" (Jeremiah 31:3).

You see, when you read these words of God from His Word, your name is written on them because God is speaking directly and personally to you. Charles Haddon Spurgeon explains the personal nature of God's Word in his book, *Beside Still Waters*: "Continually study God's Word to see if the promises have your name written on them. Many times God has brought a promise to my heart with such freshness that I felt it was given only to me. This promise contained private marks that exactly matched the counterpart of my soul's secrets. This proves that God meant me when He spoke."[1] God's Word is fresh manna for you today. It is "living and active," ready to encourage, equip, direct, and give you hope (Hebrews 4:12, Romans 15:4, 2 Timothy 3:16-17).

I like to think of our intimate relationship with the Lord and the time we spend with Him as a dance. He invites us to lean in to His embrace and then follow His lead as He takes us on to the dance floor of life. And sometimes, we lean in closer as He speaks to us in His Word with promises, encouragements, and instructions to lead and guide us. And our dance with Him is a beautiful story that is seen by the world. I wrote about this relationship in *A Woman's Heart That Dances.*[2] Everyone is made to dance with the Lord. Even the great King David, the man after God's own heart, "danced before the LORD with all his might" (2 Samuel 6:14).

Jesus is very serious about His calling to you to draw near, sit at His feet, listen to His Word, talk with Him, and know and love Him. Intimacy with you is His heart's desire. I see this calling very clearly in an event shared by Luke in the New Testament. One day Jesus and His disciples visited some of His dearest friends, Martha, Mary and Lazarus in the little town of Bethany, about a mile and a half east of Jerusalem. Martha immediately jumped into action with the preparations for the esteemed company of Jesus and His disciples in her home. She was probably the epitome of hospitality in her day and time and took great pride in taking good care of her guests. Certainly, her care of her guests was immensely important. Her sister, Mary, was a different personality and temperament. Both of them loved Jesus. When Jesus arrived with the disciples, He began to teach. Mary drew near and sat at His feet listening to His Word. Martha became upset and distracted with all her preparations and finally went to Jesus, indignant that Mary was not helping her. She said, "Lord, don't You care that my sister has left me to serve alone? So tell her to give me a hand" (Luke 10:40 HCSB). I'm sure that Martha expected Jesus to support her and reprimand Mary. But instead Jesus gave Martha a lesson in life and priorities for His disciples. From His words, He reveals how He knows all that is going on in our hearts. There is usually more to our story than the agitation that surfaces in a difficulty. He answered her, "Martha, Martha, you are worried and upset about many things, but one thing is necessary. Mary has made the right choice, and it will not be taken away from her" (Luke 10:41-42 HCSB). The Lord confirmed to us the priority of sitting at His feet and listening to His Word. There it is in living color and I pray we don't ever forget this calling from Jesus for quiet time alone with Him in His Word.

You and I need to make a choice. Every day we decide. Will we sit at Jesus' feet and listen to His Word? Will we talk with Him, pouring out our hearts in passionate prayer? He is inviting us. He is waiting for us. He has something to say to us in His Word—it could be a word of encouragement, a moment of conviction, a life lesson, or a message of comfort. But every day, He waits for us with the calling from His Word. It is as though He is saying *will you dance with Me?*

I have discovered essentials to help me answer the call of Jesus and spend quiet time with Him every day. I go back to these basics again and again. We need to set aside a time, find a quiet place, and have a plan for quiet time. I have written about this topic in my book *Six Secrets To A Powerful Quiet Time—Discovering Radical Intimacy With God.*[3]

The morning, at the beginning of the day, is the best time for me to meet with the Lord. I take my example from the Lord Himself. Mark tells us that "Very early in the morning, while it was still dark, Jesus got up, left the house and went off to a solitary place, where he prayed" (Mark 1:35 NIV). I love the mornings and most often I have my quiet time very early while it is still dark, the house is still, and there are no outside distractions. I encourage you to actually schedule your quiet time—even write it on your calendar—so you make it a priority in your life.

Then, find a quiet place where you can be alone. Again, I take my example from the Lord. Luke tells us "He often withdrew to deserted places and prayed" (Luke 5:16). Finding a quiet place can be a challenge especially with family schedules and home layouts. If you are like me, you may not actually have a dedicated room and others may be up and about very early in the morning. I encourage you to be tenacious in the search and setup of a quiet place. I have my quiet time basket filled with my quiet time materials in our family room. I make it a point to get up earlier than my husband for quiet time. And for special times, I will go to a restaurant where I can have what I call "breakfast with the Lord."

Imagine Jesus coming to you and saying, as He did to those first century disciples, "Come away with Me by yourself to a quiet place and rest a little while" (Mark 6:31). What conversation would you love to have with Jesus? How would you pour out your heart to Him? Then, consider the topics He might want to discuss with you. The gospels of Matthew, Mark, Luke and John give you a good idea of the things that are on His heart and mind.

One of my favorite promises in the Bible is James 4:8, "Draw near to God, and He will draw near to you." I truly believe that God is passionate about our time and our intimate relationship with Him. Richard Foster, author and founder of Renovare, dedicated to renewal of the church, wrote about the heart of God in his book, *Prayer: Finding The Heart's True Home.* "Today the heart of God is an open wound of love…He longs for our presence. And he is inviting you— and me—to come home, to come home to where we belong, to come home to that for which we were created. His arms are stretched out wide to receive us…

He invites us into the living room of his heart, where we can put on old slippers and share freely.

He invites us into the kitchen of his friendship, where chatter and batter mix in good fun.

He invites us into the dining room of his strength, where we can feast to our heart's delight.

He invites us into the study of his wisdom, where we can learn and grow and stretch… and ask all the questions we want.

He invites us into the workshop of his creativity, where we can be co-laborers with him, working together to determine the outcomes of events.

He invites us into the bedroom of his rest, where new peace is found and where we can be naked and vulnerable and free. It is also the place of deepest intimacy, where we know and are known to the fullest."[4]

When you realize that you are called with an invitation from the Lord to spend time with Him, then the most important thing you can do is respond with a *yes*. Set aside everything and make sitting at His feet your great priority every day.

Something happened to me one day that taught me a profound lesson about the importance of my daily time with the Lord where I sit at His feet. I had scheduled a meeting with a dear friend at Starbucks coffee shop. Because we had not seen each other in a long time, I wanted to give her something special. So I ordered a copy of one of my very favorite books, *A Psalm In Your Heart* by George O. Wood. I have used this commentary on the psalms in my quiet time for many years and absolutely love it. When it arrived, I wrote a note on the flyleaf, and put it in a beautiful gift bag. I got to Starbucks early because I wanted to get the best table—a place that was quiet where we could talk. I put the gift bag on the center of the table so she would be immediately surprised. I waited with anticipation and excitement. I knew she would love my gift. The time came for her to arrive. Twenty more minutes went by, and still she wasn't here. *I hope nothing has happened to her.* Then the thought came, *She may have forgotten.* So I pulled out my phone and dialed her number. My friend answered and immediately exclaimed, "Oh no, was it today that we were going to meet?" I laughed and said, "Yes, let's just reschedule." After I got off the phone with her, my eyes moved to the gift in the center of the table. A pang of sadness touched my heart. *Oh, I won't get to give her the gift today!* As I pondered that thought, then I said out loud, "Lord, I wonder if you have a lesson for me in this?" I thought, *Every day I have an opportunity to spend quiet time with the Lord. He has gifts all wrapped up waiting for me. And when I don't draw near to Him, then I miss all that He had prepared for me that day. I just miss it. Thank You Lord, for teaching me a valuable lesson about my time alone with You.*

You see, every day the Lord wants to meet us in His Word. He is waiting for us even now. In Hebrews 1:3 we see that "the Son is the radiance of God's glory and the exact representation of his being, sustaining all things by his powerful word." The Lord Jesus will sustain you with His Word. In Him all things hold together, including you (Colossians 1:17). Your deeply-involved experience alone with Jesus will make you the person He wants you to be. In your quiet time with Him, He will write the story of who you are and help you understand why you are here. Meeting alone with Him is the most important time of your day.

Sometimes I just drop everything and go sit at the feet of Jesus. I open the pages of my Bible and just live in a passage, personalizing it as a prayer to the Lord, writing my thoughts in *The Quiet Time Journal*, and just thinking about what Jesus wants me to learn. I ask, "Lord, what are You saying to me here? What words are you calling me to this day? What do you want me to know?" Though I cannot see Him with my physical eyes, I imagine Him there with me with the knowledge that He is, in fact, *there with me.* My *Quiet Time Journal* has become a gathering place for me where I pour out my heart like water in the Presence of the Lord (Lamentations

2:19), think about all God is teaching me, and express in writing and creativity (photography and watercolor) all I am learning from Him. When I think about my life, I can remember many wonderful times the Lord and I have had together. Someday I know I will see Him face to face and I can't wait to thank Him for the amazing times we've shared in quiet time.

So dear friend, will you answer this calling to draw near to Jesus and sit at His feet? Will you dance with Him? Tomorrow, when you awaken, will you be a Martha, anxious and worried? Or will you be a Mary who sits at the feet of the Lord, listening to His Word? He is calling you even now to draw near and sit awhile with Him.

God I pray, light these idle sticks of my life and may I burn up for Thee.
Consume my life, my God, for it is Thine. I seek not a long life
but a full one like Yours, Lord Jesus…
Give us that vital contact of the soul with
Thy divine life that fruit may be produced and
Life-abundant living may be known again
as the final proof for Christ's message and work…
Lord, make my way prosperous
not that I achieve high station,
but that my life be an exhibit
to the value of knowing God.[5]

JIM ELLIOT

The Calling Journey Three
CALLED TO A PASSION
Matthew 4:19

Sometimes in life you get an offer you simply cannot refuse. That was the case for Peter, Andrew, James, and John when Jesus walked their way and called them to "follow Him." They knew Jesus was inviting them to something higher and greater. The scope of the call was so much larger than their present vocation. Essentially He was saying, "Would you like to sit in this boat and fish for the rest of your life or would you like to take a new road with Me and influence the world?" There is nothing so exciting as seeing lives changed for Jesus Christ. Impacting a world is the desire, the will, and the call of Jesus. And the secret for any who hear Jesus calling to follow Him is to say yes.

I WANT TO FOLLOW JESUS

Come, follow me, and I will show you how to fish for people.
MATTHEW 4:19 NLT

One day Jesus was walking along the shore of the Sea of Galilee. He saw two brothers, Simon Peter and Andrew, casting their net into the water because they were fisherman. Jesus called out to them and said, "Come, follow me, and I will show you how to fish for people" (Matthew 4:19 NLT). They left their nets at once and followed Him. A little farther along the shore, he saw two brothers, James and John, along with their father, Zebedee, sitting in a boat, repairing their nets. He called out for them to follow Him. "They immediately followed him, leaving the boat and their father behind" (Matthew 4:22).

Sometimes in life you get an offer you simply cannot refuse. That was the case for Peter, Andrew, James, and John when Jesus walked their way and called them to "follow Him." They knew Jesus was inviting them to something higher and greater. The scope of the call was so much larger than their present vocation. Essentially He was saying, "Would you like to sit in this boat and fish for the rest of your life or would you like to take a new road with Me and influence the world?" There is nothing so exciting as seeing lives changed for Jesus Christ. Impacting a world is the desire, the will, and the call of Jesus. And the secret for any who hear Jesus calling to follow Him is to say *yes*.

The Lord had a work in mind that would extend far beyond His own life on earth. How would He do it? Through simple, ordinary people like these fishermen. He designed a plan called discipleship. He issued forth a commission—the Great Commission—with these words: "I have been given all authority in heaven and on earth. Therefore, go and make disciples of all the nations, baptizing them in the name of the Father and the Son and the Holy Spirit. Teach these new disciples to obey all the commands I have given you. And be sure of this: I am with you always, even to the end of the age" (Matthew 28:18-20 NLT).

Once these simple men said *yes* to His call, Jesus began His work, first transforming them into vessels fit to serve Him, then engaging the world in and through them by His power. It is an exciting business, this thing called ministry. We don't do the work. Jesus does. That's why I like to define ministry as "Jesus Christ in action." The secret is allowing Jesus to mold and shape you as He pleases. Then, follow Him where He wants to go, and rejoice in all He does.

When Jesus called those simple fishermen to follow Him, little did they realize all that the Lord wanted to accomplish in and through them. They could never have envisioned the formation of the early church as seen in the book of Acts. But Jesus had it in mind. And He has you in mind and knows that His choice of you, a faithful man or woman, is critical for His service.

Paul describes Jesus' strategy to reach the world in his words to his disciple, Timothy: "You have heard me teach things that have been confirmed by many reliable witnesses. Now teach these truths to other trustworthy people who will be able to pass them on to others" (2 Timothy 2:2 NLT).

So what does Jesus' plan look like in real life? I love the story of Bill Bright, co-founder of Campus Crusade for Christ, and one of my heroes of the faith. At one point, Bill Bright was just an ordinary, shy young man who was an agnostic. He didn't know if God existed and he really didn't care if He did. Bright was determined to be strong and accomplish everything he set out to do. In college he was student body president and named to *Who's Who In American Colleges and Universities*. After college he moved to Los Angeles to start his own business, Bright's California Confections. He rented an apartment in Hollywood from an elderly couple who repeatedly invited him to church. "Will you come to church with us?" they asked again and again. Bright describes his response: "For a long time I would smile, thank them for the invitation, then come up with an excuse. I had seldom attended church since I left home for college. I preferred to spend my Sundays doing an amateur radio broadcast and going horseback riding in the Hollywood Hills."

The couple never gave up with their church invitations, telling him that he would love the preacher, Dr. Louis Evans, at First Presbyterian Church of Hollywood. Bill Bright could not imagine the concept of loving any preacher and so he became curious. One Sunday, after his horseback ride, he decided to drop in on the evening service. He sat in the back so no one would see him. After he left, he said "So much for church." He figured he was done with church.

Three days later, a young woman called, "I'd like to invite you to a party we're having here at the church." He decided to go, just on a whim. He was impressed. "I was in for quite a surprise. Gathered were three hundred of the sharpest young adult men and women I had ever seen. They were happy, having fun, and obviously loved the Lord. In one evening, my notion that Christianity was a women-and-children-only religion was really shaken. I had never met people like this before."[1]

Although he was busy with his growing business, He began regularly attending the young adult meetings and church services. One day after church, he went home and found the Bible his mother had given him long ago. He was interested in learning more and began reading his Bible.

Bill Bright was still consumed with developing his new business. One day he approached a wealthy businessman at church and asked him what it was like to be successful. The man gave him a surprising response: "Material success is not where you find happiness. There are rich people all over this city who are the most miserable people you'll ever meet. Knowing and serving Jesus Christ is what's important. He is the only way to find happiness."[2] Those words impressed him. After listening to so many great sermons, meeting impressive young people, and now a successful businessmen who loved Christ, Bill Bright decided to study the life of Jesus. After much study, he concluded, "Jesus is the Son of God."

One day he went to a meeting taught by Dr. Henrietta Mears, director of Christian education at the church. She talked about Paul and his dramatic conversion on the road to Damascus. Then, she challenged those who were attending to go home, get on their knees, and ask God, "Who are You, Lord, and what will You have me do?"

What happened next is best described in Bright's own words: "As I returned to my apartment that night, I realized that I was ready to give my life to God…What attracted me was God's love, which had been made known to me through my study of the Bible and through the lives of the people I had met at Hollywood Presbyterian Church…That night I knelt beside my bed and asked the question with which Dr. Mears had challenged us: 'Who are You, Lord, and what will You have me do?' In a sense, that was my prayer for salvation. It was not theologically profound, but the Lord knew my heart and He interpreted what was going on inside me. Through my study I believed Jesus Christ was the Son of God, that He had died for my sins, and that, as Dr. Mears had shared with us, if I invited Him into my life as Savior and Lord, He would come in according to His promise in Revelation 3:20. Although nothing dramatic or emotional happened when I prayed, I know without a doubt that Jesus did come into my life. I accepted Him and He accepted me. Asking Him that question, 'Who are You, Lord, and what will You have me do?' did not seem very dynamic at first, but as I began to grow in my new commitment and love for the Lord, I became more and more aware of what a sinner I am and what a wonderful, forgiving Savior He is."[3]

Bill Bright began growing in his newfound Christian faith and was eventually elected president of the Sunday school class. He met with Dr. Mears regularly along with other leaders in the church. The more he learned about God the more he wanted to know, and he decided to enroll in seminary. Running his business and attending seminary became quite challenging for him. And in the midst of his busy life, he had fallen in love with a girl from home, Vonette Zachary. He asked her to marry him, but soon realized that she did not know the Lord. He had told her that the Lord would always be first in their lives. She did not feel that was right and was not certain he was the one for her. He asked if she would meet with Dr. Mears before making her final decision. She agreed. They met together in a cottage at Forest Home Christian Camps in the beautiful San

Bernardino Mountains of California. Vonette recalls her thoughts after Henrietta Mears talked with her about a personal relationship with Jesus Christ: "When Dr. Mears finished, I thought, *If what she tells me is absolutely true, I have nothing to lose and everything to gain.* I accepted her invitation to pray together and asked Jesus Christ to come into my life. As I look back, my life began to change at that moment. God became a reality in my life. For the first time I was ready to trust Him. I became aware that my prayers were getting beyond the ceiling. No longer did I have to try to love people; there just seemed to be a love that flowed from within that I did not have to create." Vonette became as enthusiastic as Bill about Jesus Christ and they were married in 1948.

Giving their lives to Christ was their first response to Jesus' call to follow Him. But now He was going to call them to a deeper commitment in following Him and go on a road with Him that would involve reaching hundreds of thousands of people throughout the world. Bill Bright describes the beginning of this journey: "We realized that the more we learned of God's love and provision for us, the more we could trust Him. Every day, in some new and exciting way, we were learning that God's will was better than our own. We no longer had a great appetite for the materialistic goals that had previously driven us."[4] Bill and Vonette were moved together to write out a contract describing their commitment to follow Christ, a transaction of the will, and they both prayerfully signed it. They didn't know what it would mean, but they knew they no longer wanted to live for themselves, but to follow Jesus wherever He led. The Lord was going to soon give them the beginning of His adventure for their lives.

Not long after signing that contract, Bill Bright was studying for a Greek exam. Suddenly he sensed the presence of the Lord in a way he had never known. He set down his book and asked the Lord if He had something to say to him. He heard no audible voice, yet saw an idea for a ministry in his mind—fulfilling the Great Commission in Matthew 28:18-20 by winning and discipling college students for the Lord, since they were tomorrow's leaders and world-changers. He shared this with Vonette and she too was convinced this was from the Lord.

Bill went to one of his professors, Dr. Wilbur Smith, and told him what had happened. Dr. Smith came back to him the next day and handed him a piece of paper. On it was written these words: "CCC—Campus Crusade for Christ. God has provided the name for your vision. He has called you to this. Obey His call. Let me know how I can be of help." Bill and Vonette Bright left the nets of a confection business to fish for people through Campus Crusade for Christ International that includes 5300 ministries, and has reached millions of people with the gospel of Christ.

Saying *yes* to Jesus, answering His call, and following Him doesn't always mean leaving one business for another. Sometimes it means you stay where you are and follow Christ there. Sometimes He will lead you in another direction. Either way, it will always mean that Jesus will touch the lives of others in and through you. Answering the call to follow Jesus will become your great passion.

And what about Catherine Martin? When one person, like Bill Bright, says *yes* to Jesus and follows Him, others throughout the world are impacted. Indeed, Bill Bright's decision influenced me and the course of my life was forever altered. The day I said *yes* to Jesus in college was only the beginning of an amazing adventure. The summer following that decision, I wanted to grow in my new relationship with Christ. I remembered a table I always saw in the quad at Arizona State University. It had a sign that mentioned Christ. *I'm going to check out that table the first day I get back to school.* I walked up to the table and looked into the eyes of the friendly girl that was standing there. "Hi, I'm Catherine. I want to learn more about your organization and how to get involved." She said, "My name is Leann. Let's set up an appointment." I replied, "I don't want an appointment. I want to go to a Bible study and get involved." She said, "Well we need to meet first." I was frustrated but agreed. Oh, how thankful I am for the strength and determination of Leann Pruitt McGee, a staff member with CCC at ASU, that first day. I met with Leann and that was the beginning of a discipleship relationship where I learned what it means to follow Jesus as His disciple. She taught me how to have a quiet time, how to share my faith, how to pray, how to study the Bible, and how to teach others the same things. Soon I learned that as I spent quiet time with the Lord, He was going to lead me as I walked through the day. I needed to watch for Him and follow Him. Every day became an exciting adventure. I never knew what to expect from the Lord. Sometimes I would meet people who were discouraged and I could encourage them. Sometimes I needed encouragement and would receive a note in the mail. That was the beginning of what I have come to discover as "the great adventure of knowing God."

During my time with Campus Crusade for Christ as a student at Arizona State University, I attended a Christmas Conference at Arrowhead Springs in San Bernardino, California. We learned how to share the gospel at the conference, and then immediately we were challenged to put those lessons into practice, traveling door to door talking with people in San Bernardino. I was terrified at the thought of knocking on someone's door to tell them about Jesus. I was also excited to see what God would do. *I'm going to do this no matter what.*

We went in groups of two in different neighborhoods. I knocked on the door of the first house in our assigned neighborhood. A lady answered the door and invited us in. I gulped, thinking, *Well, this is it. I am really doing this.* We sat down in her living room and I began sharing the four main points of the gospel using the *Four Spiritual Laws.* "God loves you and offers a wonderful plan for your life. Man is sinful and separated from God. Therefore, he cannot know and experience God's love and plan for his life. Jesus Christ is God's only provision for man's sin. Through him you can know and experience God's love and plan for your life. We must individually receive Jesus Christ as Savior and Lord; then we can know and experience God's love and plan for our lives." I read all the verses that supported each of the four points of the gospel. The woman listened intently. Then, with much fear and trembling, I asked, "Would like to pray to receive Christ?" She looked directly into my eyes, and said with confidence, "Yes!" I was shocked. I couldn't believe it. "Are you sure?" I asked. "Yes!" she responded. We prayed together and she repeated the prayer after me. As we were leaving, she said goodbye. We walked out of her house, amazed and excited at the same time. That was *it* for me. I had tasted the excitement of "Jesus Christ in action" and I knew there was no other life for me. I was hooked forever. I no longer wanted to live for the things of this world, but for eternal things that lasted forever. Jesus had grabbed my heart in an unalterable way and I was His.

Someone asked me once what I love most about following the Lord. "Watching Him in action! That's what I love," I responded. That's what ministry is all about. *Jesus Christ in action.* The amazing thing is that He includes us in His work. Sometimes people ask me how I can be involved in so many things: speaking, writing, leading women, teaching for a Christian university, president of Quiet Time Ministries. And I start laughing. "It's not me. It's Him. I just get to follow Him as He does a work I could never do by myself."

Many years have come and gone since my time with Campus Crusade for Christ. The excitement of Christ in action is still just as compelling for me. I love watching Him at work. I remember the time I had the opportunity to talk about Christian beliefs in a world civilization class at a local secular college. After I spoke, the students had the opportunity to ask me questions. They asked things like:

How can I know truth?

Is there anything I can do to be saved?

Whose name can be written in the book of life?

Why is God a Triune God?

Does God choose us or do we choose Him?

What about people who have never heard the gospel?

As you might guess, we had a rousing discussion about Jesus Christ. It was a microcosm of a world hungry to know Jesus. I left that room excited and passionate again about following Jesus and watching Him in action. There have been many days of excitement just like that.

Sometimes it's just the seemingly small things, like receiving an encouraging communication. After first launching the Quiet Time Ministries website many years ago, I received an email from a lady in South Africa asking if she could print my testimony and pass it out to students at all the universities there. Of course, I responded with a resounding "Yes!" Imagine the opportunity to be an instrument for Jesus to touch lives clear across the world.

Of course, there are times when things don't always seem to work out in ministry. But when they don't, it's always because the Lord has something else in mind. He is leading in a new way. And I just need to trust Him and follow Him. I remember the first time I decided to lead a Bible study in my home in San Diego. I advertised for the study and a number of people said they wanted to attend. When the day came for the study to begin, I sat waiting for people to arrive. No one showed up. I was devastated and brokenhearted. I called my friend Judy, sobbing, "Judy, no one showed up for my Bible study." "Oh honey, let me pray," she responded. I just couldn't believe that no one showed up for my Bible study. I wanted so much to lead a Bible study. Out of the blue, two days later I received a phone call from someone at our local church. She informed me that there was a church Bible study that had lost their leader. Then, she asked, "Would you consider becoming the leader of this group?" I couldn't believe it. I immediately said *Yes!* and proceeded to watch that Bible study grow over the years. Thus began my adventure in leading Bible studies that continues to this day. I knew I had the desire to lead. I just did not realize that the Lord wanted me to lead more people than could possibly fit in my home.

Many years ago I was asked to give a message at a local retreat in San Diego. It was the first time I had ever spoken at a retreat and I was able to choose the topic. "I'll speak on 'The One Thing In Life' from my life verse in Psalm 27:4." So the day came and I walked up to the stage and looked out over the audience of hundreds. *Okay, here goes.* I was shaking, but excited because it was the first message I ever presented on quiet time. And so I began with these words: "How can we develop an intimate relationship with the Lord? How can we cultivate time alone with God? This is going to be our question for today. And we are going to answer it by looking at the life of someone who was intimate with God. Someone who had a relationship with God that was characterized by the kind of intimacy God wants with us. That person is David, the shepherd boy who became king of Israel, the one whom God called 'a man after My own heart.' That impresses me! You know why? I want to be a woman after God's own heart. Let me tell you about David…" The more I shared the message, the more passionate I became, until I soon preached those words with excitement and determination.

After I delivered that message, people surrounded me and asked me countless questions. It was a decidedly unexpected response for such a simple message. I remember walking out to the parking lot and telling the Lord, "I loved that, Lord. It would be incredible if I could do this full-time." Not long after that, the Lord gave me the idea for Quiet Time Ministries. And the ideas for messages and quiet time resources cascaded and developed, one after another. There was no one urging me on except the Lord. Of course, that was all I needed. Christ is sufficient. For me, it seemed almost effortless to produce these books and resources because the ideas were so clear in my mind. Although it did ultimately require hard work and perseverance, the Lord was more than enough and He encouraged me, day by day, year after year. Quiet Time Ministries began to grow larger than I had ever imagined. I received requests to speak at conferences and retreats. As a result, I have been privileged to receive numerous incredible opportunities to encourage others in their quiet times with the Lord over the years.

For a number of years I had been thinking about writing something to give others the actual experience of quiet time with the Lord. I experimented with many ideas. Finally, one day, all those ideas came together and I saw the format of the books of quiet times in my mind. It was so real to me that I sat down and wrote three chapters of *Pilgrimage Of The Heart* in less than two weeks. Since that time I have now written nearly thirty books, many of them quiet time studies. I receive letters and emails from people all over the world, expressing their joy in drawing near to God using these books.

That's *my* story. I share it because I want to ask you about *your* story. I wonder what plans Jesus has in mind for you. He is calling you to follow Him. Do you hear Him calling? Do you sense that He has come your way and is saying "Follow Me"? How can you respond? Dear friend, just say *yes Lord, I will follow You*. You will begin to discover who you are and why you are here. As He leads you in life, surrender to His lead. Always remember that in a dance, only one can lead, and the other follows. And then, every dance tells a story. You will discover the story as you engage in this great adventure of knowing Him. There are lots of hills and valleys, but the view is breathtaking.

Doors have opened for ministry that I could have never imagined as I have walked, day by day, with the Lord. The joy for me is to follow Christ and watch what He is going to do in and through me. He is the One who leads, going where He desires to do His work. That is really the heart of Christian ministry. Jesus leads, we follow.

When we walk with the Lord in the light of His Word,
What a glory He sheds on our way!
While we do His good will, He abides with us still,
And with all who will trust and obey.

Refrain:
Trust and obey, for there's no other way
To be happy in Jesus, but to trust and obey.

Not a shadow can rise, not a cloud in the skies,
But His smile quickly drives it away;
Not a doubt or a fear, not a sigh or a tear,
Can abide while we trust and obey

Not a burden we bear, not a sorrow we share,
But our toil He doth richly repay;
Not a grief or a loss, not a frown or a cross,
But is blessed if we trust and obey.

But we never can prove the delights of His love
Until all on the altar we lay;
For the favor He shows, for the joy He bestows,
Are for them who will trust and obey.

Then in fellowship sweet we will sit at His feet,
Or we'll walk by His side in the way;
What He says we will do, where He sends we will go;
Never fear, only trust and obey.

JOHN H. SAMMIS, TRUST AND OBEY, 1887

EMBRACING THE ETERNAL PERSPECTIVE

So we don't look at the troubles we can see now; rather, we fix our gaze on things that cannot be seen. For the things we see now will soon be gone, but the things we cannot see will last forever.

2 CORINTHIANS 4:18 NLT

What is it that enabled Amy Carmichael, a woman who saved young girls from temple prostitution in India, to write some of her best books in the last twenty years of her life while bedridden due to a devastating injury? How did Darlene Deibler Rose, a newly married missionary in the West Indies, sing hymns in a dark jail cell while imprisoned for her faith? How could Betsie and Corrie ten Boom, two sisters who were arrested for protecting Jewish people in their home, teach Bible studies to hundreds of women at Ravensbruck concentration camp in World War II? How in the world was Elisabeth Elliot, whose husband was martyred for his faith in Ecuador, able to go back into the jungle and share the gospel with the very tribe of Auca Indians who had murdered her husband? They all shared one secret in their ability to rise above their circumstances—an eternal perspective given to them by Jesus through the power of His Holy Spirit.

An eternal perspective is the ability to see all of life from God's point of view and to have what you see affect how you live in the present.[1] You discover the eternal perspective in the Bible, God's Word where you are called to a whole new way to see, think, live and experience. It's a new day for you who know Christ when you learn to see. When you have the eternal perspective, you see by faith, you think about the things of heaven, you live the abundant life, and you experience personal, spiritual revival. I have written about the eternal perspective in my book, *A Heart To See Forever —Embrace the Promise of the Eternal Perspective.*

Paul outlines our calling to the eternal perspective in 2 Corinthians 4:16-18. "That is why we never give up. Though our bodies are dying, our spirits are being renewed every day. For our present troubles are small and won't last very long. Yet they produce for us a glory that vastly outweighs them and will last forever! So we don't look at the troubles we can see now; rather, we fix our gaze on things that cannot be seen. For the things we see now will soon be gone, but the things we cannot see will last forever." These are some of the most important verses in the Bible because they show us our calling to the eternal perspective—a whole new way to see life, think about things, and live moment by moment.

I didn't always know about the eternal perspective. One day, I was listening to a lecture on the cultural context of the book of Revelation, taught by my favorite seminary professor, Dr. Walt Wessel. I was so excited to be in this class because I knew very little about Revelation and was hungry to dive in and study a book that has been difficult for so many. While Dr. Wessel was talking, I was thinking about the seven churches of western Asia Minor. I thought, *I wonder why Revelation is so difficult to understand?* The context really hinges on these seven churches and their problems. Jesus told John to "write the things which you have seen, and the things which are, and the things which will take place after these things" (Revelation 1:19). I thought, *What a perfect outline for the book of Revelation—the things John saw, the things which are, and the things which will take place after these things.* Why did the Lord give us the book of Revelation? I listened to Dr. Wessel describe the persecution of Christians by the Roman emperor Domitian. The problems facing the churches were our problems today—compromise, suffering, worldliness, despair, discouragement, financial challenges, idolatry, unbelief, illness, and immorality. Merrill C. Tenney, in his commentary on Revelation, writes, "In hours of darkness, Revelation has given courage to its readers, enabling them to endure persecution and death for the sake of Christ." Sitting in class that day, it call came together for me. The Lord wanted to give suffering believers in the church the eternal perspective, so that they could know the rest of the story of life, and stand strong in their present troubles. In that moment of realization, I wrote out the definition of an eternal perspective—*the ability to see all of life from God's point of view and to have what you see affect how you live in the present.* The eternal perspective became the focus of the study I wrote on Revelation—*A Heart To See Forever.*

Can you imagine actually having hope in the very worst of times just like those seven churches of western Asia Minor back in the time of persecution by Domitian, the cruel Roman emperor? And yet, because of our calling to an eternal perspective, we are spiritually revived in God's Word through the power of the Holy Spirit every day and experience newness of life within. Our circumstances may not change. But we have changed. We are brand new, again and again each day, as the Holy Spirit works in us. And so we find inner strength we never had before. The eternal perspective shows us that our present troubles are small and won't last very long. This is especially encouraging in trials that have plagued you for years. Oh yes, one day those trials will come to an end. That's a promise from God and you can count on it. With this calling to an eternal perspective we discover that we can see invisible things by faith. We open the pages of

God's Word and are given a glimpse into the whole new realm of God's kingdom. Though we may feel alone, we discover that God is with us always even if we can't see Him with our physical sight (Isaiah 41:10). We learn that He will provide for all our needs even though we don't have the resources or answers (Philippians 4:19). And even when we are weak, we can see by faith that we are strong and can do all things through Christ who gives us strength (Philippians 4:13). Oh, there is a whole world, invisible yet real, and open to us with the eternal perspective.

The eternal perspective is all about faith. One day the disciples were caught in a storm on the Sea of Galilee. Their boat was being tossed around in the waves and they were convinced they were going to die. Suddenly, they saw Jesus walking on the water and exclaimed, "It is a ghost!" He encouraged them, "Take courage, it is I; do not be afraid" (Matthew 14:27). One disciple was brave enough to take the Lord at His Word. Peter said, "Lord, if it is You, command me to come to You on the water." The Lord told him, "Come." Peter climbed out of the boat by faith in the word of the Lord, and oh yes, he walked on water toward the Lord. But then, Peter saw the wind and the rain, and he began to sink. He cried out to the Lord, "Lord, save me!" Immediately the Lord stretched out His hand and took hold of him. He said, "You of little faith. Why did you doubt" (Matthew 14:31). With the eternal perspective, the Lord is calling us to have a walk on water faith where we get out of the boat, listen to His Word, and look up at Him instead of looking at the wind or the rain.[2]

What does the eternal perspective look like in real life? Amy Carmichael is one of my favorite heroes of faith, who lived out the eternal perspective. As a young girl in Ireland in the mid-19th century, she would take time at night for evening prayer. But then she would smooth out a place on her bed, and say out loud, "Lord Jesus, will You come sit beside me, so we can talk?" Her mother taught her, "Amy, when you pray to the Lord, He will answer you."

Amy was so convinced when she first learned the power of prayer that she knelt before the Lord that night and prayed for the thing she wanted most of all: "Lord, will You change my eyes from brown to blue?" Oh how she longed for the beautiful Irish blue eyes. The next morning she jumped up and ran to the mirror, fully expecting that God had answered by changing her eye color. Looking into the mirror, Amy let out a wail. "Mother, my eyes are still brown. God didn't answer!" "Amy, *no* is an answer also. God must have given you brown eyes for a reason," her Mother explained. Even in her lesson on prayer, she saw with an eternal perspective and learned that God's ways are higher than our ways.

She heard the call to see, live, and think with the eternal perspective and acted on it with every new opportunity. As a teenager in Belfast, Northern Ireland, she made her way into the slums to reach out to young girls who worked in the mills. She set up Bible studies to feed their hunger for God. She took her ministry to the slums of Manchester, England, where the streets were dangerous and conditions were terrible. And yet, her passion to spread God's Word to those in need flourished in this most desperate of places.

One day Amy Carmichael heard Hudson Taylor, founder of China Inland Mission, give a message about missions, saying "a million are dying a month without God." She was drawn in by his words and heard the call of Jesus to go out into the world. She applied to China Inland Mission but was rejected for health reasons. And yet, she knew that God would equip her and give her strength even in her weakness. How could she know this? Because she saw the truth of it—the eternal perspective—in God's promises in His Word. She didn't see the way the world saw. She saw what God sees. Her mind was fixed on God's view—His perspective outlined in the Bible. She stepped out in faith in God's Word. And she was excited to follow Jesus wherever He led. And lead He did. She had been turned down for missionary work time after time due to health reasons. She determined to go when the Lord led and said, "If any mission anywhere will take me, I'm going." In 1894, Amy was to receive a calling that would change her life forever and take her in the direction of her life work with the Lord.

A friend invited Amy to join the Church of England Missionary Society in Bangalore, India. Amy traveled to India, learned the Tamil language, studied the Hindu caste system, and shared the gospel of Christ with others. She wrote that she found the Indian people "a series of contradictions. They are loving and lovable, cruel and needing-all-grace to love, bright and dull, eager and lazy to a degree perfectly incomprehensible at home. They are trustworthy and utterly the opposite, courteous and quite barbarous. They are everything you can imagine except, perhaps straightforward."[3] You can see her heart for the Lord and passion to carry out His will in her words, "I long to be led to the truly seeking soul."[4]

Then, in 1901, something happened that was to change Amy's life and ministry forever. She and a small band of women who had joined her in a ministry of itinerant evangelism had moved to Dohnavur, a small village in India. The women had witnessed little girls who were sold and then given by their families to service in the temple as prostitutes. Amy was sitting one morning having her early tea. A Christian woman named "Servant of Jesus" appeared in the doorway with a disheveled little Indian girl. "This is Preena" she said. Preena ran to Amy, jumped into her lap, looked into her face and said, "My name is Pearl-eyes, and I want to stay here always. I have come to stay."[5] Preena called her "Amma" which means "mother." In her conversations with Preena, Amy learned about the sex trafficking that was going on with young girls.

Amy's mission station in Dohnavur became a home for many young girls—some were rejected by their family due to their faith in Christ. Others were seeking sanctuary from the temple where they had been given by their families to be prostitutes. Soon there were more than 50 in her adopted family and she came to be known as Amma, the Tamil word for "mother."

In India, she discovered the reason why God did not give her blue eyes. She blended in with the culture with her dark hair and eyes. God had made her just right for what He was calling her to do. And for the next fifty-five years, she wore the traditional sari, and served as Amma to hundreds of young girls. Some of these girls became beloved co-laborers in her work at Dohnavur Fellowship, her orphanage in India.

One day as she was walking the land of Dohnavur, she took a bad fall. Her injuries kept her isolated to a single room and often bedridden for the last twenty years of her life. But that did not keep her from ministry. She studied, and wrote books and poetry. She was prolific during her ministry, writing nearly forty books during her lifetime.

Amy never returned to England after arriving in India. How could it be possible that such a gifted woman could spend her entire life in an obscure corner of the world in India? Amy didn't live for what she could see, but for things invisible because of the calling to an eternal perspective. She said, "Faith does not eliminate questions. But faith knows where to take them."[6] According to Elisabeth Elliot, Amy longed to have "a single eye for the glory of God. Whatever might blur the vision God had given her of His work, whatever could distract or deceive or tempt other to seek anything but the Lord Jesus Himself she tried to eliminate."[7]

She loved God's Word and lived in it every day of her life. She didn't think about the things of the world, but instead thought of heavenly things with Jesus her Lord. She said, "If the life of a man or woman on earth is to bear the fragrance of heaven, the winds of God must blow on that life."[8] When the Lord Jesus makes His home in us and we are filled with the Holy Spirit, there is no mistaking that life. It's a heavenly life where the winds of God have been blowing through the mind and soul.

She was constantly revived by Him and given everything she needed each day as she walked with the Lord. She engaged in the great adventure of knowing God and lived an abundant and fruitful life. She simply was not ruled by the temporal but by the eternal, not by sight but by faith, not by the physical senses, but by the eternal spiritual senses within. She said, "Our feelings do not affect God's facts. They may blow up, like clouds, and cover the eternal things that we most truly believe. We may not see the shining of the promises—but still they shine!"[9]

When speaking of her ministry, Amy Carmichael remarked, "Missionary life is simply a chance to die." Amy saw by faith that it was no longer she who lived, but Christ who lived in her. And the life she lived was by faith in the Son of God who loved her and gave Himself up for her (Galatians 2:20).

I first learned of Amy Carmichael from Elisabeth Elliot, the wife of Jim Elliot, the missionary martyred for his faith, who knew her and wrote her biography, *A Chance To Die*. Amy has always been a hero of the faith for me. I have read many of her books and have meditated on her devotional writing in my quiet times. Every time I read something she has written, I think, *Lord, I want to have a passion and perspective like Amy*. In fact, Amy's books, *Thou Givest, They Gather* and *The Edges Of His Ways* have been the tools God used to teach me how to glean spiritual treasure from God's Word and write my insights in my journal. I remember reading about how Amy noticed the word "trust" in the Bible. She looked up its meaning in a Bible dictionary and discovered the expanded description "to lean upon, to place the weight of my confidence upon." She then wrote about how this helps her learn to put her trust in God into practice by leaning upon the Lord and His lovingkindness. Amy has taught me to take time to notice spiritual truth in God's Word from single words and small phrases. As I take time in the Bible like this I am given the eternal perspective and move from the temporal to the eternal. Amy Carmichael has been one of the key mentors who has discipled me in my relationship with the Lord. She was also, in a sense, the spiritual mother for Elisabeth Elliot. Elisabeth learned so much about the faith from her. I can see how that could happen. It has been true for me as well. Amy Carmichael has taught me to have the eternal perspective and live by faith with every choice and direction I take in life.

So I want to ask you, have you answered the calling to see with an eternal perspective and live by faith? What will help you to have an eternal perspective and see and think with your spiritual senses? The most important thing you can do is live in God's Word every day. I just cannot stress this principle enough. It is most important that you develop and cultivate your quiet time with the Lord. I realize I have said this before, but now I want to say some things that are still on my heart. The world just does not encourage time alone with God. Even the Christian world makes light of it. And I am going to tell you it is absolutely the most important and essential thing you will do every day.

When you lose your quiet time you lose more than you can imagine. You will begin to see and think like the world. You will find yourself anxious and worried about everything. Your peace will fly out the window because you will forget those things that are true and right. Oh friend, the best thing you can do when you lose your quiet time is to drop everything and get alone with God and get back your time with Him.

I had an interesting conversation with a pastor who had walked through a very deep valley and had found some of my studies in a bookstore. He said they were the only studies he could find that helped him to really get back to God's Word. And then, he reflected that his troubles all began when he stopped having his quiet time.

And that leads me to this encouragement. How is your quiet time and what do you do in your quiet time? Are you actually living in God's Word? You see, many people I know read a page in a devotional and call that quiet time. That's not the kind of quiet time that I'm talking about. It is a quiet time, yes, but not quiet time where you live in God's Word and draw near to the Lord.

I'll never forget the day in one of our Bible studies where I was leading discussion and a woman stood up and said, "I was amazed to read a passage in the Bible and actually experienced God speaking to me in His Word!" She described how the words seemed to jump off the page and into her heart. They were so much more significant and meaningful to her and she was convinced God wanted her to know the truth she gleaned from them. You see, that's what the Holy Spirit does when He takes the Word of God and applies it to your heart. The Bible is one of your best friends. Get to know it better than you know any earthly friend. It's where you will find God's eternal perspective.

When you live by the eternal perspective, your eyes will be fixed on Jesus, and you will follow Him wherever He leads. Living with an eternal perspective is essential to heart revival, a transformed and victorious life, and becoming the person God wants you to be. You will experience the joy of Jesus—not the absence of suffering, but the presence of God. We are called to experience joy and it flows directly from the eternal perspective we gain from the word of the Lord. Jesus says, "I have told you these things so that you will be filled with my joy. Yes, your joy will overflow" (John 15:11 NLT).

I have discovered that one of the main ways the Lord grows our eternal perspective is by removing earthly props and supports so we will see the heavenly, eternal truth in His Word. His Word shines much more brightly in the darkness of disappointment or loss. G.D. Watson, a 19th century deeper life author, in his little book, *Soul Food*, describes God's ways: "He allows all sorts of disappointments—the death of bright hopes, the removing of earthly friendships or destruction of property, the multiplied infirmities of the body and mind, the misunderstanding of dear ones, until the landscape of religious life seems swept with a blizzard, to compel the soul to house itself in God alone."[10]

There is a true story about a man who set sail off the coast of Massachusetts in a small motor yacht. All of a sudden fog engulfed the sailing vessel. One wrong move and his tiny craft would be crushed like paper by the huge ships that occupied the same waterway. The man described his terror and loss of perspective, "It was though the windows were painted black and I was forced to fly by instruments only." The Word of God helps you "fly by instruments only" and maneuver through the fog of trials and difficulties in life, growing your eternal perspective.

My friend, Melinda, has been traveling through the fog of a life-threatening heart problem over the last two years. She so trusts in God and His promises that she said "the storms of life are God's brilliant disguises." That is the cry of one who truly lives by the eternal perspective and is fully assured of God's purpose and His presence. It is a red letter day when you can step out in faith and recognize the presence of the Lord even in life's deepest darkness.

When you turn to God alone, and look to His Word in desperation, His eternal perspective shines like a beacon into your life, and your faith in Him grows and expands as never before. This turning to God is a raw act of faith enabled by the indwelling Holy Spirit without any feeling or visible awareness or trace of His presence in the face of extreme adversity. This is the highest form of faith. S.D. Gordon, author and lay minister in the 20th century, writes of this faith experience of God as the difference between *realizing* (sight) and *recognizing* (faith): "There is something a little higher up than realizing. It is yet more blessed. It is independent of these outer conditions, it is something that abides. It is this: recognizing that Presence unseen, so wondrous and quieting, so soothing and calming and warming...Some *One* is present, a warm-hearted Friend, an all-powerful Lord. And this is the joyful truth for weeping hearts everywhere, whatever be the hand that has drawn the tears; by whatever stream it be that your weeping willow is planted."[11] When we can come to the place where we believe and trust God and His Word without any earthly sight or support, then nothing can shake us and we will stand strong in Him.

One day I was taking a walk with the Lord and I confess I was frustrated with all the adversity in my life. As I was walking and talking with the Lord, I started complaining to Him. "Lord, I am tired of all these trials. I'm tired of not knowing where certain things I need are going to come from. And I'm tired of faith. I want the sight." Well as soon as I finished that last statement, I stopped. It was as though the huge hand of God stopped me in my tracks. *Catherine, what in the world are you saying?* That thought literally went through my mind, as though I was speaking to my own heart and soul. And then this thought came. *Catherine, you have more sight than most people. And it's because you know more of God's Word than most people. That IS your sight!* Whoa! I'll tell you, the Lord brought me up short right then and there. I started laughing at myself. Then I told the Lord how sorry I was for complaining about things that weren't even true. I am so thankful for how the Lord took me straight to His eternal perspective that day. I was able to go on with Him joyfully as He continued to lead me in life. In that moment, I once again experienced personal spiritual revival—a restoration of heart and soul so I could continue to experience God's plan and purpose as I walked with Him.

Amy Carmichael writes, "If you would live in victory over the circumstances, great and small, that come to you each day...and if you want God's life and power to well up from the depths of your being...then you must refuse to be dominated by the *seen* and the *felt*."[12] Real sight comes from the calling of God that we hear and discover in His Word.

The Lord is so very faithful to give us His eternal perspective day-by-day and moment-by-moment. He is calling us to His eternal perspective. Just open His Word and there it is for the taking. Amy Carmichael knew it. Elisabeth Elliot knew it. And you can know it too.

From prayer that asks that I may be
Sheltered from winds that beat on Thee,
From fearing when I should aspire,
From faltering when I should climb higher,
From silken self, O Captain free
Thy soldier who would follow Thee.

From subtle love of softening things,
From easy choices, weakenings,
(Not thus are spirits fortified,
Not this way went the Crucified,)
From all that dims Thy Calvary,
O Lamb of God, deliver me.

Give me the love that leads the way,
the faith that nothing can dismay,
the hope no disappointments tire,
the passion that will burn like fire;
Let me not sink to be a clod:
Make me Thy fuel, Flame of God.[13]

AMY CARMICHAEL

SHARING GOD'S HEART

Delight yourself in the Lord; and He will give you the desires of your heart.
PSALM 37:4 NIV

elen Roseveare heard about missionary work in faraway places when she was just 8 years old in Hertfordshire, England in the early 1900s. And her family must have engaged in conversations about it in some way because both her father and brother ended up living and working in Africa as teachers. Driven to scholarly excellence, Helen studied medicine at Cambridge University. Some young women from the Cambridge Inter-Collegiate Christian Union befriended her. She began attending Bible studies and was led to read the Bible for herself. And yet, she was still searching. She didn't understand what God was all about; she was drawn to these women who seemed to have a peace and joy that was elusive to her.

Helen was searching for God and one night after a heated argument with some women, she ran up to her room and threw herself on the bed: "I…rushed upstairs, bitterly ashamed of having been drawn into the argument and losing control of myself. Suddenly, I flung myself on my bed, in a flood of tears and loneliness. With an overwhelming sense of failure and helplessness I cried out to God (if there was a God) to meet with me and to make utterly real and vital to me Himself. I raised my eyes, and through my tears read a text on the wall: 'Be still, and know that I am God' (Psalm 46:10). That was all. Immediately the whole burden fell away in a moment. Be still and know God, whose name is "I am."…Stop striving to understand with the intellect. Just be still, and know him. In that moment, a great flood of peace and joy and unutterable happiness flooded in, and I knew that He and I had entered into a new relationship.[1] For the first time, she experienced the peace and joy of a relationship with God. It was at that very moment Helen Roseveare fell in love with Jesus and was filled with an overwhelming desire to serve Him wherever He led. And that desire or calling remained a constant for her entire life never, diminishing or fading away.

A Bible teacher wrote Philippians 3:10 in Helen's Bible. That verse became one of Helen's life verses, "That I may know Him and the power of His resurrection and the fellowship of His sufferings; being conformed to His death." In these words, we see that there is a sharing we have with Jesus—a sharing of everything—and that includes His power and His suffering. Through the course of Helen Roseveare's life, she experienced the truth of sharing everything with Jesus in more ways than she could have ever imagined—more power, His higher ways and thoughts, and greater suffering. From the moment she stepped into a relationship with Jesus, she discovered her heart became burdened with needs greater than her own. She knew she was called to missions and that calling included her medical training. But she did not know at the outset all it would involve and how it would carry her outside of herself into uncomfortable places with sub-optimal conditions. Helen described her calling from God in these words: "He who was calling me on to service overseas was standing there, gently smiling, promising His presence and companionship and enabling, telling me to look forward and upward, not backward or inward."[2]

Through Worldwide Evangelization Crusade, Helen was assigned to establish medical services and training in the remote village of Ibambi in the Belgian Congo. The Belgian Congo was a Belgian colony in Central Africa between 1908 and 1960 in what is now the Democratic Republic of the Congo.[3] She had spent years of training as a physician and now, at the young age of twenty-seven, she was going to what seemed like the end of the world to practice medicine in a place that had very little equipment or personnel. The conditions were nothing like what she was used to in her training in Britain. And this was not certainly easy for her. Now she would truly begin to share the heart of her Lord. What was His dream for His girl, Helen? She would discover it, little by little. And through struggle and wrestling, she learned to surrender and dream His dreams.

Helen Roseveare describes the reality of surrendering to God, sharing His heart, and doing all things for the sake of the gospel: "When I began to realize that over 200 patients were being treated daily…and 75% or more were responding immediately to the initial treatment given, I began to see that it was not necessarily a lowering of standards to treat malarial symptoms without laboratory confirmation: rather it was a necessary adaptation to circumstances…These same 200 patients daily, having received something that aided their physical pain to subside, were then much more open to listen to the preaching of the gospel."[4]

Helen established forty-eight rural health clinics, a training center, and a hospital. With her as the leader, the training college and hospital were built from the ground up. Here was where Helen especially struggled. So many necessary roles competed with the primary one of medical missions. Again and again, she had to surrender to Jesus at the foot of the cross to discover what was on His heart for her in the place where He had led. Sometimes that meant she had to drop everything and draw near to Him in a quiet place where she could refresh and renew. Sometimes she needed to just be still and know that He was God.

At the end of her life, in her last video message, Helen Roseveare spoke of sharing the heart of Jesus. She said, "The very first night I was saved I had the overwhelming desire that I wanted to serve Him. I would do anything he asked, I would go anywhere he sent me, and I wanted to let Him know Him to know I loved Him. That has honestly never changed for me. It's the root motivation for me…All of us have the privilege of being called to be His servants. That's just so wonderful. Jesus said that He Himself, did not come to be served but to serve and to give…We are called to serve Him. We serve Him because we love Him. Whatever we are doing, we are doing for Jesus. Think in those terms. Put Jesus first. And when you feel as though you've reached the end of your tether, He is there. He knows. He's been through it all. He's there to help you. Even if you can't see any point in what you are doing, nevertheless, it's for Him and He knows what He is doing and why. It does all fit in. It's amazing."

Helen Roseveare had such a great sense of the privilege to share in the sufferings of Jesus and to be chosen to serve Him. Even near the end of her life when she had a greater longing to go home to heaven, she would smile and say, "He knows when. I'm resting in the wisdom and guidance of my Lord."

I've spent many hours reflecting on Helen Roseveare's life, her example of a surrendered heart to God's ways and His will, and her passionate commitment to sharing His heart and serving Him. I see in her life a journey of learning and growth developing in her a willingness to follow Jesus.

One of the greatest discoveries I made early on in my own relationship with the Lord was that God had ideas in mind for me that were far different from my own initial desires. After I came to the Lord and I became deeply involved with Campus Crusade for Christ, I was filled with a great desire to disciple women on college campuses. I applied and was accepted as a staff member with Campus Crusade for Christ. My dream was to go to a college campus somewhere and train women the way Leann Pruitt McGee, my CCC mentor, had trained me at Arizona State University. The one thing I had not counted on was that God might have something else designed for me that was higher and better in His story for me. There is a verse I did not yet know or understand in Proverbs, "The mind of man plans his way, but the Lord directs his steps" (Proverbs 16:9). And God was taking me in a direction that had not even entered my mind. That's where the adventure of a lifetime usually begins.

When you apply for staff with Campus Crusade for Christ, you go through a series of interviews, tests, and applications. Then, each applicant is placed as God leads and the placements are then communicated to the new staff members. When the placement letters came out for my staff assignment, I was shocked. It read: "Secretary, Josh McDowell Ministry." I was absolutely devastated. The last thing in the world I wanted to do was be a "secretary" and this placement did not fit into my plans at all.

Right away, I was forced to think in a new way. If God was leading in this direction, then I had to surrender to His dream for me, and think in a whole new way. I can't even begin to tell you how difficult this was for me. I called my mother on the phone sobbing, "Mother, this is the last thing I would have ever wanted. I'm devastated." My mother tried to calm me down, but I was inconsolable.

I hung up the phone. *I've got to get out of here and go to a place where I can think. I need to talk with the Lord.* So there I was in Fort Collins, Colorado, in a seemingly foreign place where I literally did not know anyone. Sobbing uncontrollably, I walked to my little used Fiat in the parking lot and I looked up at the majestic Rocky Mountains. *I want to go to the mountains where I can talk with God about this.* So I got in my car, pulled out of the lot, and drove at least 35 miles towards Rocky Mountain National Park, crying so hard I could barely breathe. My dreams were utterly shattered. Then, some words from Oswald Chambers came to my mind about how sometimes God will withdraw conscious blessings to teach us to walk by faith. I had read somewhere else that when our dreams are shattered, our vision is broadened. *If God is in this, then what does He want me to do?* I pulled my car over at a rest stop where I could get out in the open air looking up to God's vast creation there in the mountains. I said out loud to God, "God, I don't want to be a secretary, because I don't see how that can lead to my dream of sharing the gospel and discipling women. But I do want Your will. If this is Your way, then even if I don't understand, I surrender to You and trust that You are causing all of this to work together." Oh, that was such a hard prayer. But after I prayed it, with tears still rolling down my cheeks, I experienced a newfound peace from God.

Perhaps, the hardest thing I ever did in my life was get in my little car and drive to Dallas, Texas, to serve the Lord in the Josh McDowell Ministry. On the other side of that time, I can see what God was doing. I didn't know that the Lord was going to lead me into Quiet Time Ministries where I would begin writing books and delivering messages at retreats and conferences to hundreds and hundreds of women. But God knew all along that was His dream for me. And what better way for me to learn than to place me with one of the greatest Christian speakers and writers of all time, Josh McDowell. I just couldn't see it then. So the most important choice I made was to surrender, say *yes* to the Lord, draw near to God, and pour my heart into knowing and loving Him. And that decision continues to be the most important choice I make every single day. Surrender. Always surrender. Why? Because I am still, and always, in that place of needing to dream God's dreams and share His heart. In the same way that I didn't understand His ways many years ago, I still do not immediately see or understand what He is doing in my life. But I can always share His heart. And I can follow Him in new ways to dream His dreams.

Going in God's direction has helped me know and understand how He has made me. He is faithful to lead me to places and ministries and jobs where I either learn those things that are definitely not my gifts or discover new gifts I didn't even know I had.

I walked through the door of the temporary employment agency. I was desperate for a job. My husband and I had moved to a new city and we needed the second income. "I'm here to see if you can find me a job," I said with concern in my voice. The receptionist handed me an application and said, "Once you fill it out, we will test you to see what you can do." I filled it out, listing all the computer software I knew and my past job experience, then handed the form back to her. As I sat there waiting, all these disparate thoughts went through my mind: *I can't believe I'm sitting here at a temp agency, desperate for work. How in the world will this work out? I'm never going to get a job. We're going to end up on the street. Lord, what are You doing here?* It truly is amazing the false stories I can tell myself in hard times. "Catherine, follow me." The businesslike voice of the woman broke the flow of anxious thoughts flooding my mind and brought me back to reality. I followed the woman into another room filled with computers. "We would like to test your typing skills and also your ability to use QuarkXpress." I replied, "Well, I know Adobe InDesign but I've never used QuarkXpress." She said, "Well, we want to see how you do on it anyway." I got kind of excited about this new challenge with desktop publishing software I had never before used, though I thought it was a little unorthodox. The typing test was a piece of cake. I've been typing since I was in high school and using the keyboard is like playing the piano for me. Now came the time for the QuarkXpress test. I answered each question by thinking, *How can I take what I know about InDesign and apply it to this software?* I discovered it was actually easier than I expected.

The results surprised me and the lady at the temp agency. She said, "You aced QuarkXpress like a pro. We didn't actually expect that kind of a result. We are going to be able to easily get you a job." And in fact, I did get a job within just a few days.

That event at the employment agency is when I began to understand I had a gift for computers and software. God has made me that way so I can do certain things He has in mind for me. Since that time I've been able to use that knowledge in publishing books and designing websites. I love working on the computer and that's a good thing since I spend most of my time writing books, articles, blog posts, and messages.

In my first experience of leading a Bible study, when the Lord moved it from my home to the church, I learned something new and important from the Lord about myself, and my spiritual gifts. I learned that I have the gifts of exhortation and teaching and that the Lord did want me to teach His Word. I have always tried to be actively involved in teaching Bible studies. And the teaching in Bible studies has also led to speaking at conferences and retreats where I have the opportunity to teach God's Word and encourage others in their relationship with Him.

What is God's dream for you? How will you respond when God leads you in unexpected ways? Will you surrender to Him like Helen Roseveare? We are called to share God's heart and dream His dreams not our own. Maybe the very place where you are that you so desperately want to escape is exactly the place God is calling you for His purposes. Begin an aggressive course with the Lord of dreaming God's dreams. Open the pages of your Bible to discover what is on His heart.

Then, share His heart. Keep your mind focused on His desires and purposes. This will include the salvation of others, sharing the gospel, and the kingdom of God. One thing you notice when you read the Gospels is that Jesus preached a lot about the kingdom of God. You see, our minds are often filled with earthly things that are literally fading away. The kingdom of God lasts forever and it is the realm where we live in eternity. It goes on and on and on and on. Heaven is much more attractive to me now because so many people I love live there. I can't wait to see Jesus. And I am so looking forward to seeing my mother and father. And then, I have many beloved friends there. Oh what a day it will be. And Jesus has a place prepared for me even now. So our minds need to be filled with the kingdom of God and heaven much more than the things of earth. When that happens, we are dreaming God's dreams.

David wrote, "Delight yourself in the Lord; and He will give you the desires of your heart" (Psalm 37:4). Those words do not mean He will always give you what you want. They mean He will literally fill your heart with His desires. You will begin to dream His dreams as you know and love Him. Moses was one who wanted to share the heart of God. He asked the Lord, "Let me know Your ways that I may know You" (Exodus 33:13). Ask God to show you His ways and You will grow in your knowledge of Him.

When you surrender to God and allow Him to transform you, you will dream God's dreams and experience His will for your life, realizing again and again why you are here. Paul writes: "And so, dear brothers and sisters, I plead with you to give your bodies to God because of all he has done for you. Let them be a living and holy sacrifice—the kind he will find acceptable. This is truly the way to worship him. Don't copy the behavior and customs of this world, but let God transform you into a new person by changing the way you think. Then you will learn to know God's will for you, which is good and pleasing and perfect" (Romans 12:1-2). Again and again, the Lord has led me to give myself to Him. And He has been faithful to use His Word to change me by changing the way I think. I am led from my own ways and thoughts to His higher ways and thoughts (Isaiah 55:8-9).

Something that has helped me share God's heart is asking Him to give me a life verse. When the Lord gave me Psalm 27:4 as my life verse, I memorized it, and have pursued an intimate relationship with the Lord ever since. That life verse has helped me share God's desire for intimacy with me. Everything I do in life flows from that intimate relationship. The same will be true for you when you carry one main verse with you throughout life to guide and direct you, and help you focus on the desires of God.

How can you know the dreams God has for you? Pay attention to the places where God has led you and the things He has asked of you. What do you love to do? Where are your talents? What are your gifts? In fact, if you have doubts, I recommend you ask family members or good friends. They will help you to see things you may not even know about yourself. Then, I encourage you to take a page in your journal and write out those things you see so far in your life. I have discovered that writing in my journal helps me in sharing God's heart and dreaming His dreams. I believe that one of the best ways to know and understand your gifts and talents is to step out in faith and serve the Lord in the areas that are most interesting and exciting to you. Where do you gravitate? What is on your heart when it comes to serving the Lord?

Paul taught the Corinthian church that there are varieties of gifts, ministries, and effects from the Lord (1 Corinthians 12:4-6). Each of us is given one or more gifts for the purpose of serving and helping each other in the church, the body of Christ (1 Corinthians 12:7). We see the gifts of Word of wisdom, word of knowledge, faith, healing, prophecy, tongues, interpretation of tongues, apostles, teachers, deeds of power, forms of assistance, and forms of leadership in 1 Corinthians 12:8-10,28). There are gifts of prophecy, ministry, teaching, exhortation, giving, leading, and showing mercy in Romans 12:6-8. And finally, in Ephesians 4:11 are apostles, prophets, evangelists, pastors, and teachers. W.O. Carver in his Ephesians Commentary, *The Glory of God in the Christian Calling*, points out that each one of us "is equipped with and individual share and quality of the grace of God…each member stands out distinct from all the rest in the mind and in the giving of the Christ; yet the purpose is in every case making each one able to contribute his part to the great design of perfecting the growing Body."[5] Only God, through His indwelling Spirit, could work in us individually as Christ lives in us and yet accomplish a unity through "one body and one Spirit" (Ephesians 4:4).[6]

Our gifts are not only given to us, they are entrusted to us from the Lord. Peter gives us more insight into who we are—"stewards of the manifold grace of God" (1 Peter 4:10). And our use of our gifts is a stewardship entrusted to us by the Lord (1 Corinthians 9:17). So our calling is a high calling, not just happenstance or accidental. We live with intention as we carry out our calling from the Lord each day.

Sharing God's heart and dreaming His dreams will lead us in unexpected directions. I want you to know there will be times that He will take you where you don't want to go. Always remember, God is not out to disappoint you. He wants the very best for you and is able to cause all things to work together for good in the lives of those who love Him and are called according to His purpose (Romans 8:28). In Jeremiah 29:11 we hear God's heart for us when He says, "For I know the plans I have for you," says the Lord. "They are plans for good and not for disaster, to give you a future and a hope." God often moves us from one place to another through a bend in the road. We don't always like the bend in the road and sometimes even try to avoid it. The most important thing we can do is step back and ask, "Lord, what is on your heart? Will you help me focus on You and follow Your guidance?" When God moved us from San Diego to Palm Desert, that bend in the road devastated me. *Lord, You are making a big mistake and now my ministry is over*, was my first thought. But as I shared before, that one move was the beginning of my writing books and increased the growth of Quiet Time Ministries.

God is faithful to lead us in the power of the Holy Spirit. Paul said, "For all who are led by the Spirit of God are children of God" (Romans 8:14 NLT). J. I. Packer explains how God's Spirit leads us into God's will: "The Spirit leads by helping us understand the biblical guidelines within which we must keep, the biblical goals at which we must aim, and the biblical models that we should imitate, as well as the bad examples from which we are meant to take warning. He leads through prayer and others' advice, giving us wisdom as to how we can best follow biblical teaching. He leads by giving us the desire for spiritual growth and God's glory. The result is that spiritual priorities become clearer, and our resources of wisdom and experience for making future decisions increase. He leads, finally, by making us delight in God's will so that we find ourselves wanting to do it because we know it is best."[7]

Having God's Spirit at work in us is a winning proposition at all times. Jesus told His disciples that He would not leave them as orphans, but that He would give them His Spirit, and would come to them (John 14:13). You can count on the Holy Spirit to lead and guide you, helping you dream God's dreams for your life.

When we go about our day, sharing the heart of God means being open to the opportunities that unfold before our very eyes. We are a fragrance of Christ to God among those who are saved and those who don't know the Lord (2 Corinthians 2:15). The beautiful aroma of Christ spreads through you and touches the lives of those around you. And it will sometimes happen when you least expect it in the most unusual place.

One day many years ago I was perusing the shelves at my favorite Christian bookstore in San Diego. I noticed a young man looking at some of the books. He turned and spoke.

"Excuse me miss. Could you help me?" he asked.

I said, "Maybe. What do you need?"

He said, "My girlfriend is a born again Christian. It's her birthday and I want to give her a special gift. By the way, what is a born again Christian?"

I could not believe I was even hearing this question. I looked around and thought this must be Christian Candid Camera. I mean, how many times do you go somewhere and have someone ask you the easiest lead-in to sharing the gospel?

I asked, "Do you really want to know?"

He said, "Yes, I've been wondering about this for a long time now."

So I spent the next fifteen minutes telling him about Jesus and all that Jesus had done on the cross for him. And then I talked about our need to be born again spiritually. Finally, I asked the golden question. "Would you like to receive Christ, establish a relationship with Him, and be born again?"

He looked into my eyes with a big smile and said, "Yes, I would."

Again, I could hardly believe this was happening. But the Lord Jesus was not remotely surprised. It was on His heart for that day. His dream was to touch this young man's life and have a relationship forever with him.

We sat down at a little table there in the Christian bookstore and I prayed a simple prayer with him. After I prayed, he too prayed, asking the Lord to come into his life, forgive his sins, and make him the person He wanted him to be. It was a beautiful moment I'll never forget.

When we finished praying, I told him, "You just gave your girlfriend the best birthday present imaginable. She is going to be so excited about what has happened here. And your life is going to be changed forever."

I often think about how Jesus was on His way to Galilee one day. And the biblical text tells us this important fact: "He had to go through Samaria on the way" (John 4:4). Now, here's the question. Why in the world did Jesus have to go through Samaria? This was an unusual, out of the way action on His part. I'll tell you exactly why He went to Samaria. Because there was a precious woman who was going to be trudging down a dirt path to a well as she did every day to draw water. And Jesus knew her heart and her desperate life. And He wanted to give her living water so she would never be thirsty again (John 4). That's just how important even one person is to Jesus.

Dear friend, this same Jesus lives in you. And sometimes He will take you out of your way just to touch the life of one person. Will you dream His dreams and allow Him to touch lives in and through you in this lost and hurting world? Will you be open to His opportunities each day? Ask the Lord, "What is on Your heart today?" Sharing His heart means realizing the need of others, giving His love away, and sacrificing to do His will. If your answer is *yes* to His call to share His heart, then get ready for the adventure of your life. There are lots of hills and valleys, but the view is absolutely breathtaking.

THE CALLED-OUT ONES

…Christ also loved the church and gave Himself up for her.
EPHESIANS 5:25

Charles Haddon Spurgeon, a minister in London in the 1800s, has been called the Prince of Preachers. Carl Henry, a 20th Century theologian, called him one of evangelical Christianity's immortals. Spurgeon was born in 1834 and was part of a family of ministers, but he did not give his life to Christ until age sixteen. One year later he became pastor of his first church. His calling as an itinerant preacher was certain, he loved preaching, and he served as a pastor until the day he stepped into heaven in 1892. In his book, *Lectures to My Students*, he revealed his true thoughts of preaching, "We must feel that woe is unto us if we preach not the gospel; the word of God must be unto us as fire in our bones, otherwise, if we undertake the ministry, we shall be unhappy in it, shall be unable to bear the self-denials incident to it, and shall be of little service to those among whom we minister."[1] The churches he served included New Park Street Chapel and the Metropolitan Tabernacle in London. He was so gifted that his reputation quickly spread and every hall was filled to capacity when he preached. His sermons were published in *The [London] Times* and even in *The New York Times*. One of Spurgeon's critics remarked about Spurgeon: "Here is a man who has not moved an inch forward in all his ministry, and at the close of the nineteenth century is teaching the theology of the first century, and…is proclaiming the doctrines of Nazareth and Jerusalem current eighteen hundred years ago." Spurgeon smiled and said, "Those words did please me!"[2] Spurgeon so loved the church that he established The Pastors' College in 1856 (later changed to Spurgeon's College) to train others to become ministers.

In his sermon, *The Church As She Should Be*, Spurgeon spoke of the high calling of the church: "It is her honor and joy to stand well in the love and esteem of her royal spouse, the Prince Emmanuel…It is evident that the Divine Bridegroom gives his bride a high place in his heart, and to him, whatever she may be to others, she is fair, lovely, comely, beautiful, and in the eyes of his love without a spot. Moreover, even to him there is not only a beauty of a soft and gentle kind in her, but a majesty, a dignity in her holiness, in her earnestness, in her consecration…She is every inch a queen: her aspect in the sight of her beloved is majestic."

You are called to be part of the church, described by Spurgeon as a "majestic queen." And this high calling means that you never stand alone, but always in the context of the community of believers in Christ. Even if you think you are alone, you are not, because you are part of the church, also known as "the body of Christ." Paul tells Christians that "all of you together are Christ's body, and each of you is a part of it" (1 Corinthians 12:27 NLT).

I love the church. In retrospect, I guess I have always had a calling for the church even before I knew I loved the church. So the first thing I did after I surrendered my life to Christ while at Arizona State University was call my friend Nancy, because I knew she was definitely a Christian. "Nancy, you're never going to believe it. I just gave my life to the Lord," I blurted out. "I want to live for Him. Will you help me grow in my new relationship with Jesus?" Nancy was floored, the phone silent for a moment. Then she said, "Catherine, why don't you come to church with me? You'll meet other Christians and they will encourage you in your faith." Why not? So that first Sunday, I met Nancy at Bethany Bible Church in Phoenix, Arizona. As we walked up the sidewalk to enter the church, my heart was racing with excitement, and not a little trepidation. I loved that people were greeting each other and there were a lot of smiles. Of course, at my insistence, Nancy and I sat near the front. The pastor, Dr. John Mitchell, spoke with passion directly from a passage in the Bible, a real preacher. I just remember being so encouraged and challenged and I couldn't get enough; I could have stayed there all day. I was actually sad when the service ended. This was the new me. Then, Nancy said, "I want you to go with me to Bible study this week. It's at Earl and Mary Ann Runte's house. You'll love it because you'll meet a lot of young people who love Jesus." *Meet new people, I'm a party girl, I'm there.*

The days flew by in my mind. I was nervous but excited. We arrived at the Bible study and the front door was wide open. The first person to greet me was Earl Runte. He shook my hand enthusiastically, studied my face for a moment, and said, "Welcome, I'm Earl. I'm so happy you came to Bible Study." I responded, "Thanks, I'm Catherine, and I'm looking forward to it," not having the faintest idea what was ahead. Nancy and I sat next to some other girls who were soon to become my good friends. We all sat there attentively with open Bibles as Earl taught from a passage of Scripture. I thought, *This must be what heaven is like. The Lord is right here. I can't wait to know Him better.* Thinking back, I really loved those times. In fact, I had perfect attendance. It was a whole new life as a babe in Christ. I just couldn't wait to get to church each week and to attend those Bible studies.

Indeed, the church has been instrumental in my life. Right from the beginning. When I was in Hawaii at that summer project with Campus Crusade for Christ, the Lord led me to a wonderful church there in Oahu called Kapahulu Bible Church. It was a fairly small church and I loved the intimacy. But the first Sunday I attended was a brand new church experience for me, togetherness without pomp and circumstance. After the service, I asked the couple sitting next to me, "Okay, so where do we go for Sunday school and Bible study?" thinking of an adjacent large church building. They laughed and said, "Stay seated, it's right here. And the pastor is going to take us deeper into a passage of Scripture." I knew right then and there I was in for a treat. I took so many notes I had to get a special notebook just for Sundays. As a result of that summer, I grew even deeper in my relationship with the Lord thanks to that blessed little church in Hawaii.

Everywhere I have lived, the first and most important decision I made was, "Where will I go to church?" When I lived in Dallas, Texas, on staff with Campus Crusade for Christ, I attended Fellowship Bible Church, led by Dr. Gene Getz. His was a church steeped in the traditions of the church as a family. There I learned the importance of biblical fellowship, and I grew in leaps and bounds spiritually as a result of his outstanding and thoughtful messages. Years later in San Diego, California, I had the great privilege to attend College Avenue Baptist Church, a church heavily into Bible studies, especially women's Bible studies. There I first spread my wings and began to fly as a leader in ministry. I led Audrey Weatherell Johnson's Bible Study Fellowship studies, Kay Arthur's Precept inductive Bible studies, organized Christian conferences, and experienced the responsibilities of church leadership in an up close and personal fashion. I formed teams of women who served together with me to teach hundreds of women how to observe, interpret, and apply Scripture to study the Bible. These formative times are treasures in my heart.

When the church is the church as Jesus intends for it, then it radically transforms all who come in contact with it. What is the church and why do I love it so? The church in the general sense of the term is from the Greek word, *ekklesia*. It is a combination of two words: *ek—out of* and *kaleo* which means *to call*. When you combine those words into *ekklesia*, the Greek word for church, it means *called out ones*. This Greek word gives us tremendous insight into the church and reveals another dimension of your calling. The church is *called out of the world*. There is a separateness in lifestyle, belief, and conviction that is true of the church. The church is to be unstained by the world. It is to be holy. When the church is truly the church, it shines with the holiness of its bridegroom, the Lord Jesus Christ. Peter, the first leader of the early church, encouraged those who follow Christ to "be holy in everything you do, just as God who chose you is holy. For the Scriptures say, 'You must be holy because I am holy'" (1 Peter 1:15-16 NLT). Paul encouraged the church to "live clean, innocent lives as children of God, shining like bright lights in a world full of crooked and perverse people" (Philippians 2:15 NLT). Those in the church are given a great purpose as "a chosen race, a royal priesthood, a holy nation, a people for God's own possession, so that you may proclaim the excellencies of Him who has called you out of darkness into His marvelous light; for you once were not a people, but now you are the people of God; you had not received mercy, but now you have received mercy" (1 Peter 2:9-10).

Jesus Christ is the one who calls those who are part of the church. When He called Peter to lead the church, He said, "I also say to you that you are Peter, and upon this rock I will build My church; and the gates of Hades will not overpower it" (Matthew 16:18). Jesus is in the process of building His church even now. And as He builds, He also brings together physical groups within the church—local congregations who meet together in community. There was the church in Jerusalem (Acts 8:1), Asia Minor (Acts 16:5), Rome (Romans 16:5), Corinth (1 Corinthians 1:2), Galatia (Galatians 1:2), Thessalonica (1 Thessalonians 1:1), and in the home of Philemon (Philemon 2). There were churches in western Asia Minor described in Revelation 2-3—the churches of Ephesus, Sardis, Pergamum, Thyatira, Philadelphia, Laodicea, and Smyrna. These early believers did not have special buildings the way we do today. They met in homes according to Romans 16:5 and Philemon 2. And when they met, they worshipped (1 Corinthians 11:18), had fellowship (Acts 2:45-46), received instruction and teaching (Acts 2:42), and sent out missionaries.

There are a number of figures in the New Testament that are used for the church: The body of Christ (Ephesians 1:22-23), the Bride of Christ (Ephesians 5:23-25), a building (Ephesians 2:19-22), a priesthood (1 Peter 2:5, 9, Revelation 1:6), a flock (John 10:14-16), and branches (John 15).

Why so many different figures for this wondrous idea from God called the church? I believe it is so that you might know and understand your high calling as a member of the church of the Lord Jesus Christ. The church is all about people. And the Lord Jesus means for the church to be filled with people.

What happened with me early on in my relationship with the Lord is a perfect example of the church being the church. Nancy grabbed my hand and took me to Bethany Bible Church. She took me to the weekly Bible study. She showed me the way to grow as a Christian. That was all I needed to catch on fire for the Lord. I took off. I got involved in Campus Crusade for Christ. I read the word of God, prayed and established a regular quiet time. And I grew as a disciple of Jesus Christ. I believe it was all because of the influence of the church, the body of Christ and community of believers (Acts 2:42-47).

So when you become a Christian, one of the most important things you can do is find a church and become a part of that church community. Jesus is calling you to be part of His body, the church. However, you don't want to join just any church. Look for a church that holds the word of God as authoritative, commanding our beliefs and actions. Find a pastor who loves Jesus and preaches God's Word. Join an in-depth Bible study that helps you know God and grow in your relationship with Him. And serve the Lord in a ministry there that uses your gifts for the good of others and the glory of God.

I love the church so much. And I long very much for you to realize your high calling and love the church as well. Here are some reasons why I love the church.

I love the church because Christ loves the church. He loves the church as His body that He nourishes and cherishes and as His bride who will one day be presented to Him in marriage. He loves you as His bride.

I love the church because of the way it functions as a body with many members who each are gifted and designed to exercise those gifts in a way that brings glory to God.

I love the church because of its purpose to reflect the glory and the existence of Christ. When the church is truly the church, people are going to be drawn to Christ.

I love the church because it is the context where I discover my own purpose in life and then live it out. It is in the very community of believers in Christ that I am able to function and discover who I am and why I'm here.

I love the church because it is my family. I discover in Romans 8:15-17 that I am adopted into the family of God where I am His child. Whenever I am with believers in Christ, I am with my family.

I love the church because of the fellowship (*koinonia* in the Greek) I am privileged to experience. *Koinonia* is the experience of an intimate, loving relationship with others. Another word for fellowship is community where there is a real sense of belonging and participation with one another.

I love the church because it is where I find accountability (Proverbs 27:17). Accountability allows us to challenge and encourage one another as iron sharpens iron.

I love the church because it is where I see God at work! I love watching God at work and when I am with others who love Christ, I see His handiwork everywhere.

I love the church because it is where I am encouraged. The writer of Hebrews encourages us to not forsake "our assembling together as is the habit of some, but encouraging one another and all the more as you see the day drawing near" (Hebrews 10:25).

The church is filled with people, but those people are not perfect. It is recounted that a man came to Charles H. Spurgeon one day looking for the perfect church. The famous preacher told him he had many saintly people in his congregation, but a Judas could also be among them. After all, even Jesus had a traitor in the company of His apostles. He went on to say that some might be walking disobediently, as had been the case among the believers at Rome, Corinth, Galatia, and Sardis. "My church is not the one you're looking for," said Spurgeon. "But if you should happen to find such a church, I beg you not to join it, for you would spoil the whole thing."

Christ has called the church out of the world. We are in the world but not of the world. And yet, there is much of the world seeping into the church. Tozer once said, "The Church has surrendered her once lofty concept of God and has substituted for it one so low, so ignoble, as to be utterly unworthy of thinking, worshiping men. This she has done not deliberately, but little by little and without her knowledge; and her very unawareness only makes her situation all the more tragic." He goes on to say that "The low view of God entertained almost universally among Christians is the cause of a hundred lesser evils everywhere among us…With our loss of the sense of majesty as come the further loss of religious awe and consciousness of the divine Presence. We have lost our spirit of worship and our ability to withdraw inwardly to meet God in adoring silence…The words, 'Be still, and know that I am God,' mean next to nothing to the self-confident, bustling worshiper in this middle period of the twentieth century."[3] Tozer wrote those words in 1961 and yet they are descriptive of much of the church even in present day.

Unfortunately, I have witnessed firsthand what Tozer describes of the worldly church. I have watched church leaders filled with so much power that they presume to bully staff members and even parishioners. What does it matter to these "leaders" to move staff and parishioners around like chess pieces. What does it matter to these "leaders" to arbitrarily dismiss staff and parishioners from long years of service without the respect and courtesy of prayer and consultation. Indeed, I have watched in horror as worldly pastors and church staff go about the wholesale dismantling of thriving church ministries, patterning methods solely after the world without ever asking the Lord what He has in mind. And, alas, as a result, over the years, I have had to counsel and encourage many disillusioned "wounded warriors"—my dear friends working in the church—as they have lost a sense of who they are and why they are here as a result of their worldly church experience.

Anne Graham Lotz, in her book, *Wounded By God's People*, describes a devastating experience at her church home at that time that hurt her to the core. She was greatly wounded to the point where she left and she didn't even want to attend church for awhile. She and her husband experienced one rejection that was a result, as she describes it, of "political power struggles of a denomination." It was a battle over the issue of the Bible as the inerrant, inspired authoritative Word of God. Not an arguable point for the biblically sound Anne Graham Lotz. She describes how that rejection by their church impacted her: "I will tell you very candidly that being rejected by that church hurt. And it hurts to this day. We were wounded."[4]

Another church situation involving Anne's husband as the lone elder standing his ground with a young wounded pastor who was being asked to resign without any biblical reason sent them to a heartbreaking position Anne labels as "believers in exile." They witnessed "nightly elder meetings that functioned more like a kangaroo court than a group of faithful men seeking God's will."[5] She describes how the people who attended the church had no idea what went on behind closed doors. The "cover-up" of a "farewell dinner, prayers, and a generous severance package" had succeeded in achieving the elders' agenda. Anne wrote a letter to the elders and never even received a response. When that young pastor left the church, so did Anne and her husband. And for one year, they didn't attend any church.

Anne sums it up. She and her husband may have tried to run from the church, but they could not outrun God and His love. And then, Anne asks some poignant questions for wounded church warriors: "Dear wounded believer-in-exile, what is your story? What chapter is being written today? Is your spirit lying in the dust of your wilderness wandering? Can you hear His voice calling to you?"[6] The times when those you trust in the church have wounded you deeply are also the times when the Lord is still with you, calling out to you with His passionate, steadfast voice heard clearly and succinctly all through the pages of His Word.

I heard a message one day where the speaker said, "I recently spoke with some Christians visiting from another country. They were amazed how much the church in America tries to accomplish in their own power instead of going to God and relying on the Holy Spirit." I've never forgotten that statement and it is certainly a challenge to me to constantly turn to God for strength and power in ministry.

I recently read about a church that was looking for a pastor who would stand in the pulpit and read other current famous pastors' sermons. Their advertisement began with these words, "This offer is going to be nothing like any other church job post." And they were right. This church did not want to hear a message from God given to their pastor. They wanted the pastor to copy the words of messages by other men who were hearing from God and writing what they learned from the Word. This strikes at the heart of why I have written *The Calling*.

I want you to know who you are and why you are here, and then live it out day by day. I want you to know that God speaks to you in His Word through the power of the Holy Spirit. We need to constantly be reminded of our calling as a "called-out one," filled with the Holy Spirit, surrendered to Christ, and prayerfully allowing Him to have His way in our lives. Always remember that Jesus has something He wants to do in and through you, and His work in you will benefit and build the church.

I have a little rock in my quiet time basket that has the words painted on it, "no earthly reason." It's patterned after some words related to the work of D.L. Moody. One day a newspaperman decided to go and hear Moody speak, attempting to discover why he was so popular. His article the next day pointed out all the shortcomings of Moody and summarized the experience by writing, "I find no earthly reason for this man's success." One of Moody's assistants read the article and took it in to show Moody. Moody smiled and said, "That's the secret."

Oh friends, may we discover the secret of the church—Christ Himself. We are attached to Him, like branches to the Vine. Apart from Him, we can do nothing. But with Him, we will bear much fruit.

As part of the church, you are called out of the world to shine for Christ and bring glory to God. That is why it is essential that you know who you are and why you are here. Then, you can faithfully serve as God intends, as a called-out one. It's all about the calling—called by Christ. The words of the hymn say it best, "The church's one foundation is Jesus Christ her Lord."

The church's one Foundation
is Jesus Christ her Lord;
she is His new creation,
by water and the Word;
from heav'n He came and sought her
to be His holy bride;
with His own blood He bought her,
and for her life He died.

The church shall never perish!
Her dear Lord, to defend,
to guide, sustain, and cherish,
is with her to the end;
tho' there be those that hate her
and false sons in her pale,
against the foe or traitor
she ever shall prevail.

Yet she on earth hath union
with God the Three in One,
and mystic sweet communion
with those whose rest is won.
O happy ones and holy!
Lord, give us grace that we,
like them, the meek and lowly,
on high may dwell with Thee.

S.J. STONE. THE CHURCH'S ONE FOUNDATION, 1866

Christ also loved the church and gave Himself up for her, so that He might sanctify her, having cleansed her by the washing of water with the word, that He might present to Himself the church in all her glory, having no spot or wrinkle or any such thing; but that she would be holy and blameless.

EPHESIANS 5:25-27

THE POWER OF AN INFLUENTIAL LIFE

Remember those who led you, who spoke the word of God to you; and considering the result of their conduct, imitate their faith.

HEBREWS 13:7

The faith of Henrietta Mears always went well beyond the attainable to the extraordinary. She used to say: "When I consider my ministry, I think of the world. Anything less than that would not be worthy of Christ, nor of his will for my life." In describing her ministry calling, she said, "It is my business as a Sunday school teacher to instill a divine discontent for the ordinary. Only the best possible is good enough for God. Can you say, 'God, I have done all that I can?'"

In the same manner, God has called out to me strongly and often about ministry from one very special verse in the Bible, Hebrews 13:7. He says, "Remember those who led you, who spoke the word of God to you; and considering the result of their conduct, imitate their faith." When I first read those words, I thought, *I need to look for spiritual mentors who will be examples for me to follow, with a faith I can imitate. And then, I need to have the kind of faith that others can imitate.* I took those words so seriously that I began writing the names of those whom God placed in my life as faithful men and women who were examples for me over the years.

I think, first of all, of my mother. There is no one more precious to me who is a greater example than this hero of the faith. After my mother went home to be with the Lord, I found an old family photo album. There is one snapshot that speaks to the heart of my mother's essence. When I saw it, tears quickly came to my eyes. There she is, standing by the car, somewhere in her late twenties, holding my little brother and me by the hand, smiling and looking directly into the camera. This image shows me her determination and her heart. Indeed, she held us in each of her hands all of our lives. Even after her stroke, I remember a tender moment when she reached out and put her hand on top of my hand. She loved me unconditionally, demonstrating the infinite love of Jesus Christ. She taught me literally everything from tying shoelaces to writing a book. And she was faithful to Jesus her entire life, even to the day she stepped into heaven. She showed me how to love Jesus, to live for Him, to have a life of integrity and excellence, and to give "my utmost for His highest," as the title of Oswald Chambers' popular devotional so aptly describes our Christian commitment. She is at the top of my Hebrews 13:7 list.

Leann Pruitt McGee, a faithful staff member with Campus Crusade for Christ, will always have a place on that list of influential people in my life. While at Arizona State University, she is the one who first taught me how to have a quiet time and how to be a disciple of the Lord Jesus Christ. Most importantly, by living example, she showed me how to be a "faithful [woman] who will be able to teach others also." In a nutshell, she helped me understand how to pass on to others all we are learning in the Word, and then encourage them to do the same (2 Timothy 2:2). I am forever indebted to her.

Then there is Jim Smoke, best-selling author of *Growing Through Divorce*, speaker, and life coach. When Pastor Jim Smoke served alongside me at a local church, he took me under his wing and he encouraged me in my writing. The first day I met him, he walked into my office and said, "Catherine, I want you to bring me a copy of every book you've written." I thought, *What in the world is he thinking? I've only written a handful of books (NavPress).* What I didn't realize was that he intended to help me with my writing and book publishing. The day I finished writing *Six Secrets to a Powerful Quiet Time* (the self-published *Radical Intimacy* version), I had just arrived home after work and my cell phone rang. It was Jim, real excitement in his voice. "Where are you, Catherine?" Without waiting for a response, he proclaimed, "Well, I've got Bob Hawkins, Sr. here, the founder of Harvest House Publishers. He's seen your NavPress books of quiet times and he wants to meet you. How soon can you get here?" Oh, what a memorable day that was! Years later, through the full force of Jim's influence in my life, I had written over twenty books, many for Harvest House Publishers. I learned something so important from him. Take time with every person and pursue influencing them with great purpose and intention for the sake of the gospel. That's what Jim Smoke did with me. He would often walk into my office with a book in his hand and give it to me, saying, "Catherine, you need to read this book." We had many intense theological discussions related to my faith and my love for the Lord Jesus. Ah, how time passes. Beloved Jim is now with the Lord and I greatly miss him and I can't wait to see him in heaven.

Shirley Peters, a pastor's wife in San Diego, came from her church (Tim LaHayes', Scott Memorial Baptist Church) to attend my Bible study at College Avenue Baptist Church in San Diego. It was the early 1990s. Soon we became fast friends. One day I said, "Shirley, I have an idea for a ministry where I will teach others how to have a quiet time. I will call it Quiet Time Ministries." Several weeks later, out of the blue, Shirley stood up at a retreat where I was speaking and said, "Everybody, we need to pray for Catherine because God has given her an idea for a new ministry." And then she prayed for me, and the "worldwide impact" of Quiet Time Ministries. You could have knocked me over with a feather; I was overwhelmed and greatly humbled. And God honored her prayer as He built Quiet Time Ministries to reach the world. Shirley was such a shining example of a lover of God and His Word. Every time I was with her, she would open her Bible, and talk about a verse of Scripture that stood out to her. Then she would ask me what I thought it meant. I smile because she surely knew its meaning. But she wanted to hear what I had to say. Oh, how I loved her presence in my life. I am looking forward to seeing her in heaven with a great passion.

There are many others who are on my Hebrews 13:7 "heroes of the faith" list, and this list grows longer each year, as I write more and more names in my Bible. I have included authors, speakers, and Christian heroes of the faith from years past who have had a profound impact on my faith. Indeed, there is a powerful discipleship that takes place when we read biographies. John Piper, author, pastor and founder of Desiring God Ministry begun in 1994, writes, "Christian biography is the means by which the body life of the church cuts across the centuries…Biographies have served as much as any other human force in my life to resist the inertia of mediocrity. Without them I tend to forget what joy there is in relentless God-besotted labor and aspiration."[1] Piper points out that Hebrews 11 is our divine mandate to read Christian biographies because of the very nature and implication of that chapter filled with heroes of the faith, one after another. Perhaps my favorite biography is *Shadow of the Broad Brim* written by Richard Day about the life and legacy of Charles Spurgeon. Then, beyond biographies, there is a powerful influence from great men and women of God by reading the books they have written. There are many books that have changed my life forever and have become an integral part of the story of my life. Perhaps my favorite book by a Christian author is *The Making of a Man of God* by Alan Redpath. I have included a list of my personal "heroes of the faith" favorites in the Appendix. You'll love them!

Who is on your "heroes of the faith" list? And who will place *your name* on their list? What books will you read this year to grow in your relationship with the Lord? Following examples and being an example are equally important aspects of *your calling*! Jesus calls you to look for those examples in Hebrews 13:7 and He calls you to be an example in John 13:35 (and other places), and He calls you to pass on to others what you have learned in 2 Timothy 2:2.

As the example of an influential life of faith touches your life, there is a ripple effect that is created. Their influence touches you and then your life touches others. It is the work of Jesus Christ as He moves through them to you and then through you to someone else. The ripple effect may sometimes be seen very clearly as God uses your faith to touch the life of someone else. But you may never know the ripple effect of your life of faith on earth until you are face to face with the Lord in heaven, for "we walk by faith, not by sight" as Paul reveals in 2 Corinthians 5:7.

Dr. Francis Dixon, a minister at Landsdowne Baptist Church in England in 1946, asked for testimonies at his church one day. A young man named Peter stood up and shared his story. "This is how I was saved. I was in the Royal Navy. I was walking down George Street in Sydney, Australia, and out of nowhere stepped a little old gray-haired man and he said to me, 'Excuse me, sir, but could I ask you a question? I hope that it won't offend you, but if you were to die today, where would you spend eternity? The Bible says that it will either be in Heaven or it will be in Hell. Would you think about that, please? Thank you, God bless you, and Toodle-oo!' Then the man left. I had never been confronted with that question – I couldn't get it out of my mind; I got back to London, I sought out a pastor, and I became a Christian."

Several weeks later there was a revival in that same church and Noel, part of the revival team, shared his testimony. "This is how I came to know Christ. I was in the Royal Navy and I was walking down George Street in Sydney, Australia and out of nowhere stepped a little old gray-haired man. He said to me, 'Excuse me, sir, but could I ask you a question? If you were to die today, where would you spend eternity?…What he said bothered me and later, I sought out a Christian and I was converted to Christ."

So twice in less than month, Dr. Dixon had heard this same testimony and he was quite intrigued. But that was only the beginning of his adventure with the little old gray-haired man who had a habit of sharing the gospel and ending his words with *Thank you, God bless you, and Toodle-oo!* A few months later, Dr. Dixon traveled to Australia, and along the way, as he spoke to many different groups, he shared the amazing story of these two testimonies. At the first group meeting, when he shared the testimonies, a man in the audience stood, waving his hands, and said that the exact same thing had happened to him. He met the man, was compelled by his words, and ended up giving his life to Christ.

Dixon shared the story at another revival meeting in Australia and later, a deacon from the church, came up to him and said he, too, had met the little old gray-haired man, heard his words, and had become a Christian as a result. When Dixon got back to his home church in England, he excitedly told the amazing story of all these people who had come to know Christ. A woman in the congregation shared that she too, came to know the Lord because of that little old gray-haired man.

Again and again, wherever Dixon shared the story, even in varied cultures like India and Jamaica, there was always someone who had experienced the same encounter. Finally, Dixon decided he just had to see if he could find this little old gray-haired man who would ask his profound question, "If you were to die today, where would you spend eternity?" and then say, "Thank you, God bless you, and Toodle-oo!"

He told a friend in Australia about his experience and asked if he had any idea about who this man was. His friend replied, "Oh, yes! Everybody knows him. That's Mr. Frank Jenner. He did that for twenty-three years! But he's very old now and he's in the hospital confined to his bed." Dr. Dixon asked his friend to take him to see Mr. Jenner. What an amazing thing to finally see this servant of the Lord face to face. He introduced himself and then recounted the whole story to this simple humble man. Mr. Jenner began to weep uncontrollably. Dr. Dixon asked him what was wrong. Mr. Jenner replied, "This is the first time I have heard of anyone coming Christ because of my witness." After all those years of faithful sharing, he had never known any of the results until that very moment.[2]

Just think about how an obscure conversation you may have one day with someone about the Lord can have a profound influence and result in a ripple effect that may touch the lives of thousands. I discovered this at the young age of seventeen when I walked to the local convenience store in my neighborhood in Phoenix, Arizona. As I was making my purchase, I started talking with the cashier about the Lord. He said, "Hey lady, don't talk to me about Him. If you want to tell someone about God, then you should talk to that kid over there." I looked in the direction where he pointed and saw this seventeen-year-old kid with long hair and a basketball. I walked over and started talking with him. It turned out he was a Christian but was not walking with the Lord. We sat on the curb in front of the store. I talked to him about surrendering control of his life and being filled (controlled and empowered) with the Holy Spirit. We probably talked for about a half hour. And then I left. About a year later I was leading a time of sharing at a retreat in Prescott, Arizona. I asked, "Who would like to share what God is doing in your life?" A hand shot up in the back. And then, the guy who had raised his hand asked, "Do you remember me?" I said, "No." He then said, "Remember talking to a kid out in front of that store over a year ago?" Of course, I remembered immediately. He said, "That was me. After you left, I gave my life to the Lord and now I'm attending Moody Bible Institute." I was absolutely astounded. I hold this occurrence in my heart to this day. How exciting it is when the Lord works in and through us to touch the lives of others.

There is always a ripple effect when Jesus is at work influencing lives through you. One of the best examples I know was the day in 1854, when a Sunday School teacher named Edward Kimball in Detroit, Michigan, learned that he was going to die. Since he knew he had little time left to live, he set out to lead all of his Sunday School students to the Lord. He led one seemingly uninterested and non-religious student to the Lord in the back room of a store. That student's name was D.L. Moody.

Of course, D.L. Moody went on to become a great evangelist, and founder of The Moody Bible Institute, Chicago, Illinois, in date. One day Moody was preaching in the British Isles and a teacher, a young woman, was moved by his message. She went to her Sunday School class and shared Moody's testimony with her students. Then, she also told her preacher about Moody's message, and that, as a result, every one of her students had given their lives to the Lord. That preacher's name was F.B. Meyer, Baptist pastor and author of more than 75 books including *Our Daily Homily* and *Paul, The Servant of Jesus*.

That report by the teacher had moved F.B. Meyer to realize what it meant to be brokenhearted over sin and of the great need to point others to Christ. Ultimately, F.B. Meyer came to America and preached at Moody's school in Northfield, Massachusetts. During his message he gave a heartfelt challenge: "If you're not willing to give up everything for Christ, are you willing to be made willing?"

That remark by F.B. Meyer moved the heart of a young preacher named J. Wilbur Chapman. He became a great evangelist during the when?. When Chapman returned to the pastorate, he turned over his ministry to the YMCA clerk who had been his advance man. His name was Billy Sunday, later to become a great evangelist in America at the beginning of the 20th century.

In 1924, Billy Sunday conducted a revival meeting in Charlotte, North Carolina. Out of that meeting a group of laymen formed a permanent organization to continue sharing the message of Christ in their own city. Eight years later, in 1932, that group of men brought an evangelist named Mordecai Ham to their area to conduct city-wide evangelistic meetings. One evening during one of the meetings, a tall, lanky 16 year old stepped out of the choir and gave his life to Jesus Christ. His name—Billy Graham. And everyone knows the impact that one Billy Graham has had on the lives of millions worldwide through the Billy Graham Evangelistic Association.

This is the ripple effect of Jesus Christ and His power to work in and through lives of influence who were great examples of faith!

Never underestimate the influence your faithful life can have on others around you. I think again about Dr. Henrietta C. Mears, Christian educator, author, and evangelist in the 20th century, whose life impacted three great men of God who went on to have a powerful influence for Christ: Bill Bright (Campus Crusade for Christ), Richard Halverson (Chaplain of the Senate), and the great evangelist Billy Graham. Billy Graham said of Henrietta Mears, "I doubt if any other woman outside my wife and mother has had such a marked influence [on my life]. She is certainly one of the greatest Christians I have ever known!" Surely, Henrietta Mears had no idea how influential her life would become and the countless lives that would be transformed as a result. And most assuredly the Lord will influence others in and through your life.

Dear friend, will you answer the call of Jesus to follow the example of others on a daily basis? And will you live your life as an example of a faith that can be imitated so that you will live an influential life for the sake of the gospel? Leave the final result to God. Heaven will tell the story of the ripple effect that occurs as a result of the story of your life — who you are and why you are here.

The Calling Journey Four
CALLED TO A CROSS

Matthew 16:24

So do not be surprised when a totally, utterly, one hundred percent impossible comes your way. It is irrefutable proof that you are on the right road with Jesus. He is calling you to "a new and greater dependence on Him." If you develop a passion for the impossible, you will experience the great and mighty power of your Lord at work in and through you. The Lord intends to do the impossible; He is calling you to the impossible. This is your calling.

THE FELLOWSHIP OF HIS SUFFERINGS

That I may know Him and the power of His resurrection and
the fellowship of His sufferings, being conformed to His death;
in order that I may attain to the resurrection from the dead.
PHILIPPIANS 3:10-11

One special calling revealed in God's Word tests our faith and tries our very soul. It is singular, momentous, and noteworthy. It cuts to the quick. We are called to enter into the *fellowship* of Christ's sufferings. When Jesus is leading us on the journey He has in mind, calling us out on the water to walk with Him by faith (Matthew 14:29), there are times when the wind blows hard and the waves are tempestuous. And as we walk with Him, hand in hand, across the raging sea, we will *share* trials and tribulations together with Him. Never alone. Don't give up, dear friend, the suffering with all its aches and pains and torment, is a deep and *privileged fellowship* drawing you into an intimacy with Jesus you never would experience without the trial. It's a calling. It's your calling.

Jesus says, "Here on earth you will have many trials and sorrows. But take heart, because I have overcome the world" (John 16:33). Jesus will lead you to the other side of the stormy waters, across the parched deserts, and through the dense jungles, each laced with fear, doubt, and despair. Jesus will never leave you. How is this possible? You can count on all His promises to be with you and help you. Memorize these verses so that they roll off your tongue at the first hint of panic.

- Isaiah 41:10 [NASB]: Do not fear, for I am with you; Do not anxiously look about you, for I am your God. I will strengthen you, surely I will help you, Surely I will uphold you with My righteous right hand.

- Matthew 28:20 [NASB]: …I am with you always, even to the end of the age.

- Hebrews 13:5-6 [NASB]: Make sure that your character is free…being content with what you have; for He Himself has said, "I will never desert you, nor will I ever forsake you," so that we confidently say, "The Lord is my helper, I will not be afraid. What will man do to me?"

Andrew Murray, 19th century South African writer, pastor, and teacher, in his book *The Secret of Spiritual Strength* writes, "The secret of the Christian's strength and joy is simply the presence of Jesus."[1]

The apostle Paul experienced many trials in the course of his life with the Lord. He expressed his view of the journey in his letter to the church at Philippi: "That I may know Him and the power of His resurrection and the fellowship of His sufferings, being conformed to His death; in order that I may attain to the resurrection from the dead" (Philippians 3:10-11). What does this mean? Our intimacy with Jesus includes a sharing in His sufferings. The important point here is that they are *His sufferings*. We often take the view from our own vantage point and call them *our sufferings*. When you step back and realize that the things you are experiencing are "His sufferings," you realize your calling is to a deeper intimacy with Him. When you view suffering in this way, with an eternal perspective, then you realize sharing in His sufferings is a privilege. And this sharing in His sufferings is a calling in your life because the Lord is leading you and asking you to fellowship with Him in this way. Amen.

So then, how does the Lord help you journey through times of suffering? He gives you His promises in His Word to show you how He is helping you, and also as a strength and encouragement of all that you can know to be true in the trial. In a time of suffering, you can often feel as though you are alone and there is no hope. Those feelings, however, based on earthly sight, are simply not true. God tells you the real truth in His promises. So the most important action you can take in your trial is to open your Bible and discover the truth revealed in God's promises so that you will have hope.

"The Scriptures give us hope and encouragement as we wait patiently for God's promises to be fulfilled" (Romans 15:4). God's promises in His Word give you hope. You will quickly discover that hope when you hear God say, "Do not fear, for I am with you; Do not anxiously look about you, for I am your God. I will strengthen you, surely I will help you, surely I will uphold you with My righteous right hand" (Isaiah 41:10). In that one promise alone, God is assuring you that He is with you, He will give you strength, and He will help you. God has an answer to every impossible situation because He is "able to do immeasurably more than all we ask or imagine, according to his power that is at work within us" (Ephesians 3:20 NIV). He promises to always provide for us (Philippians 4:19), give us strength for all things (Philippians 4:13), and even weave the impossible into something good (Romans 8:28).

One of my favorite promises from God's Word is the promise of grace in 2 Corinthians 9:8, "God is able to make all grace abound to you, so that always having all sufficiency in everything, you may have an abundance for every good deed." This is one of the best promises in the entire Bible. In this one little verse, all wrapped up in an all-sufficient package, you see that God's grace gives you *everything* you need for *every* circumstance of life. Memorize this verse; write this verse on your very soul. Count on it, dear friend. You have what you need, every second, every hour, every day, all the time. Of course, it's one thing to discover the promise. It's quite another to accept that promise. In your quiet time, when God gives you a promise from His Word, then you should make a big deal about it. Write it in your journal in a favorite promises list. Memorize it. Say it over to yourself as you stand in the bank line, buy your groceries, take care of your family, and work at your business. "[Accepting] the promises of God requires surrendering your heart, letting go of your ways, and saying yes to His ways…The truth that helps me [Catherine Martin] surrender my own ideas and plans is Isaiah 43:18-19 (NLT): 'For I am about to do something new…'"[2]

Your trust in God grows in proportion with your knowledge of who He is, what He does, and what He says.[3] This is where we often get discouraged in the midst of trials because things sometimes go from bad to worse. We can't see any possible answer for our situation. How can we trust God when all we see is the trial? Our eyes must turn to God. David wrote in Psalm 9:10, "Those who know Your name will put their trust in You." This important verse promises that the more you know God—who He is, what He does, and what He says—the more you will trust Him.

One hero of the faith who knew great suffering was Jeremiah, who has been called the Weeping Prophet by some commentators because of his many tears over the course of his life. He shared the heart of God as a prophet and wrote lamentations out of the brokenness of his heart. He heard God speak may times, and came to know God in such depth that he said, "The Lord's lovingkindnesses indeed never cease, for His compassions never fail. They are new every morning; Great is Your faithfulness. 'The Lord is my portion,' says my soul, 'Therefore I have hope in Him'" (Lamentations 3:22-24). The Word of God was so vital to Jeremiah that he said, "Your words were found and I ate them, and Your words became for me a joy and the delight of my heart; For I have been called by Your name, O Lord God of hosts" (Jeremiah 15:16).

So in the difficult trial when you need to find a greater hope and a deeper trust, take time to know God. I have been so desperate at times that I grabbed my Bible, journal, and a few precious books and sought refuge in a restaurant or a park, and then sat with the Lord for a few hours. I've poured my heart out to Him and then I asked Him to encourage my heart. He has *always* given me a verse to hang on to in my trouble. He has *always* given me a devotion from one of my books to encourage my soul and lead me deeper into His Word.

The more we rely on God's promise, the more we will live it out by faith. God's promise urges us to get out of the boat to walk on water with the Lord as the wind blows and the storm rages about us. We can, as the Lord says, find courage because He has overcome the world. There is nothing so great, that He is not greater still. There is no trial that Jesus in you cannot overcome. He is an overcomer and He is your strength. He lives in you. And in Him, there is triumph and victory. Walking by faith in the promises of God means you memorize, pray, and personalize the promises of God. Walking by faith in the promises of God "moves you from what God says to hope, that confident expectation in the fulfillment of God's promise…I [Catherine Martin] like to think of trust as Total Reliance Under Stress and Trial."[4]

One hero of the faith who knew the fellowship of Christ's sufferings and experienced radical intimacy with the Lord was 19th century Christian poet, Annie Johnson Flint. We briefly touched on her challenges in life in an earlier chapter, but now I want to go a bit deeper. Everything seemed to be against her from the beginning. She lost both her parents at a young age, but was adopted by a wonderful Christian couple, Mr. and Mrs. Flint. She was raised in a Christian home and came to Christ at a Methodist revival meeting. By the age of ten, Annie discovered that she could write poetry and was thrilled to be able to express herself in verse. When she finished high school, she stayed home to care for her adopted mother who had failing health. Annie taught primary school while living at home. Then something happened that altered the course of her life. She began experiencing the devastating symptoms of arthritis. She wrote about the depth of her painful experience as only she could in a stanza in one of her poems: *Shut in, with tears that are spent in vain. With the dull companionship of pain; Shut in with the changeless days and hours, and the bitter knowledge of failing powers.* She went to more than one doctor but soon struggled even to walk. She had to quit teaching and found herself growing more and more helpless over the next three years. Wrestling to surrender her dreams and desires in the wake of her arthritis, she wrote these words: *I dare not pray for any gift upon my pilgrim path to Heaven: I only ask one thing of Thee: Give Thou Thyself and all is given. I am not strong nor brave nor wise; Be Thou with me—it shall suffice.*

One day, Annie's aunt came to her and said, "Annie, I've visited a sanitarium in Clifton Springs where I think you can find help and healing." So Annie moved to the Clifton Springs Sanitarium,location, where the doctors determined she would be an invalid for the rest of her life. She was indeed confined as an invalid for forty years before going home to be with the Lord in 1932. She was dependent on the care of others and found herself in a helpless, needy position.

In the allegory she wrote, Annie hints at how she felt in having to give up her own desired direction in life in favor of God's will and way. She writes, "Then I hid my face in my hands and cried, 'I cannot! I cannot! Ask me something else! Give me some task to do." She describes the moment of surrender. "Then came a day when the Higher triumphed, and with broken voice and streaming eyes, I held out my Dearest Wish, crying, 'Take it, take it! Thy will be done!' Then the Vision broke in splendor, and I heard the Voice saying, 'Thou hast fought a good fight. Now thou art indeed mine; and behold! thy reward is even now beside thee.'"[5]

Annie was right where God wanted her for He had something great in mind that He wanted to do in and through her. And so, the journey began as she shared in the sufferings of her Lord.

He led her to put pen to paper and write poetry, line upon line, that would speak and minister to hurting hearts. Only a hurting heart could reach hurting hearts. Annie could have never written what she did not know. But because she was walking the road of suffering with her Lord, she was able to say things in her verse that others could have never even dreamed of saying.

One day a friend wrote to Annie, "I feel so blue and downhearted. I don't see why God has allowed such hard things to come into my life." Annie wrote these words back to her friend:

> God hath not promised skies always blue,
> Flower-strewn pathways all our lives through;
> God hath not promised sun without rain,
> Joy without sorrow, peace without pain.
> But God hath promised strength for the day,
> Rest for the labor, light for the way,
> Grace for the trials, help from above,
> Unfailing sympathy, undying love.

Annie found such solace in her poetry writing. God used her poetry to give her a means of support throughout her life. Here was a helpless invalid with no way to work a job and yet God gave her an income through her writing. Two card publishers discovered Annie and printed some of her poetry. That was the beginning. Her poetry enjoyed a wider audience as they were published in *Christian Endeavor World*, *The Sunday School Times*, and *The Evangelical Christian* magazines. Throughout her life, her own faith was challenged, and she learned how to trust God, especially when sales fell off and doctors' bills mounted. She could write about the challenges because she intimately shared in the sufferings.

Annie Johnson Flint looked at her suffering as a "taking up" of the cross in response to Jesus' words, "Then Jesus said to His disciples, "If anyone wishes to come after Me, he must deny himself, and take up his cross and follow Me" (Matthew 16:24). In these words, we find a calling from the Lord to take up our cross and follow Jesus. We ourselves are called to a cross. The cross in our lives can be many different kinds of suffering where we yield and surrender to the Lord and rely on His grace.

Annie speaks of the cross allegorically in the only prose piece she every wrote.

"And it came to pass, as I travelled along the Highway of Life, that I saw in the distance, far ahead, a mountain, and on it One standing, upon whose face rested a divine compassion for the grief of the world. His raiment was white and glittering, and in His hand was a cross. And He called unto the sons of men, saying 'Come! Come! Who will take up his cross and follow me, that he may be like unto me, and that I may seat him at my right hand and share with him things glorious and beautiful beyond the dreams of earth and the imaginings of men?' And I said, 'What is my cross, that I may take it up?' And a Voice answered, 'There are many crosses, and thine shall be given thee in good time.'"[6]

God settled any doubts and worries Annie had with an important verse about His promises in 2 Corinthians 1:20. "For as many as are the promises of God, in Him they are yes; therefore also through Him is our Amen to the glory of God through us." In response to that verse, Annie wrote these lines of poetry expressing how all her questions and ours are answered by God:

'Is God-?' 'Does God-?'
Man's 'Why?' and 'How?'
In ceaseless iteration storm the sky.
'I am'; 'I will'; 'I do'—sure Word of God,
Yea and Amen, Christ answers each cry;
To all our anguished questionings and doubts
Eternal affirmation and reply.

I often think about Annie Johnson Flint when the fiery trial rages in my own life. Her suffering was not easy and her pain grew worse as her arthritis increased. A visitor remarked that one glance at the bed in Annie's room revealed nine soft pillows carefully placed on her bed in such a way to help her endure the pain through the night. Only Annie and God truly knew and shared the reality of her suffering. But I will tell you that any poem you read written by Annie Johnson Flint will minister to you especially when you are brokenhearted or crushed in spirit. Why? Because Annie knew the fellowship of Jesus' sufferings and can speak of His comfort and strength in deeper ways because of all she endured. Her words reach a place in you that others just cannot touch because they have never walked the road she was on with her Lord.

My mother had the same rare privilege, as she was bedridden from advanced stages of multiple sclerosis in the last ten years of her life. I never knew such a strong and vibrant woman of faith like my mother. She was my best friend. And when you walked in her room, there was a joy and love I never have found anywhere else except with the Lord. My mother studied to be a concert pianist but in later years could not play the piano because of the way her fingers became bent and twisted. My mother helped me understand the fine art of surrender and faith and joy and hope in the sharing of the sufferings of her Lord.

One day I was talking with her on the phone and she said, "Catherine, I never knew I was going to be in a wheelchair and ultimately bedridden. But God has given me such a good life and I am content." The secret to my mother's victory was her identification with Jesus and His sufferings, especially His sufferings on the cross. A wooden cross was hanging on the wall across from her bed and she looked at it every day. Whenever I visited my mother, she always talked about Jesus and the cross. Because He was obedient to the point of death on a cross (Philippians 2:8), He would give her His overcoming strength as He shared the road of suffering with her in this life. She took great comfort in the words of Hebrews 4:15-16—"This High Priest of ours understands our weaknesses, for he faced all of the same testings we do, yet he did not sin. So let us come boldly to the throne of our gracious God. There we will receive his mercy, and we will find grace to help us when we need it most."

I have the cross that was in my mother's room as her faith is now sight and she is face to face with her Lord. The cross is a reminder to me that He is leading me through every suffering, and I am sharing with Him in the fellowship of His sufferings. Jesus says, "If anyone wishes to come after Me, he must deny himself, and take up his cross and follow Me" (Matthew 16:24). I learned from my mother that I can walk victoriously with Christ through difficult times in life. And then, those looking on will see the power and glory of the Lord at work. When we are weak, as the apostle Paul discovered, then we are strong and God's power is perfected in our weakness (2 Corinthians 12:7-10). Sometimes, that is exactly what God wants others to know as a result of our life with Him.

So then, you discover in the fellowship of Christ's sufferings, that difficult times are no match for the King of Kings and the Lord of Lords. He does indeed make the clouds His chariot and walks upon the wings of the wind (Psalm 104:3). The raging storm and waves of the sea are no match for the Lord Jesus as He walks on the water as though it is a paved road (Matthew 14:25). And then, He calls out to us in our most desperate hour, "Take courage, it is I; do not be afraid" (Matthew 14:27). Octavius Winslow, a contemporary of Charles Haddon Spurgeon, writes, "Listen then, to the voice of Jesus in the storm…In every stormy wind, in every darksome night, in every lonesome hour, in every rising fear, the voice of Jesus shall be heard, saying 'Be of good cheer; it is I; be not afraid.'"

And so, dear friend, in the dark and stormy seas at night, cast yourself on the Lord and learn to lean hard on Him. As Peter said in his little letter on suffering, "Cast all your cares on Him, for He cares for you" (1 Peter 5:7). In this way you are trusting in God. Trust really means *total reliance under stress and trial.*[7] You can truly cast your burden on the Lord because He knows and understands the burden better than any, for you are sharing it with Him. It is His burden and He alone can carry it. Lean on the Lord and all your burdens roll onto Him. That is the great *privilege* of one who is called into a fellowship of His sufferings. You are so close to Him in a radical intimacy, that everything you thought you had to carry no longer weighs heavy on you, for it is all carried and managed by Him and Him alone. And then you will have, as both Job (Job 35:10) and Annie Johnson Flint learned, a song in the night.

> We make our songs in the day of our gladness,
> When life is all laughter and joy and delight,
> When never a shadow has clouded our sunshine;
> But God giveth songs in the night!
>
> He giveth songs in the night of our sorrow,
> When tears are our drink and when grief is our meat,
> Till we silence our weeping and still our repining
> To list to those cadences sweet.
>
> God giveth songs in the night of affliction,
> When earth has no sun and the heavens no star;
> Like a comforting touch in the desolate darkness
> His voice stealeth in from afar.
>
> He giveth songs—and His music is sweeter
> Than earth's greatest voices and gladdest refrains;
> Our loveliest melodies shade to the minor,
> But His keep their full major strains.
>
> He giveth songs when our music is over,
> When our voices falter and our tongues are mute;
> When trembling hands drop from the lute and the harp-strings,
> And hushed are the viol and flute.
>
> Give us Thy songs, O Thou Maker of music!
> Teach us to sing, O Thou Bringer of joy!
> Till nothing can silence the notes of our triumph
> And naught our rejoicing destroy!

ANNIE JOHNSON FLINT, SONGS IN THE NIGHT

So then, since we have a great High Priest who has entered heaven, Jesus the Son of God, let us hold firmly to what we believe. This High Priest of ours understands our weaknesses, for he faced all of the same testings we do, yet he did not sin. So let us come boldly to the throne of our gracious God. There we will receive his mercy, and we will find grace to help us when we need it most.

Hebrews 4:14-16 nlt

THE WORLD, THE FLESH, AND THE DEVIL

…greater is He who is in you than he who is in the world.

1 JOHN 4:4

I n the 1600s, a Puritan pastor, William Gurnall, wrote an important book, *The Christian In Complete Armour*, published with the help of a benefactor. This book was reprinted more than once in his lifetime and is available even now. None other than renowned preacher Charles Spurgeon loved Gurnall's book and remarked: "Gurnall's work is peerless and priceless; every line is full of wisdom; every sentence is suggestive. The whole book has been preached over scores of times, and is, in our judgment, the best thought-breeder in all our library." 20th century American Christian evangelist David Wilkerson suggested that every Christian leader, teacher, pastor, evangelist or Christian worker should have *The Christian In Complete Armour* and read its message. John Newton, who wrote *Amazing Grace*, said, "If I might read only one book beside the Bible, I would choose *The Christian In Complete Armour*."

How is it that a book from the 1600s can apply to someone living in the twenty-first century? It is because the theme is timeless and the challenges addressed by the book occur in our lives right now. The book is written from Paul's words in Ephesians 6 about spiritual warfare and our calling from Jesus to put on spiritual armor in our fight against the devil (Ephesians 6:11-12). Here's the point. We are in a spiritual battle whether we realize it or not. And when we are in a trial where we trust God to provide every need with His unseen resources, we are on the front lines of the battle. It is the opportune time for our enemy to come against us and knock us down.

In the very beginning of all Gurnall writes on the subject of spiritual warfare, he points out the heart of our need and how the fear in our desperate situation defeats us. "Some of my dear friends must be quaking in their boots to see their enemies so strong and themselves so weak, so numerous while they are so few, so well equipped and expert at arms while they are just raw recruits."[1] He writes that Paul must have been thinking these thoughts before writing about spiritual warfare in Ephesians 6:10-18. "He [Paul] must have known a fear-wracked soul is too preoccupied with its present distress to listen to advice from anyone, even a well-meaning friend. Fear immobilizes its victim—like the distraught soldier who runs trembling to his foxhole at first rumor of an attack and refuses to come out until all threat of danger is passed." And then, Gurnall explains the antidote for fear given by Paul in Ephesians 6:10-18. "The outcome of the battle rests on God's performance, not on your skill or strength."

Are you afraid, dear friend? Do you get out of bed in the morning anxious and worrying even about the trials and tribulations you may or may not face? Does your mind race with artificial fears—stories and scenarios—that have not even been realized yet? Enough! Be encouraged! You are called to have a courageous heart in the daily battles you face in life. The battles are not yours, but the Lord's. Your power ("strong in the Lord") and strength ("strength of His might") belong to and reside with the Lord, not measly old you (Ephesians 6:10). Give it up for God! God gives you *divine provision* in the form of spiritual armor. Your armor includes truth, God's righteousness, peace, faith, and salvation. Your offensive weapon is the sword of the Spirit, the Word of God, and constant prayer. You are a spiritual gladiator!

That's the good news, now for a reality check. We need to know that we have real enemies: the devil, evil rulers, and authorities in the unseen world, mighty powers in the world, and evil spirits in the heavenly places (Ephesians 6:11-12). During our time on earth we are living *in the midst of the world*, an evil and relentless force ("the spiritual forces of wickedness") that is God's sworn enemy. In other words, the evil is all around you. John, the beloved apostle, explains how the world fights against God. The world offers "a craving for physical pleasure, a craving for everything we see, and pride in our achievements and possessions" (1 John 2:16 NLT). Never fear, God has a plan. We are in the world, but we are not to be of the world nor love the things of the world (1 John 2:15 NLT). That's the strategic battle plan so that we will "be able to stand firm against the schemes of the devil."

How does this apply to *the calling*? We are the called-out ones. Called-out from the world, even to take up your cross daily and follow Christ (Luke 9:23 NASB). The calling in our lives necessitates that we make decisions about the world and how we live in it. This is not a legalistic lifestyle, but a *forming of convictions* to help us walk day by day in the tangled maze of the world. How will you live? Make your decisions ahead of time. Preplan your thoughts and actions. Are you living for God or living for the things of the world? Are you obsessed with money and possessions, or are you committed to the Lord? Of course, you can run a lucrative business and still live wholly for Christ in every choice you make. You can also have no income and be more obsessed with money than you are with the Lord. Your convictions for Christ are the crucible on which you live your life.

I write these things from harsh personal experience. I grew up in a family where we had very little money. My mother worked three jobs just so we could have food and clothing. My greatest fear has always been having no money and no income. Along with that, I have secretly harbored at times a fear of being homeless. I believe our enemies—the world, the flesh, and the devil—strike at the core of those things that make us most afraid. And for me, that fear is provision for basic needs. Our ministry needs and personal needs rely primarily on ministry donations, resource sales, speaking engagements, and teaching opportunities. I don't even know how God will provide from month to month, and I must constantly trust Him moment by moment for every provision. I believe all of us need to rely on God to provide for us and take care of us. But for me, I struggle with this in the most basic of ways. Fear and worry strike panic in my heart at times. Most times, however, I am filled with peace and trust.

What are your fears? Our fears open up the door for the enemy to tempt us to believe lies that come in the form of simple statements that run through our minds and stories that fill our hearts. No wonder the Lord constantly says, "Don't be afraid" in many of His promises (Isaiah 41:10). What will I choose to believe—the lies and stories or the truth from God's Word? Here is where the spiritual battle takes us right to the front lines. We need to remember what Jesus has told us about the devil—he is a liar and the father of lies (John 8:44).

So what are the lies and stories I believe and what can I do in the face of those lies and stories? If my mind has jumped to the story that I'm not going to have enough, that I'm not going to make it, and that I'm going to be homeless, then I am absolutely believing a lie. How do I know? Because God's Word says that the Lord will provide my needs and will never leave or forsake me (Philippians 4:19, Hebrews 13:5-6). My home is in the Lord and He will take care of me (Isaiah 41:10). He promises. Always remember that "greater is He who is in you than he who is in the world" (1 John 4:4).

In Paul's words to the church at Ephesus, he tells us we need to put on the full armor of God so we can stand firm against the schemes of the devil (Ephesians 6:11). He points out the importance of the shield of faith and the sword of the Spirit, the Word of God. I cannot emphasize this biblical principle enough. When the lies come at me like fiery arrows, I have got to set aside the fear and panic, and take up the shield of faith in prayer and belief. Then, I absolutely must find out what is true from God's Word and fill my mind with those truths.

Paul makes it very clear that we are called to be serious about the spiritual battle in life. He told the Corinthian Church "though we walk in the flesh, we do not war according to the flesh, for the weapons of our warfare are not of the flesh, but divinely powerful for the destruction of fortresses. We are destroying speculations and every lofty thing raised up against the knowledge of God, and we are taking every thought captive to the obedience of Christ" (2 Corinthians 10:4-5). We need to realize that even the flesh becomes an enemy causing us to crave the things of the world instead of the things of God. The mind set on the flesh is hostile to God and can never please God (Romans 8:6-8). If we know God, then we are not in the flesh but in the Spirit (Romans

8:9). So it is *spiritual* warfare and we war according to the *Spirit*. That means we absolutely and assuredly rely on faith and God's Word as offensive weapons.

Jesus has shown us how to handle the lies of Satan when He was tempted by the devil out in the wilderness (Luke 4:1-13). After 40 days of fasting in the wilderness, Jesus was hungry. It was then that the enemy came to tempt Him. Always remember that the enemy will throw his lies and stories at you when you are most vulnerable. But you are not alone—the battle is the Lord's and He can overcome the enemy. The devil threw three different lies at Jesus. Jesus answered every single lie with "The Scriptures say…" and then would state truth from the Word of God. This is what we must learn to do. It may seem like a powerless thing to do—state truth from God's Word. But it is like taking a sword and cutting down every lie. I have learned and I am still learning to do this moment by moment and day by day.

My fear may not be your fear. Wherever you are weak and vulnerable, open the pages of God's Word and find out what God has to say to counteract the lies and false stories you are tempted to believe.

It's amazing how the truth can expose a lie and put it to rest. I saw this in a new way one day when I heard Brene Brown, research professor at University of Houston, at a leadership conference I was required to attend, share an experience exposing her own vulnerability.

In her book, *Rising Strong*, Brene Brown writes about this same event that occurred during a summer vacation with her husband, Steve, and her children at a lake in the Texas Hill Country. She and her husband went for a swim in the lake. Out there in the water together, Brene felt overcome with savoring the moment and love for her husband, and said, "I'm so glad we decided to do this together. It's beautiful out here."[2] She expected something sweet in return. Instead, her husband just brushed her off. She tried again, and he just made a brief comment of agreement. And then, he swam back to shore. Well, Brene was just fit to be tied—and angry. The more she thought about the whole event, the more she started personalizing it and creating stories in her mind: *What's going on? I don't know if I'm supposed to feel humiliated or hostile. I wanted to cry and I wanted to scream.*[3]

Brene decided to question her husband with her thoughts. She basically told him the stories that were running through her mind—either he thought she was getting old, couldn't swim very well, or didn't look so great in her swimsuit. And that's when the truth came out. He said, "I don't know what you were saying to me today. I have no idea. I was fighting of a total panic attack during the entire swim…Last night I had a dream that I had all five of the kids on the raft, and we were halfway across the cove when a speedboat came hauling toward us…I grabbed them off the raft and pulled them as deep as I could go."[4] It was just a dream. But once in the water with Brene, he could only feel the panic from the story that had haunted him in the night. Once Brene realized that the stories she had believed weren't remotely true, her anger was gone, and peace once again ruled in her heart

When I heard Brene Brown share her own story about "stories," I immediately applied it from a biblical standpoint thinking, *Stories! How often have I myself believed a story that absolutely is not true? This is going to be important for my own growth and walk with the Lord.*

In her book, *Rising Strong*, Brene Brown speaks primarily about stories from a secular view and talks about how to handle them. She focuses on the importance of uncovering "the story I'm making up" and believing. Now, she is talking from the vantage point of a research professor and social scientist at the University of Houston Graduate college of Social Work. From my own perspective as a theologian and teacher of God's Word, I think there is an even greater spiritual side to the untrue stories we believe. Where do the stories come from? I believe that the enemy of our souls, the devil, feeds us one false story after another, trying to defeat us with fear and panic. And sometimes we don't even realize that we have believed a false story filled with lies. Kay Arthur encourages us to frisk every thought that comes to our mind determining whether it is true or false by asking the question, "Who is that knocking at my door?" I can't quote it accurately, but I seem to remember Charles Stanley, the beloved preacher and senior pastor of First Baptist Church in Atlanta, Georgia, always saying that "when the devil tells you a story, you let it go in one ear and out the other." Thank you Kay and Charles! Wise words, indeed!

As I mentioned in a previous chapter, when my husband and I moved from beautiful San Diego to Palm Desert (where it's 120 degrees in the summer) and I knew absolutely *no one*, I immediately leaped to the extreme, "I've lost the smile of God. All is lost! My life is over! There is no hope!" But that was a false story that left me defeated and depressed for a year until I finally decided to live in the Psalms. I learned that you can never calculate any situation without God. And when you factor the Lord into your situation, all is never lost. Your life does not depend on your plans or the answers you expect. Your life depends on God and God alone. If your plans don't work out, then you can know that God is doing something that has not yet entered your mind. Little did I realize that moving to Palm Desert was the beginning of writing books and a much larger ministry than I had ever imagined.

Always remember that the devil is the father of lies "seeking whom he may devour" (1 Peter 5:8 KJV). He would love to have you believe the lies and all kinds of false stories. He can't destroy your salvation, but he will attempt to destroy your peace of mind and fellowship with Christ. He wants you to have the lies and stories become the authority for your belief instead of the Word of God. He would love to have you looking at temporal things and believing earthly sight instead of God's Word.

It comes down to the authority for your belief. Will it be what you see, how you feel, the lies and stories, or will it be God's Word? That is the critical issue, dear friend. It's all about being "transformed by the renewing of your mind" in the Word of God (Romans 12:2 NASB).

Just think about the Brene Brown story. How ridiculous would it have been for her to continue believing what she felt and thought instead of what her husband had explained to her? Once she knew the truth, the lies dissipated. In the spiritual realm, the same is true. Once you know God's Word, the Spirit of God will take those truths and cause the stories and lies to dissipate. The fear, worry, and despair that often accompanies those stories and lies also dissipate. But if you never take the sword of the Spirit which is the Word of God and cut away the lies and stories, your fear and panic and worry will thrive and grow.

Jessie Penn Lewis, a Welsh evangelical speaker in the 1800s, in her book *War on the Saints*, wrote, "The Holy Spirit needs the believer's use of truth to work with in energizing and strengthening him for conflict and victory."[5] She said that generally the devil does not work "in the open but always behind cover…generally the wiles [of the devil] are primarily directed against the mind, or thoughts, and apart from yielding to known sin, most of the workings of Satan in a believer's life may be traced back to a wrong thought or belief, admitted into the mind."[6] Her words show the importance of the Word of God and the power of the Holy Spirit in counteracting lies and stories that enter our mind.

Paul tells us to fix our thoughts "on what is true, and honorable, and right, and pure, and lovely, and admirable. Think about things that are excellent and worthy of praise" (Philippians 4:8 NLT). This is a great offensive move in the spiritual battle. God is calling us to pay attention to our thoughts and fix them on what we know is true and right. Those things can be found in the Word of God. Gurnall points out that "Scripture is a garden which grows a comforting promise for every sorrow. And a wise Christian gathers one of every kind and writes them down as a doctor keeps records of tried and proven prescriptions for diseases."[7]

And then, pay attention to your relationship with the world. "Don't copy the behavior and customs of this world, but let God transform you into a new person by changing the way you think. Then you will learn to know God's will for you, which is good and pleasing and perfect" (Romans 12:2 NLT).

As you fix your thoughts on truth, the Lord will transform you into a new person. He is going to make you bold, courageous, and confident. The disciples in the first century church were such great examples of God's transforming work. These fearful men who ran for their lives when Jesus was arrested, became faithful followers who ultimately gave their lives for Christ. What can account for such a transformation? God did a mighty work in them through the power of the Holy Spirit. As God gave them strength and power in their calling to spiritual battles and warfare, He will do the same for you. This is your calling.

Deliverance from the power of the evil one comes through definite resistance on the ground of the Cross.

J.O. FRASER IN WAR ON THE SAINTS BY JESSE PENN LEWIS

A PASSION FOR THE IMPOSSIBLE

With people this is impossible, but with God all things are possible.
MATTHEW 19:26

As you walk the road of life with Jesus, you have discovered that occasionally there are annoyances, obstacles, and difficulties. Bumps in the road that are temporary distractions, but not beyond your skills at repair. But more often that not, certainly more often that you would like, on that road with Jesus, you must face the impossible. It is only when you see the way becoming totally, utterly, one hundred percent impossible that you can *know* you are on the right road in your journey. You are exactly where Jesus wants to be *for such a time as this* (Esther 4:14, Acts 26:29). The Lord intends to do the impossible; He is *calling* you to the impossible.

One day Jesus was talking about the difficulty of salvation for people. Jesus said to his disciples, "I tell you the truth, it is very hard for a rich person to enter the Kingdom of Heaven. I'll say it again—it is easier for a camel to go through the eye of a needle than for a rich person to enter the Kingdom of God" (Matthew 19:23-24 NLT). Realizing the impossibility in light of what Jesus was saying, the disciples asked, "Who can be saved" (Matthew 19:25). Jesus replied with an important truth about God that we absolutely need to know for our own lives. "With people this is impossible, but with God all things are possible" (Matthew 19:26). God is the God of the impossible.

Jeremiah, a prophet whose life is seen in the Old Testament, was called to serve the Lord at a young age. God's calling to Jeremiah actually sent him into a state of panic. He basically told God that there was no way he could do it—"I can't speak for You! I'm too young" (Jeremiah 1:6). God responded to Jeremiah by telling him to go where God sent him and say what God told him to say. Then, a beautiful thing happened right in the midst of the calling in Jeremiah's life. The LORD reached out and touched Jeremiah's mouth. And then God made His promise to Jeremiah, "Look, I have put my words in your mouth! Today I appoint you…" (Jeremiah 1:9-10). This would prove to be important over the years for Jeremiah. God knew what He had in mind for Jeremiah, for He was sending Jeremiah to speak for Him to a rebellious people. Jeremiah was called to be God's object lesson to the people of God, showing them the error of their ways, and reaching out to them with love to woo them to Himself. God knew there would be suffering in the days ahead. But God also knew there would be a radical intimacy with his precious servant, Jeremiah.

One of God's greatest statements to His people through Jeremiah is, "I have loved you with an everlasting love; therefore, I have drawn you with lovingkindness" (Jeremiah 31:3). When Jerusalem was under siege by the Babylonians, the king imprisoned Jeremiah. The king was not happy at the prophecies of Jeremiah who had not given him good news about the outcome. During that time, God gave Jeremiah these encouraging words. "I am the Lord, the God of all the peoples of the world. Is anything too hard for me" (Jeremiah 32:27 NLT). And then God proceeded to give Jeremiah a promise of future good where He would bring His people back after they were scattered into exile; they would be His people, and He would be their God (Jeremiah 32:37-42). This promise seemed totally, utterly, one hundred percent impossible in the midst of war and ruin and devastation. Yet God gently and patiently reminded Jeremiah that He could perform the impossible, that nothing was too hard for Him.

God promises His power for you when you encounter impossible situations. The promise for God's work in your impossible situation is all the more difficult to believe because of the ruin and devastation threatening you. Harry Truman once said something like, "If you hear about a guy losing his job, it's a downturn; if the guy across the street loses his job, it's a recession; if you lose your job, it's a depression." It is all the more personal and devastating. With impossible situations, you can't see any "possible" way God can fix this circumstance. But, surprise—you are not God! Always remember that God knows more than you and His ways are just beyond your comprehension at times (Isaiah 55:8-9). Paul experienced this truth more than once in his life, and he told the Ephesians that God is "able to do immeasurably more than all we ask or imagine, according to his power that is at work within us" (Ephesians 3:20 NIV).

Paul was so convinced of this assurance and promise in his own impossible trial that he developed a passion for the impossible. Paul was given what he called a thorn in the flesh. It was so bad for Paul that three times he begged God to remove it. He recounts his cries to God, "Three different times I begged the Lord to take it away" (2 Corinthians 12:8). He knew God could remove it and he was devastated when He didn't do it. But then, God taught Paul something that gave him a new view of the impossible situation. God said, "My grace is all you need. My power works best in weakness" (2 Corinthians 12:9). Basically, He was telling Paul that the thorn in the flesh was not the end of Paul's story. Yes, it was impossible. Then God told Paul something he didn't know. God's power is best displayed in an impossible situation. Paul was so excited at the realization of this truth from God that he exclaimed, "So now I am glad to boast about my weaknesses, so that the power of Christ can work through me. That's why I take pleasure in my weaknesses, and in the insults, hardships, persecutions, and troubles that I suffer for Christ. For when I am weak, then I am strong" (2 Corinthians 12:9-10 NLT). Paul had developed a passion for the impossible because he could not wait to see what the Lord Jesus Christ was going to do in and through him.

I am developing a passion for the impossible, though I will be the first to admit I am not always passionate about impossibilities. However, I'm growing in the excitement of having a challenge that has no earthly answer. Yes, sometimes impossible situations freak me out and throw me into a panic. I believe some people actually thrive on impossibilities. They are the ones who run to a disaster, rather than away from it. That would not be me. And yet, I have seen God do such amazing miracles when I am in an impossible place that I experience the excitement anticipating His power at work in my life. Lilias Trotter, 19th century missionary in Algiers, wrote, "We love to see the impossible done. And so does God." A. W. Tozer, 20th century author and pastor wrote: "Anyone can do the possible; add a bit of courage and zeal and some may do the phenomenal; only Christians are obliged to do the impossible."

A "financial" bend in the road came my way a number of years ago—I was in a desperate place, a dark night of the soul. My situation felt totally, utterly, one hundred percent impossible! My heart was broken, our bills mounted, and a need for more income was immediately apparent. I thought to myself early one morning as I talked with the Lord. *I am absolutely terrified Lord. How are we going to make it personally, financially, or emotionally? I am in despair, Lord. I can't see any possible answer or any visible means of support. What are we to do?* When I stand back and think about it now, I smile because of the irrational thought on which I based my despair. I was thinking that because I couldn't see the answer, therefore, there must be no answer. That thought is ridiculous, counterproductive, and straight from the enemy himself. But God was in the process of changing the way I think. And God was beginning the journey for me of developing a passion for the impossible. If God wants to do the impossible, then things need to be impossible. I didn't know that at the time, but I know it now.

The beautiful stanza from Annie Johnson Flint's poem came to my mind. "Have you come to the Red Sea place in your life, Where in spite of all you can do, There is no way out, there is no way back, There is no other way but through?" I thought, *I am exactly in that place—the Red Sea Place.* The Red Sea place is the place where your faith is tested, and you experience what might be called a crisis of the heart.[1] The questions in front of you are very real: "How am I going to make it? Where is the answer? Is God real? How can I believe God's Word?" The Red Sea place comes at many defining moments in life—a need for salvation and forgiveness of sin, times of financial struggle, difficulties in a job, loss of career, difficult relationships, illness, and loss of loved ones.

My Red Sea Place, the impossible situation I now faced, became the impetus for a new study in God's Word for me. I opened to Exodus and began living in God's Word. What I saw in Exodus began a journey of healing and heart transformation. I experienced many *Aha!* moments as I lived in Exodus. One truth has stood out to me above all others—God's passionate, unfailing love for me, His child. I saw the truth of His words in Jeremiah 31:3, "I have loved you with an everlasting love." I realized that the greatest truth that stands out in the Bible, from Genesis to Revelation, is God's passion for His people—His extravagant, immeasurable, unconditional, amazing love. His love is so great that He goes to any length to save them, rescue them, deliver them, provide for them, sustain them, and protect them. He is adamant and resolute in His love and has a definite plan and purpose in mind.

In the impossible situation, the best truth to discover is God's love for you. And it is usually the very truth we forget. His love gives us everything we need. Jeremiah was led to God's amazing love in his impossible situations. He wrote of his experience in Lamentations 3:21-24—"This I recall to my mind, therefore I have hope. The Lord's lovingkindnesses indeed never cease, for His compassions never fail. They are new every morning; Great is Your faithfulness. 'The Lord is my portion,' says my soul, 'Therefore I have hope in Him.'" When you see the greatness of God's love, you realize that even if everyone else forsakes you, God will never forsake you.

Through my own journey in Exodus, I experienced a divine rescue and I found the way through and the way out. It was a sacred journey, one that I will never forget. God showed me that He rescues us so that we can know, love, and serve Him. Losses become gains. God causes all things to work together for good when we surrender them into the hands of the One who loves us and lives with us moment by moment from now until we enjoy our life with Him in heaven. That is the truth from God's Word. And Jesus promises that when you know the truth, "the truth will make you free" (John 8:32). Oh yes, dear friend. God is greater than any impossible that you are experiencing right now. He loves you with passion, power and purpose. And He wants you to walk in freedom.

Ultimately the Lord led me in a new direction in ministry and has faithfully provided for us, one step at a time. And out of that impossible situation came a new quiet time study that the Lord led me to write: *One Holy Passion—A Sacred Journey in Exodus to God's Amazing Love*. In that study, I was able to write about the Red Sea Place and the wilderness because I had walked through it myself with the Lord. I realize now that I could have never written about the impossible situation had I not lived it as a firsthand experience.

Even today, I face new impossible situations where my faith is tried and tested. And in the midst of these new and more difficult impossible trials, I know God has a plan. Recently, in my quiet time in the Word, the Lord gave me a new perspective about facing impossible situations. I saw the word impossible (im·pos·si·ble) in an entirely new way: "I'm possible." I need to begin to think that way in all my impossibles—that indeed *I am possible* in the midst of it all. Every impossible place clears the way for a new miracle from God and a display of His power. There are enough promises in God's Word to support every miracle needed to take care of us in every impossible trial. And so, the impossible actually puts God on notice and high alert. Here is a place and situation where His power will most certainly save the day. Is God enough for such an impossible need and demand? Oh yes, He is. "He counts the number of the stars; He gives names to all of them. Great is our Lord and abundant in strength; His understanding is infinite" (Psalm 147:4-5). And we can know most certainly that the God who called stars, planets, and universes into being with His commands is able to handle your impossible situation.

Charles Haddon Spurgeon writes: "Nothing will happen that God has not foreseen. No unexpected event will destroy His plans. No emergency will transpire for which He has not provided. No peril will occur against which He has not guarded. No remarkable need will take Him by surprise. He declares the end from the beginning, from ancient times things that are not yet done (Isaiah 46:10). God fills His own eternal now. He sees everything, the past, the present, the future...He who is at the helm is Master of every wind that blows and of every wave that breaks its force on the ship."[2]

What impossible situation has God called you to face? What will God do? Perhaps only He knows. You may not know. And He almost certainly will do something that is only in His mind. So it most likely will not be something you see or have planned in your own mind. And that is where I sometimes get most uncomfortable. Maybe you do, too. I like to *see* it. I like to *know* it. It seems all the more definite, assured, and fait accompli when "I'm in control." How foolish; I laugh at myself. Am I to face the impossibles in life as a doubting Thomas, where I say, "Unless I see the [fill in the blanks], I will not believe." That's not walk on water faith. That's not a passion for the impossible! That's not my calling.

However, faith calls for new eyes that see the unseen and know all that God promises in His Word. Abraham was a champion at this kind of faith in an impossible situation. Abraham had the promise from God that he would become the father of many nations. And yet, he was old and did not have any children. It was totally, utterly, one hundred percent impossible. Here's how Abraham demonstrated faith in his impossible situation. "Abraham's faith did not weaken, even though, at about 100 years of age, he figured his body was as good as dead—and so was Sarah's womb. Abraham never wavered in believing God's promise. In fact, his faith grew stronger, and in this he brought glory to God. He was fully convinced that God is able to do whatever he promises" (Romans 4:19-21 NLT). You see, Abraham admitted the impossibility. But he believed God's promise, fully convinced that God can accomplish all things. The impossible is never too great for our great God.

As a result of all we know about our God, we need to cultivate a brave and confident heart.

Bravery, confidence, and courage are a calling from God. Hear His voice calling you even now: "So do not throw away this confident trust in the Lord. Remember the great reward it brings you! Patient endurance is what you need now, so that you will continue to do God's will. Then you will receive all that he has promised" (Hebrews 10:35-36 NLT). With a brave and confident heart, we can trust God to provide, show us what to do, and lead us in the way we should go.

Mrs. Charles Cowman, co-founder of the Oriental Missionary Society in the early 1900s, shares these words of truth from Carrie Montgomery: "If we have the faith that believes to see, it will keep us from growing discouraged. We shall 'laugh at impossibilities,' we shall watch with delight to see how God is going to open up a path through the Red Sea when there is no human way out of our difficulty. It is just in such places of severe testing that our faith grows and strengthens."[3]

Mrs. Charles Cowman certainly knew many impossibles. She shares them again and again her books, *Streams in the Desert* and *Springs in the Valley*. She experienced a particularly devastating Red Sea place when she received an ominous doctor's report, "No more public services for you. Your heart is gone. To disobey may be to drop dead." But she knew that nothing was impossible for God. As she drew near to God, she received a profound promise from Him—that He is the resurrection and the life (John 11:25), that her life belonged to Christ, and that He lived in her (Galatians 2:20). "The Lord is urging me to a new and greater dependence on Him. I've decided I'm going to trust Him for His strength and keep on speaking and ministering for Him." She was encouraged to depend on His life in her for all that He called her to do until the day she stepped into heaven. She felt as though the Lord was encouraging her, and personalized the famous Francis Havergal hymn: "Take My life and let it be everything, My child, to thee! Take Me for thy spirit's wealth, Take Me for thy body's health." Miraculously, she experienced His power as she continued her speaking ministry and no longer felt weak and sick. She finished the manuscript for *Springs in the Valley*, and ministered at many future speaking engagements. At her Red Sea place, Mrs. Cowman a passion for the impossible and was led to a new and deeper trust in God. That was her calling.

So do not be surprised when a totally, utterly, one hundred percent impossible comes your way. It is irrefutable proof that you are on the right road with Jesus. He is calling you to "a new and greater dependence on Him." If you develop a passion for the impossible, you will experience the great and mighty power of your Lord at work in and through you. The Lord intends to do the impossible; He is *calling* you to the impossible. This is your calling.

Mrs. Charles Cowman writes: If there is a great trial in your life today, do not own it as a *defeat*, but continue, by faith, to claim the victory through Him who is able to make you more than conqueror, and a glorious victory will soon be apparent. Let us learn that in all the hard places God brings us into, He is making opportunities for us to exercise such faith in Him as will bring about blessed results and greatly glorify His name.[4]

My goal is God Himself, not joy, nor peace,
Nor even blessing, but Himself, my God;
'Tis His to lead me there, not mine, but His—
'At any cost, dear Lord, by any road!'

"So faith bounds forward to its goal in God,
And love can trust her Lord to lead her there;
Upheld by Him, my soul is following hard
Till God hath full fulfilled my deepest prayer.

"No matter if the way be sometimes dark,
No matter though the cost be ofttimes great,
He knoweth how I best shall reach the mark,
The way that leads to Him must needs be straight.

"One thing I know, I cannot say Him nay;
One thing I do, I press towards my Lord;
My God my glory here, from day to day,
And in the glory there my Great Reward.

MRS. CHARLES COWMAN IN STREAMS IN THE DESERT

FAILURE, REGRET, AND IMPERFECTION

So now there is no condemnation for those who belong to Christ Jesus.
ROMANS 8:1 NLT

When my father discovered he had incurable cancer, one of his first responses was intense regret for mistakes when he was younger in life. He confessed to me in a tender moment at his beside in Lake Havasu City, Arizona, , "Catherine, I missed your growing up years and also your brother's early years." I stared at my folded hands, unable to meet his gaze. The divorce had come when I was only five, my brother only three. We had felt abandoned, cast aside, worthless, desperate for fatherly attention. And now, it was evident my father felt an overwhelming sense of failure and remorse, something he had carried with him as a heavy burden. I was stunned, taken aback, then silent to gather my thoughts. He had never spoken like this before. Finally, my voice trembling, I looked up at his sunken eyes and gaunt tense face and said, "Dad, we love you so much. We're just so thankful that we have gotten to know you, love you, and enjoy so many incredible years with you." His chest heaved in gasps, tears streaming down across a ghostly pallor, and I leaned into his open arms and I told him how much I loved him.

The most beautiful part of those last months with my father was witnessing the work of Christ in his life. Now here was a man who had run from God most of his life. He was a very successful businessman in his earlier years and he saw no real need for God. He lived passionately and wildly in what many would call "the good life." He had expensive cars, a private airplane, and many beautiful homes. Unfortunately, I did not really know my father until much later in life—after I was married. He made a point of coming to my wedding, and, for some reason, perhaps relief from responsibility for me, he began visiting my husband and me in San Diego. And so, we would spend more and more time together, golf weekends, dinners out, ordinary family stuff. And slowly inexplicably, over the years, we became fast friends. And surprise, I discovered something I had never known about myself. Though I was very much like my mother: I was also very much like my father.

As I spent more time with my father, we would have these deeply spiritual conversations. I discovered he had his own ideas about spirituality. When I would talk to him about how God loved him, he would say, "Cath, God may be fond of me, but He really loves you!" And then he would confess that he didn't believe in God the way I did. In fact, he used to jokingly say I was going to get him into heaven. And I would tell him that Jesus was the only way to God.

Remembering, there was this time, during the holiday season, that I had watched a very powerful sermon online by a well-known pastor, Stephen Furtick, of Elevation Church. Without even thinking much about it, a spur of the moment decision, I sent a message link to my father just for encouragement. I really didn't even think my father would actually watch it. But I didn't want to miss the opportunity to share the biblical truths. It was not until about a week later that I received a call from my father that went to voicemail. His message, "Cath, you are messing with me. Call me. I want to talk to you about that message." My heart started racing. I thought, *Really? He actually watched the message?* I just couldn't believe it. I immediately called my father, I could not get in a word edgewise; he could not stop talking about that message.

So, sometime later, on Christmas day, I received another voicemail from my father. His voice firm and quiet, he said, "Cath, you're going to want to call me. I did something you are going to want to know about." I had absolutely no idea what he was going to tell me. When I called later that day, I got one of the best stories I have ever heard. My father had been listening to all of that same pastor's messages on Christmas Day. Pastor Furtick was sharing the gospel on how to become a Christian. Then the pastor issued the invitation. My father recounted the pastor's words, something to the effect, "If you want to become a Christian and pray with me, receiving Him into your life, then stand and express your desire for Christ. Even if you are watching this from home, you should stand right where you are and pray with me." Silence for a few moments. Then, his voice rushed, my father said, "Guess what, Cath? I stood and prayed that prayer!" I was still silent. My father concluded, "You know what, Cath? When I sat back down, I knew I was different." When I heard my father's story, I was just stunned. I knew in my heart that he had truly given his life to Christ. It was just one year later that he found out he had cancer. But oh, how God worked in his life during that one year. I witnessed an amazing transformation. I truly saw the words of Paul come to life in my father: "Anyone who belongs to Christ has become a new person. The old life is gone; a new life has begun" (2 Corinthians 5:17 NLT).

I spent a lot of time with my father during the last six months of his life. I remember one moment etched in time when he couldn't sleep because of his suffering. He knew I was there in the room and he said, "Cath, just think about this. When we come to know the Lord, He gives us His righteousness. I've been thinking a lot about righteousness these days. I'm realizing the amazing gift of righteousness in light of our own sin and imperfection. The incredible part is that He doesn't make us pay for it. He gives it to use freely out of His heart of love and grace. What a deal! Who in the world would turn that gift away?" I smiled when my father shared that profound truth. I loved hearing his words. My dad truly got it. He understood, and he knew Christ. Not long after that, he went home to be with the Lord. And though I greatly miss him, I know that I shall see him someday in heaven.

I watched the Lord transform my father right before my very eyes, and take all my father's failures, regrets, and imperfections, and use them for His glory. The Lord calls out to us triumphantly with those words in Romans 8:28 where He promises to cause all things to work together for good to those who love Him and are called according to His purpose. What He is really saying is that He will use the very things we wish removed from our lives—failure, regret, and imperfection—as tools for good. And the amazing truth is that God's power is actually displayed best in the very weaknesses we wish would disappear (2 Corinthians 12:9). God has actually chosen "the foolish things of the world to shame the wise" and "the weak things of the world to shame the things which are strong" (1 Corinthians 1:27).

There is a special woman in the New Testament who is a good example of how the Lord can work something beautiful out of failure, regret and imperfection. One day while Jesus was teaching at the temple in Jerusalem, the scribes and Pharisees brought an accused woman and put her in front of Jesus and before the crowd. They challenged Jesus, "Teacher, this woman has been caught in adultery, in the very act. Now in the Law Moses commanded us to stone such women; what then do You say?" Would Jesus be forced to make one of His blasphemous claims of being God, perhaps saying something like "Your sins are forgiven." That would be a direct claim to being God because only God can forgive sins! More pieces of evidence against Him! A snare, a perfect trap! Yet, stiff-necked, as whited sepulchers, the scribes and Pharisees presumed to accuse against the all-powerful force of the King of Kings and Lord of Lords, Yahweh, and the Eternal Creator! How foolish! Jesus bent down and wrote on the ground with His finger. The scribes and Pharisees kept demanding an answer. Finally, Jesus responded, "He who is without sin among you, let him be the first to throw a stone at her" (John 8:7). Then He bent down and again continued to write on the ground, perhaps the names of the scribes and pharisees in the dust. So how did they respond to Jesus' words about casting the first stone? One by one, the accusers left, the older ones leaving first, then followed by the younger ones.

Ultimately, we are confronted with the heart of Jesus for the adulterous woman, caught in sin, facing the harsh reality of failure, regret, and imperfection. Jesus spoke to the woman. "Where are your accusers? Didn't even one of them condemn you?" "No, Lord," she said. And Jesus said, "Neither do I. Go and sin no more" (John 8:10-11 NLT). Do you see His heart of mercy and grace for you, no matter what you have done, or where you have been in life? Jesus invited that woman to a new life. The great truth is that when we come to Christ, there is therefore now "no condemnation to those who are in Christ Jesus" (Romans 8:1). This is our calling.

There's a frequently overlooked item many miss in the story of the adulterous woman : "…they began to go out one by one, beginning with the older ones…" The older ones were the first to walk away. Oh, I love the irony that the Lord included this detail in the story. I believe the older ones walked away first because they were more aware of their sins having lived a longer life. They knew their sins and knew them all too well. Their sense of guilt must have been greater. I believe as we age, we encounter a greater sense of failure, regret, and imperfection. The answer? We need to realize the matchless, immeasurable grace of God.

We fail. We are imperfect. But *in Christ*, we are tall and strong. *In Christ*, we experience glorious grace in our imperfection. Our life is hidden with Christ in God. Does that mean we just can do anything we want? Not at all. He is calling us—inviting us—to a beautiful abundant life. But to have this abundant life, we travel on the road and take the journey that gives us the experience of that life. If we want to go to experience the history of Italy and enjoy its beauty, then we must actually travel there. The same is true with our spiritual journey. The way to abundant life and the experience of knowing Christ more and more is to be filled with the Spirit, walk with Him, talk with Him, and surrender to Him moment by moment. We'll fail a thousand times—yes— but we are forgiven and we live in the garden of grace. So we get up and keep going. We grow in the grace and knowledge of our Lord and Savior (2 Peter 3:18). But if we choose to walk the road of sin and debauchery, we're on the wrong path. You can't get to Italy by driving on a dirt road somewhere in California. That road doesn't take you to Italy. So no matter what wrong road you may have gotten yourself on, stop and turn around, and get on the right road. The turning around on the road is called *repentance*. Then, you need to keep going in grace, one step at a time with Jesus. He will take you in the right direction on the right road throughout your life. Just stay close to Him, every step of the way.

I have struggled often with failure, regret, and imperfection. I can make a mistake and then beat myself up in my mind and my heart for days. My husband remarked one day, "Catherine I would like for you to go a whole day without putting yourself down." That was an eye-opening statement.

In her book, *The Gifts of Imperfection*, research professor Brene Brown speaks of the importance of letting go of certain things in order to embrace courage, bravery, and worthiness. The Lord encourages us to "lay aside every encumbrance" in order to run the race set before us (Hebrews 12:1). We need to let go of what people think, perfectionism, the need for certainty, comparison, anxiety, self-doubt, and control. We truly do need to make a decision about how we will live and be tenacious to own our calling to Christ in the midst of our imperfection. Otherwise, we will live in this pattern of shame, self-humiliation, and disappointment.

I remember reading a very important statement by 19th century Bible expositor, William

Newell, many years ago. He wrote: "To be disappointed in yourself is to have believed in yourself." He pointed out the need for us to see ourselves "in Christ only." I love those words and accept them as part of my calling.

I have a beautiful crystal cross, given to me by Beverly, who is so dear to my heart. It sits on a pedestal with the words written on it, "Through The Cross." When you set the cross in a position where the light shines through, then the light creates beautiful colors. So it is with us. When our lives are seen through the cross of Christ, we are beautiful and perfect in every way, because through the cross, we are "in Christ only." Oh yes, we are called to this cross of the Lord Jesus Christ and we need to see ourselves *in Christ only*.

Paul teaches us how to live with imperfection. He says, "I don't mean to say that I have already achieved these things or that I have already reached perfection. But I press on to possess that perfection for which Christ Jesus first possessed me. No, dear brothers and sisters, I have not achieved it, but I focus on this one thing: Forgetting the past and looking forward to what lies ahead, I press on to reach the end of the race and receive the heavenly prize for which God, through Christ Jesus, is calling us" (Philippians 3:12-14 NLT). Jesus is calling us to *press on*.

There is an advantage to failure in our weakness, guilt and regret, and imperfection as we live life. God does His work and everyone recognizes the Lord's hand in our lives. In Paul's first letter to the immature church at Corinth, he addressed the truth about how God works in imperfect people. He said, "For consider your calling, brethren, that there were not many wise according to the flesh, not many mighty, not many noble; but God has chosen the foolish things of the world to shame the wise, and God has chosen the weak things of the world to shame the things which are strong, and the base things of the world and the despised God has chosen, the things that are not, so that He may nullify the things that are, so that no man may boast before God" (1 Corinthians 1:26-29).

At the end of the day, at the end of our life, when all else fails, we are called from God to boast in Him and Him alone. We are called to recognize His greatness and power in our own weakness, grace in our failures, forgiveness and mercy in our regrets, and Christ's righteousness and life in our imperfections. That's the advantage. That's our salvation. That's our victory! It's His life *for* ours! It's His life *not* ours! It is no longer we who live, but Christ who lives in us. So, dear friend, we lay every failure, regret, and imperfection at the foot of the cross, fix our eyes on Jesus, and keep running with endurance the race set before us (Hebrews 12:1-3).

WHEN YOU FORGET YOUR CALLING

And we know that God causes everything to work together for the good of those who love God and are called according to his purpose for them.

ROMANS 8:28

There are days when I *forget* my calling. I forget who God is; I forget who I am in Christ; I forget why I am here. I descend into the pit of fear, doubt, and mistrust, and so many other ugly emotions, where I wallow in the miry mud, the dangerous quicksand, of disbelief. I *feel* as though I'm not good enough for God to love me; I *feel* that God is on the far side of the universe disinterested in me, and I *feel* that I am absolutely, positively certain I cannot make it even one more day in life. I lose my sense of purpose and I fail to remember God's promises. I have a feeling that you have felt the same way at times. So what can we do when the world seems to be crumbling in on top of us?

How do I arrive at this position of amnesia where all looks hopeless? Always remember that the devil is "the father of lies" (John 8:44) and he is your enemy, who "prowls around like a roaring lion, looking for someone to devour" (1 Peter 5:8 NLT). So walking by faith in God's Word, the truth in every situation, is imperative in spiritual warfare.

If I have lost my quiet time and I have not spent daily time with God in His Word for awhile, then I'm sure to fall into the pit soon enough. Then, a difficult trial can send me there quickly, if I am not careful and disciplined to remember all that is true and walk by faith in God's Word. Of course, some of the most difficult times for me come when someone has tried to demean and demoralize me through words or actions. I have experienced this latter trigger more than once, and sometimes it has come from places where you would least expect such discouragement—leaders in the church or people I trusted in my life.

In recent years, the most difficult times of my life have followed great losses. Loss of job, finances, health, loved ones. I have frequently felt like Job after losing everything dear to him: "Then Job arose and tore his robe and shaved his head, and he fell to the ground and worshiped. He said, 'Naked I came from my mother's womb, and naked I shall return there. The LORD gave and the LORD has taken away. Blessed be the name of the LORD'" (Job 1:20-21).

I do not shave my head like Job, but I do withdraw, feeling as though I have lost the sense of who I am. I take a step back, feeling wounded and broken in heart and soul. Roy Hessian writes in *The Calvary Road* that "to be broken is the beginning of revival," and when uncertainty, disbelief, and depression strike, I know personal spiritual revival is just around the corner for me.[1] The Lord took me quite recently on a wild journey with an emotional, rollercoaster change of church venue; and combined with the loss of both my parents, I found myself smack dab in the middle of a valley, what I call "the valley of the shadow." In Psalm 23, David spoke of walking in the valley of the shadow of death where he would fear no evil because the Lord was with him. I know the encouraging truth of King David's words because I have experienced the Lord's close companionship in my own valley.

The Lord is calling you, always speaking to you, as He makes His home in your heart. You can count on Him, through the indwelling Holy Spirit, to speak words that are exactly what you need to hear, exactly when you need to hear them. Jesus promised, "the Helper, the Holy Spirit, whom the Father will send in My name, He will teach you all things, and bring to your remembrance all that I said to you" (John 14:26). These aren't words from a far off place, issued by a pontificating, armchair guru, but by our omnipotent Creator, God Himself. God uses what we know as the Word of God found in the Bible to speak truth into every circumstance of our life. That is what He most recently did for me! I have already shared about my intensive study in Exodus during a time of doubt and despair that led to writing of the A Quiet Time Experience, *One Holy Passion*. But how did I actually get to that Red Sea Place in the Bible, and what did I do about it? How can you apply my learning experience to your life?

In my lowest time in the valley, I realized God was writing a story in my life and this was yet another chapter in the drama. He was living His life in and through me, and this was where we were at the moment—in the valley of the shadow at the Red Sea place, where there is no way back, and no way out, only going through with the Lord. Through prayer and the Word, He also assured me I wouldn't be in that valley forever, though I surely felt like I would never move on. He helped me remember it's no longer my life, but His life, and He intended to move us on in His time and His way. But then the Lord accomplished something very special and custom-designed just specifically for me.

It all began with a feather on the ground in my back yard. After a long day of writing, I was sitting with my husband on our back patio. It was a hot summer evening. As I surveyed our desert landscape, barrel cactus, succulents, and decorative rock, I spotted this beautiful striped feather on the ground near our grapefruit tree. I jumped out of my chair and walked over to the feather, leaning down to take a closer look. Just then, the eerie feeling came to me that I was not alone. Something was looking at me. I just couldn't escape that feeling. I looked up into our palm tree, and I just about fell over with what I saw no more that ten feet close upon me—a beautiful, great-horned owl was looking directly into my eyes. If you've ever seen a great-horned owl up close and personal, then you know how big and beautiful their eyes are, large black pupils and shimmering golden irises. Well, this predator was not a bit put off, and with all its territorial command, was staring straight at me, inspecting me.

I backed up slowly and made my way into the house, grabbed my Nikon D810 camera, my 80-400mm telephoto lens, and my tripod. As a myPhotoWalk devotional photographer, I knew this is one of those rare photographic opportunities given by God, and I was determined to capture as many images as possible before this wild bird flew away. When I arrived back in place and setup, I noticed Mr. Owl hadn't moved even an inch. It was still looking directly at me, as though making a connection with me. It did not appear afraid or nor affected in the least by my presence. So I began capturing photographs of this amazing creature and the results proved incredible. When I processed them on my computer, I couldn't believe how this owl seemed to be posing for me, looking directly into my camera lens. So what was this visit from the owl all about? I was soon to discover at least one of God's purposes in it all.

The next morning, I couldn't wait to get up and see if my owl was still there. I slowly walked out to the palm tree and looked up. Much to my surprise, there were now two owls! I just couldn't believe this *sovereigndipity*—my word for the unique sovereign hand of God in circumstances that are not coincidence. Again, I took many photographs and those owls never moved. Later that afternoon I discovered the reason why.

So I was sitting at my dining room table working on the *One Holy Passion* manuscript, and I noticed a flurry of frenzied activity in the back yard. At least half a dozen menacing black birds were strafing the owl's palm tree. Oh, my! Suddenly, another black bird appeared from around the corner of the house, and sped straight for the palm tree. There ensued a furious battle between the black bird and the owls, but finally the black bird gave up and flew away. The two owls seemed to change their behavior right after that fight with the black bird. They moved to another branch of the tree and appeared to be in shock. Later, one of the owls flew away, but the other owl (perhaps the mother) stayed for days. I would go out every night and just sit on the back porch and look into the eyes of that owl. That owl's eyes seemed filled with sadness. It would just stare at me as though it knew me, as though I was a friendly face. Then, the owl would go to an outer branch and just sit there, looking off into the distance. For the next six months, that owl would come and stay for a few days, then fly away and be gone for weeks at a time. The times between the visits became longer and longer and I realized that the owl might not come to the palm tree anymore. So what happened and what was God teaching me?

I believe that the owls had a nest there in the palm tree. And they were guarding that nest with some baby owls. I believe the black birds ultimately destroyed the nest and the owls were grieving that loss. The one owl kept returning, grieving the loss, or so it seemed. Barbara J. King, an anthropologist at the College of William and Mary in Virginia, and author of the 2013 book, *How Animals Grieve*, shares that "birds certainly possess the capacity to mourn." In her book, *Wesley, The Owl*, biologist Stacey O'Brien shares the story of how she adopted a baby barn owl with an injured wing and nursed it back to health. I can relate to O'Brien's story. I felt as though a friendship had developed with these owls; they seemed to know me. It was really profound to have what felt like a closeness develop with my (mother) owl as it seemingly grieved its loss. Finally, the owl let go of its grief and moved on with its life and existence. It did not stay forever in that palm tree in my back yard.

God used those owls to teach me a lesson. There is a time for grieving and closure. But ultimately, as long as the Lord has me here on earth, He has a plan and purpose for me. I need to always remember my calling. There is a time to move on. And just like those owls moved on, so I needed to take the bend in the road and move on with the Lord. For a brief time, I had forgotten that God is calling me onward. I was so wrapped up in my grief and loss over my recent "valley of the shadow" life events. Those owls helped me see the strategic significance of my calling and get on with hearing God's voice and following Him. When you forget the calling because of heartbreak or loss, you can know that the Lord has His eye on you and is faithful to lead you on. He may not send you a great horned owl, but He will send you something to help you move on.

I have learned this powerful truth of God's guidance and provision from Oswald Chambers, 20th century evangelist and teacher, in his wonderful devotional, *My Utmost For His Highest*. Oswald Chambers writes, "The first thing God does with us is to get us based on rugged Reality until we do not care what becomes of us individually as long as He gets His way for the purpose of His Redemption."[2] *But what about my hurt?* "Why shouldn't we go through heartbreaks? Through these doorways God is opening up ways of fellowship with His Son." *Ah, I see, but if I pray, why won't God just make the pain go away instantly?* "Most of us fall and collapse at the first grip of pain; we sit down on the threshold of God's purpose and die away of self-pity, and all so-called Christian sympathy will aid us to our death-bed. But God will not. He comes with the grip of the pierced hand of His Son, and says—'Enter into fellowship with Me; arise and shine.'" *God desires our fellowship in our suffering!* "If through a broken heart God can bring His purposes to pass in the world, then thank Him for breaking your heart." *Thank you, Father for your infinite wisdom and love.*

Those words by Oswald Chambers must have been such a powerful message to his wife, Biddy Chambers, when her beloved husband went home to be with the Lord, "entering into Life" as she called it.[3] She is such an example of how the Lord leads us through deep valleys as He calls us on in life. She described her own experience this way: "There was never a moment's doubt of God or of His word or ways, nor was any question allowed to perplex the mind as to what would happen now, but just an eager willingness to do God's will as He should make it clear."[4] After her husband died, she experienced a new calling that came out of her dark valley of loss. She had a gift of transcription, and indeed had faithfully transcribed all of Oswald Chambers' messages. At the Lord's leading, she took those transcribed messages and put together many books by Oswald Chambers including the inspirational devotional, *My Utmost For His Highest*, one of the top selling Christian books of all time. Charles Rae Griffin, friend of Oswald and Biddy, and founding member of the Oswald Chambers Publication Association, remarked "It is hardly possible to pay adequate tribute to the devotion of Mrs. Chambers in recording his spoken words, full shorthand notes having been taken of lectures and sermons and addresses almost without exception, so that the project once started, continuous publication of new matter would be possible."[5] Griffin used one of Oswald Chambers' favorite phrases, "Let God engineer," to describe the Lord's direction in the publishing of the lectures and sermons transcribed by Biddy Chambers. And that is such a good encouragement for us when we may have forgotten the calling. We need to look again to God and trust His guidance. God does indeed carry out magnificent plans even in the darkest valleys. I thank the Lord for the faithfulness of Biddy Chambers; *My Utmost For His Highest*, is at the top of my list of books and has faithfully mentored me for many years in my quiet time. Oh, how faithful the Lord was to work in Biddy Chambers' heart and use her for God's glory. It was her calling.

The Lord was faithful to work in my heart, where He lives through the Holy Spirit, to call me out of my recent "valley of the shadow," and lead me in a new direction. He literally pulled me out of the pit, set my feet on more solid ground, reminded me of who I am in Him, and how He wants to continue His work in and through me. What He did for me, He will do for you also.

So what will help you when you forget your calling?

First—*quiet time*. Renew and cultivate your quiet time with the Lord. Spend extra time with the Lord in His Word and in prayer. My study of Exodus day-by-day in my quiet time and all I learned became the catalyst for helping me in remembering the calling. God calls us to this time when He says, "Be still and know that I am God" (Psalm 46:10 NIV).

Second—*fellowship*. Spend time with a few good friends who will pray with you and for you. I am so thankful for a few of my good friends who faithfully walked with me through my most difficult times. They were praying for me, emailing me, texting me on my phone, calling me, and spending time with me. Those good friends were angels from God to encourage me in my most desperate hours. The Lord tells us to "encourage one another daily" (Hebrews 3:13) and "stimulate one another to love and good deeds" (Hebrews 10:24).

Finally—*community*. Choose a good, Bible-teaching church to attend each week. The church community is so important and essential for your growth and service. You will stay connected rather than completely isolating and withdrawing in your broken time in the valley. The writer of Hebrews says, "And let us not neglect our meeting together, as some people do, but encourage one another, especially now that the day of his return is drawing near" (Hebrews 10:25 NLT).

Always remember that there are seasons in the life of the calling. There are going to be seasons of joy and seasons of difficulty. But Jesus has overcome the world (John 16:33). Never forget that the Lord's calling in your life assures you that He will never leave you or forsake you (Hebrews 13:5). And He is weaving together everything in your life to for good (Romans 8:28). You can count on Him even in the darkest times of your life.

The Calling Journey Five
CALLED TO A DESTINY

1 Corinthians 2:9

Heaven is the place where your faith becomes sight. Earth is the place where you are called to faith and the eternal perspective. But dear friend, heaven is the place where you are called to open your eyes, enjoy your Lord, and never have to walk by faith again. Your faith will be sight. The veil will be pulled back and you will be face to face with your Lord. And when you see Him, I believe that you and He will have a very special moment where there is a familiar, loving, knowing of all you shared together while you were on earth. You lived by the calling you heard from Him, and now your story continues in heaven. Your joy will become complete, for you will be together with Him forever.

CHAPTER 21

A NEW KINGDOM

*For he has rescued us from the kingdom of darkness and
transferred us into the Kingdom of his dear Son.*
COLOSSIANS 1:13 NLT

W hat is this little book? An unassuming red book with a worn binding seemed to catch my eye among hundreds in my theology collection. *Oh, yes, a treasure from the Bethel Theological Seminary book sale! The Silver Lining* by John Henry Jowett, an English biblical scholar and pastor of Fifth Avenue Presbyterian Church in New York in the early 1900s. I was suddenly so drawn to this book in my research for *The Calling* that I began reading it that very day, chapter by chapter, in my quiet time. I soon found my daily thoughts drifting from earth to heaven as Jowett took me deeper into God's Word. Jowett's style of writing, the depth of knowledge, the clarity of language, transported me into the atmosphere and surroundings of the Bible, making each scene come alive. That's what Jowett's writing will do for you. Warren Wiersbe, 20th century pastor, author, and Bible teacher, called Jowett "the greatest preacher in the English speaking world."[1] Jowett had an uncanny knack for choosing exactly the right words to express deep thoughts. Wiersbe described Jowett's writing in his book, *50 People Every Christian Should Know*: "His hobby was words (he read the dictionary for a pastime) and he used them as an artist uses colors. He was a master of the perfect expression. He never used "almost the right word; it was always exactly the right word."[2] After I read *The Silver Lining*, I began searching for more of Jowett's treasures and I began using each Jowett book in my quiet time. *Thirsting for the Springs, Life in the Heights, The Passion for Souls.* All gems! Over and over, I kept thinking, *I am a citizen of another country. I breathe the air and atmosphere of that heavenly kingdom more deeply when I focus on God and His Word.* And after spending time with Jowett books in my research, I inexplicably felt more compelled to turn my thoughts heavenward to contemplate the existence and power of the kingdom of God. No time is ever wasted when I think about the kingdom of God.

After having lived in the gospels for many years and walking with Jesus there, I have noticed how surprisingly much Jesus taught about the kingdom of God. Matthew tells us that Jesus was going through all Galilee "teaching and proclaiming the gospel of the kingdom" (Matthew 4:23).

Just before Jesus ascended into heaven, He spent forty days with His disciples. And for a good part of that time, He talked with them about the kingdom of God (Acts 1:3). Indeed, the focus of the preaching and speaking in the early church seen in Acts was frequently the kingdom of God (Acts 8:12, 14:22, 19:8; 20:25, 28:23,31).

Throughout the New Testament, as I read God's Word, I hear the calling to be a member, citizen, and partaker of a new kingdom—God's kingdom. This is one of God's important messages for us today from His Word. Though I live on earth in this world, this place is not my real home. We are called to a journey heavenward, to God's kingdom. This calling to God's kingdom has important implications for how I live while one earth.

One day, many years ago, my husband announced, "Catherine, we are going to take the trip of a lifetime to romantic Italy—Venice, Florence and Rome." I was excited; I had never been out of the United States. But the first words out of my mouth were, "Oh my, what will I take? How will I pack? The day arrived to leave for the airport, me still stuffing all my worldly belongings into too many bags, and my husband walks in. "What's all this?" he laughed surveying the damage. It was then and there I realized I didn't even have enough hands to carry everything no matter how many shoulder straps I used. We rolled on the floor with laughter—and repacked. I still had too many bags.

Now, in the 1980s, travel seemed more leisurely. After a few glorious days in Venice, from the Venezia Santa Lucia railway station, we caught the local train to Florence. No bullet trains, then. How to pass the time, really the better part of a day? David and I dropped off our many bags at our seats, and we made our way to the elegant dining car.

"Would you like some of the veal?" asked the waiter with a huge platter of veal scallopini on his arm. "Yes, definitely!" I smiled. Indeed, I said, "Yes," every time the waiter walked by with a new platter. Soon my husband grinned, "Cath, you know we have to pay for all these courses." The ordering issue aside, a few hours and many local stops later, we were very, very relaxed and finally enjoying our dessert and coffee. Over the loudspeaker came the monotone announcement, "Santa Maria Novella, Firenze." I looked out the window; the station sign read, "Firenze." I panicked, "David, I think we've arrived at Florence. We have to get off right away!" We jumped up, paid our bill, and ran four or five cars to where our bags. The loudspeaker blared "Roma Termini," and the train jerked forward. My husband and I were literally throwing our bags off the train while it was moving, and then jumped off just in time. *Next time I travel to Europe, I'm not taking so many bags!*

I think life on earth as a citizen of the kingdom of God is a bit like our travel to a foreign land. At the hotels in Italy, we did not completely unpack our bags, knowing we would soon be traveling to another place. The residents of Italy spoke Italian, the menus were in Italian, and all the street signs were in Italian. And, most telling, while we were sojourners in a delightful foreign land, our thoughts often retreated to our home in San Diego. In a foreign land, we are constantly reminded that it is not our permanent home and we are on a temporary journey.

You and I are called to a new kingdom. Our calling to the kingdom of God is a calling to the reign and rule of God in our lives forever. Our homage is to Him and our home is in that heavenly country. This calling includes a place prepared for us by Jesus. And living here on earth is like living in a foreign land that is not our home. This world is not our home. At least, that's the way it should be if we are truly citizens of another kingdom. We are on a journey in this life, what I call "a pilgrimage of the heart." I have written about this topic in *Pilgrimage Of The Heart —Satisfy Your Longing For Adventure With God.* The psalmist writes, "Blessed are those whose strength is in you, whose hearts are set on pilgrimage" (Psalm 84:5 NIV). We have the heart-set of a pilgrim with our eyes fixed on Jesus, our King, as we journey from earth to our home in heaven. If we look and act more like the world than the kingdom of God, then we have assimilated into the world and we will find it difficult, if not impossible, to be a powerful ambassador for Christ and His kingdom.

While Jesus was on earth, He demonstrated the perfect way to live as one from another place and kingdom. I think we see it best in an important conversation Jesus had with Pilate after His arrest. I have always been taken with the fact that two rulers were standing there talking—one from this earth and One from heaven. One ruler was created and the other was Creator. One ruled on earth and the Other rules over all things as Lord. And though Pilate acted as though he had all power over Jesus, he didn't have any power at all. Jesus rules and reigns and His kingdom is eternal.

In their conversation, Pilate taunted Jesus about how He was delivered over by His own people. Jesus immediately corrected Pilate with the truth and moved the conversation to another plane by talking about His own kingdom. "My kingdom is not of this world" (John 18:36). Then, Pilate asked, "So You are a king" (John 18:37). And Jesus told Pilate, "You say correctly that I am a king" (John 18:37). Then Jesus turned the focus to the truth and His very voice speaking and calling to others. He told Pilate, "For this I have been born, and for this I have come into the world, to testify to the truth. Everyone who is of the truth hears My voice" (John 18:37). Pilate, either ignorantly or willfully oblivious to the real identity of the One who was speaking with him, then challenged, "What is truth?" *and Pilate walked away.* Here we see the world and heaven colliding in an irreconcilable impasse.

Our heavenly Father has "rescued us from the kingdom of darkness and transferred us into the Kingdom of his dear Son, who purchased our freedom and forgave our sins" (Colossians 1:13-14 NLT). We are citizens of heaven, where the Lord Jesus Christ lives (Philippians 3:20 NLT). We are ambassadors for Christ and have been given the ministry of reconciliation (2 Corinthians 5:18-21). God is actually making His appeal to others through us. So we are not just called to hang out here on earth until we get to heaven. God has called us to a great work as He touches lives in and through us.

We need to find out about our new kingdom—the kingdom of God—how to be a good citizen of the kingdom. Our owner's manual for the kingdom of God is the Bible. It holds the description of our kingdom and everything else we need to know. In the Bible, we learn what kingdom people look like—our character qualities—the fruit of the Spirit—love, joy, peace, patience, kindness, faithfulness, goodness, and self-control (Galatians 5:22-23). In the Bible, we learn how kingdom people think—on the things that are true, honorable, right, pure, lovely, admirable, excellent, and worthy of praise (Philippians 4:8).

When others look at us, they should be able to say, "You're not from around here, are you?" We need to look like we are from the kingdom of God. People will see, just from our appearance, that we are not like the world. The heroes of the faith in Hebrews 11 have been described as strangers and exiles on earth, seeking a country of their own, and desiring a better, heavenly country (Hebrews 11:13-16). "Therefore God is not ashamed to be called their God."

How, then, shall we live?

How can you live this calling to the kingdom of God while you are in the world? Christ makes it possible as He lives in us through the power and presence of the indwelling Holy Spirit (Galatians 2:20). The King of Kings actually rules and reigns in us and His kingship is seen in our lives. He is Lord and Master in us. We listen to the words of our King as He leads and guides us in life (Matthew 7:24-27). We are not run by the world. Instead, Christ rules our life. And He is a good and merciful King who loves us with an everlasting love (John 15:9, Jeremiah 31:3).

In his book, *The Silver Lining*, John Henry Jowett encourages us to "find a place and find an hour when you can send your imagination among the realms of the blessed, to remind yourselves of the country towards which you are going, of the inheritance to whose possession you are succeeding, and give yourself the sense of the dignity of one who has part and lot in the matter, who is a partaker of the Divine nature, and will share with the Eternal the blessedness of eternity."[3] I see this as a preparation for stepping from time into eternity where we will see the Lord face to face in glory. As we serve the Lord well here on earth, so in heaven we also serve the Lord (Revelation 22:3). Here on earth we walk and talk with the Lord in prayer (Philippians 4:6-7). In the eternal kingdom, we will see His face and be with Him forever (1 Thessalonians 4:17, Revelation 22:4).

Jesus taught in the parable of the mustard seed and the leaven (Matthew 13:31-35) that the kingdom of God is not static, but it is growing. It starts out small but grows larger than anyone can imagine. God is the One who causes the growth and He reaches out to others in and through us. John Bright, 20th century Biblical scholar, in his book, *The Kingdom of God*, describes the

Kingdom of God as "a power already released in the world." He writes: "True, its beginnings are tiny, and it might seem incredible that the humble ministry of this obscure Galilean could be the dawning of a new age of God. Yet it is! What has been begun here will surely go on to its conclusion; nothing can stop it. And the conclusion is victory."[4] What a radical call Jesus has made to us with the message in His word that we are to enter the kingdom of God! He has called us to a radical decision to love, follow, and serve Him.

John Bright speaks of how the Kingdom of God is calling out with a summons for a decision. "In New Testament theology, the Kingdom of God is not only the goal of all history and the reward of all believers, not only the norm by which all human behavior is judged, it is a new order which even now bursts in upon the present one and summons men to be its people. Its summons demands response, and that response is obedience and righteousness here and now. Christ intended his followers to live each day in the light of the Kingdom which is intruding into the world, to live each day as if the end were tomorrow."[5]

The Kingdom of God is calling to us even now to step out of the crowd and say Yes to its existence, its growth, its service, the rule and reign of God, and ultimately its victory in eternity. Bright says that the person who "refuses its call is saying *No* to his very self" and denying the very highest in their nature.[6] Respond to God today and labor in the service of the King knowing that your toil is never in vain in the Lord (1 Corinthians 15:58) and heaven will truly tell the story of what it meant to say *Yes* to Jesus and His calling to the kingdom of God.

CHAPTER 22

THE ETERNAL NOW OF TODAY

*Therefore be careful how you walk, not as unwise men but as wise,
making the most of your time, because the days are evil.*

EPHESIANS 5:15-16

Life is never going to be the same! No more Phoenix, Arizona. No more ASU. You can't stay in college forever, girl. I miss my mother and brother already. I love them so much!

On staff with Campus Crusade for Christ!

Dallas, Texas? What do I really know about Dallas, Texas?

The Josh McDowell Ministry!

A whole new life!

An adventure!

Will my Fiat make it to Dallas?

Where is my typewriter, anyway?

Life is moving too quickly.

Will my Fiat really, really make it to Dallas?

My eighteen years passed before me in the blink of an eye.

A wave of fear and sadness came over me. I sat down on my bed and cried.

That was the day—the moment—I heard God's calling through Paul's words in Ephesians 5:15-16. "Therefore, be careful how you walk, not as unwise men, but as wise, making the most of your time, because the days are evil." I heard *the calling* as loud and clear in my mind right then and there as if God Himself was speaking to me in the Garden of Eden. And those words forever became a guiding force for me. "Therefore, be careful how you walk…making the most of your time." The tears wiped away, the Lord led me to those words in His Word that have helped me become more intentional about all the moments in the days and the details of my entire life. "Making the most of your time."

Fast forward to a day many years later. My dear friend, Shirley Peters, a real student of the Word, sat down with our Quiet Time Ministries staff team and she shared an incredible story I've never forgotten. She said, "Girls, I want to share something that God did in my life when I turned fifty."

She looked each of us in the eye one at a time. "The Lord gave me the words of Psalm 90:12, 'So teach us to number our days, that we may present to You a heart of wisdom.' God used that verse to bring me to a deep commitment to pay special attention to each day and live it wholeheartedly for the Lord." She paused, letting that sink in. "Over the years the Lord reminded me of those words and helped me serve Him faithfully, and invest in those things that last forever."

We looked at Shirley with great trust and admiration. Everyone was afraid to speak, to ruin the moment.

"Shirley, what do you want to teach us with these words?" I finally asked.

"Now," her voice broke, her eyes gazing at her hands holding her Bible, "I'm 80 years old." She closed her Bible and held it up for all to see. "Thirty years have flown by. I want all of you to pay attention to how you run your race and always bring glory to the Lord. God used that verse to help me grow deeply with the Lord all these years, and He will do the same thing for each one of you." Tears came to our eyes in a rush of emotion. *Making the most of your time.*

I've never forgotten Shirley's words to us this day. Oh, how well she served the Lord, a dear friend, mentor, and faithful example in my life. Shirley and I first had the opportunity to teach together at our church in San Diego. Later she became a diligent Board Member for Quiet Time Ministries for nearly ten years. She was one of my great encouragers. So her words carried a lot of weight with me, teaching me to be careful how I spend my time because the years go by very quickly, and every moment is a gift from the Lord. Franklin Graham, son of the Reverend Billy Graham, said it well when he spoke at First Baptist Church in Jacksonville, Florida, "Time is like a river. You cannot touch the water twice, because the flow that has passed will never pass again." *Making the most of your time.*

After God first showed eighteen-year-old Catherine how precious my time was to Him that day I was packing to drive to Dallas, I became absolutely obsessed with how I spent my time. Even while working full time for Josh McDowell on staff with Campus Crusade for Christ, I began planning out all my spiritual responsibilities months in advance. This Bible study, that mentoring opportunity, another ministry idea. All too soon, it became overwhelming! The shocking challenge for me was when God took me in unexpected directions and my plans did not materialize as I had hoped. Early on, even at a young age, I was crushed by the relentless movement of time, but I soon learned the Lord had His own idea of how He wanted to spend my time. That was when I began to appreciate that it was not *my* time at all. It was *His* time.

Understanding time and how to live each day is a very important part of God's calling. Because it's no longer my life, but His life, then the days all belong to Him. If He is going to tell His story in your life, then He is going to use the moments in your days to write the chapters. The priority then becomes hearing Him speak and being sensitive to where He wants to go and what

He wants to do. It's not about me trying to become what the world wants, but staying close to Him and following Him as He leads in life. Instead of becoming consumed with the past or the future, we need to pay attention to today and live in the here and now. Paul arrived at this very truth when he said, "Forgetting what lies behind and reaching forward to what lies ahead, I press on toward the goal for the prize of the upward call of God in Christ Jesus" (Philippians 3:13-14).

There is a sense in our earthly days that we are touching eternity. I think about how the call of God in Christ is an "upward" call and that we are pressing on toward the goal for the prize of this upward call. We have a heavenly life when we use our time for eternal things. Only the use of the present moment touches the eternal result. That is the only life being lived. Jesus is living His life in and through us in the present moment. So we need to pay attention to being "all in" for the present moment. I call it "the eternal now of today." We need to live in the "now" of this moment. It is in this moment that I am investing in the things that last forever (Matthew 6:19-21). It is in this moment that I am "always abounding in the work of the Lord" knowing that my toil is not in vain in the Lord (1 Corinthians 15:58). It is in this moment I need to "seek the Kingdom of God above all else, and live righteously" (Matthew 6:33). It is in this moment I need to always pray, and pray about everything (1 Thessalonians 5:17, Philippians 4:6).

The implications of this calling to wise use of our time include saying *no* to many good things in order to say *yes* to the best. I see this lived out in a very real way in the community where I live. There are community activities available for the people who live in my neighborhood—activities like swimming, games, and clubs to join. Some people literally spend all their days playing cards. I am not saying that is a bad thing in itself. What I am saying is that if all a person does is play cards, yet leaves God out of the picture, then they are absolutely wasting one of the greatest commodities entrusted to them: *time*. And I see a lot of people living godless lives. There are many ways you can waste your time and live as though God is not a part of your life. Oh, what a wonderful day it is when a person hands the keys of their life over to God and begins to experience the amazing adventure of knowing Him and allowing Him to write His story in and through them.

Saying *no* to many good things is an imperative if we want to say *yes* to the very best. The first area I had to learn to say *no* and *yes* was my quiet time. After I learned about the importance of quiet time from Leann in Campus Crusade for Christ, I knew I wanted to make it part of my life. But I really had no idea where to begin.

I remember making my way into the cafeteria at Arizona State University, grabbing a cup of coffee, and finding a secluded table that would become my sanctuary with the Lord for the next two years. I remember that first day pulling my Bible out of my backpack. I set it on the table wondering where to begin in my quiet time with the Lord.

I saw this girl sitting two tables away with her Bible, a notebook, and another book. I watched what she did for the next half hour. She noticed me was watching her, smiled and walked over and said, "Hi, I'm Denny."

I told her I noticed she was reading her Bible and asked, "Do you do this every morning?"

"Yes, it's my quiet time."

Then I asked her the question that truly changed my life and led me on an adventure in making the most of my time.

"What *exactly* do you do in your quiet time?"

She talked with me about reading a passage of Scripture, writing in a journal, and then reading a chapter in a Christian book that would help me grow spiritually. That was enough to get me started. And soon, I was off and running. Every day I went to that cafeteria and sat at my little table and spent quality time with the Lord. Oh, I learned so much from Him. I learned how to write insights and observations in my journal. I wrote prayers and commitments to the Lord. That was just the beginning. Early on, I decided to invest many hours in learning how to spend quiet time with the Lord. I experimented. I put together my own "Quiet Time Notebook" that became the prototype for *The Quiet Time Notebook* published by Quiet Time Ministries. I spent hours in Christian bookstores, learning how to use Bible study tools so I could listen better to God in His Word. *Making the most of your time.*

So each day the priority for me is quiet time alone with the Lord Jesus. No time is ever wasted when it's spent with the Lord. I have found that my quiet time is a great secret in hearing the calling and answering God's call to make the most of my time. When I spend the first time of the day with the Lord, He orders the rest of my steps that day. I am more readily available and open to living in the eternal now of today and spending my minutes and hours for the Lord.

Another area where I've had to say *no* and *yes* in the wise use of time has been ministry. When I graduated from college, I was faced with a decision. I had an offer to go to Moody Bible Institute, all expenses paid, for an advanced degree. I also had the opportunity to go on staff with Campus Crusade for Christ where I would have to raise my own monthly support. I talked about the matter with the Lord and He reminded me again of the need to make the most of my time. I realized that going on staff would allow me to immediately invest in eternal things where I could share my faith and disciple others. I did spend four years on staff with Campus Crusade for Christ prior to marrying and moving to San Diego.

Then came another *no* and *yes* in how I would spend my time when my husband came to me with the idea of attending seminary. That was a big decision that altered the course of my life. It meant many hours of study and writing papers to get a Master's Degree in Theological Studies. One particular day, I felt bogged down in the midst of all the study. And I was out in the garage frustrated over looking for a book I needed. I was absolutely exhausted. So I stopped and I cried out to the Lord, "Why in the world am I doing this?" And then, the thought came to me, *You are doing this because the Lord wants you in seminary. You said yes and all this study is going to make a spiritual difference in ministry years from now.* I was investing in eternal things by living in the moment of now.

Even today, my decision to serve full time in Quiet Time Ministries, the ministry the Lord has called me to nurture, is based on making the most of my time, knowing that God is using all that we do for His glory. I spend the time necessary to write books that the Lord asks me to write. I say yes to Speaking Ministry engagements so that others can be touched by the Lord. And I daily walk by faith that the Lord will provide substantial donors dedicated to Quiet Time Ministries, and our mission, *Teaching Devotion to God and His Word.* These are the kinds of treasures that last forever.

A number of years ago, I had the opportunity to speak at a quiet time conference in a beautiful coastal town in southern Florida. A young woman, an attendee at the conference who had heard me speak about *Six Secrets to a Powerful Quiet Time,*[1] felt compelled to send me an email not long after the event to share an amazing story that touched my heart. "I was so excited after the conference" she wrote, "and I couldn't wait to begin quiet time with the Lord. When I arrived home, my husband was gone. He had decided to leave. But I didn't give up. I poured myself into quiet time and prayed like I've never prayed before. Guess what, Catherine? My husband came back! He gave his life to the Lord."

Making the most of your time.

Another young woman shared a story with me of how she came to an event in Phoenix, Arizona where I was speaking about having a heart that dances, a great adventure of intimacy with God from *A Heart that Dances* book of quiet times.[2] She had sat in the very front row, drinking in every word. A time, a place, and a plan. *The P.R.A.Y.E.R.™ Quiet Time Plan. The Quiet Time Notebooks.* She wasn't yet a Christian and her life was literally falling apart. Well, she gave her life to the Lord that very day and her life was changed forever. She began growing mightily in the Lord, and now she is involved in a great ministry at her church.

Making the most of your time.

I love the stories of people who have read one of my books, or participated in a Quiet Time Ministries Bible study, or heard me speak live or on multimedia, and then have grown deeper spiritually as a result. I think about all the hours spent writing books, filming messages, and ministering in far away places. And how God uses that time spent for His glory. It was worth it all. This is the deeper life in Christ. This is my calling.

That's my story. What about your story? *Who are you? Why are you here?* Do you hear the calling from God to make the most of your time? Are you numbering your days? Ask Him to teach you how. There are some eternal investments of time still to come for you that will have dramatic results much greater than you can even imagine right now. Ask God where you need to say *No* in order to say *Yes* to the best. And make sure your quiet time alone with the Lord is a priority so you can hear Him calling to you every day.

I think there are times when we are truly caught in between the *now* and the *not yet*. We are living in time and making the most of it. But there is suffering endured in the hours of time. There is sacrifice and surrender in the moments of time where we suffer for the righteous choices and may even have to let go of many good things. But the *not yet* of eternity is worth it all and someday we will know that to be true.

God uses the days and moments we live for Him in ways that we may not realize until we get to heaven. But you can be sure of this promise. You will reap what you sow (Galatians 6:7). If you sow to the eternal and allow the Lord to live in and through you, making the most of your time, you will reap an eternal reward. And someday you shall hear those words, "Well done good and faithful servant" (Matthew 25:23).

Thou hast encompassed my path, and Today thou art with me,
Thou art the Way that I walk and the Light on that Way;
Thine is the hand that is holding and leading and trying,
Thine is the voice that is bidding me haste or delay;
Who else but Thou, who seest my past and my future,
Who else can know how my steps should be ordered today?

ANNIE JOHNSON FLINT, MY DAYS

Chapter 23

WHEN GOD CONNECTS THE DOTS

Now to him who is able to do immeasurably more than all we ask or imagine, according to his power that is at work within us.

Ephesians 3:20 niv

One weekend, I was driving back home to Palm Desert, California, after a few days in Phoenix, Arizona, having spent a warm and gentle time visiting family. The Sonoran Desert was in full bloom after a rain storm, the cactus sprouting a rainbow of blooms, the Saguaro standing at attention waving goodbye as I passed. It was a lazy Sunday morning, not much traffic on Interstate 10, so I stopped at my favorite truck stop near Tonopah on the way out of town to put some coffee in me and put some gas in my car. I needed a pick-me-up. As soon as I popped the travel center doors open, I heard the loud speaker come on, a deep, booming voice, sort of a country drawl, filling the entire place.

"Hello, this is Chaplain Paul of Truck Stop Ministries, and I would like to invite you to our Sunday service at 10 am this morning." Crackle, pop, a breath sound. 'We meet in the TV room at the back of the truck stop—and all are invited. Starts in ten minutes!"

Well, I was astounded. A church service in a truck stop! Now that was something I just had to see for myself. 1 Peter 3:15 flew into my mind, "always being ready to give an account for the hope that is in you." *Was this a God-thing? A divine appointment? What should I do, Lord?* It just so happened that I had a box of my Quiet Time Ministries books in my car, recently shipped to me from my publisher. And so, I thought, *I'm going to see if I can find this church service and give Chaplain Paul a few of my books as an encouragement.* As so often happens with me, the thought and the action are born in the same moment. I ran out to my car and grabbed a small stack of books, then rushed back in to the truck stop. I ran up to the counter and asked as I caught my breath, "Where's the TV room?" They pointed down this long hallway, the stark fluorescent lighting blinking on and off as I traveled, the noise of many voices ahead of me.

Just as I got to the end of the hallway, I saw this burly looking man with a weathered face dwarfed by a gigantic cowboy hat. He had on a blue jeans jacket, an embroidered emblem announcing, "Chaplain Paul—Truck Stop Ministries."

"Are you Chaplain Paul?" I asked, stating the obvious.

"That's me." He pointed to the emblem, let out a burst of laughter, his large brush mustache curling up when he spoke.

Still catching my breath, I said, "Chaplain Paul, I heard your announcement. I'm a Christian. I've written some books, and I just wanted to give you these books as a big thank you for being faithful to the Lord."

Chaplain Paul's mouth hung open, the large grin fading into an expression of disbelief.

Was I making any sense? I continued, unperturbed. "Also, I want to encourage you with the words of 1 Corinthians 15:58, "Be steadfast, immovable, always abounding in the work of the Lord knowing that your toil is not in vain in the Lord.""

Well, I thought Chaplain Paul was going to cry. Instead, He opened his arms wide and gave me a great big hug that nearly took the wind out of me. "Oh, dear girl, thank you so much!" he exclaimed in a preacher's voice. "There are truly angels around here, there must be!"

I smiled and told him it was a privilege to meet him. And I meant it. Here was a faithful servant of the Lord in the trenches of Christian ministry.

"You know," he said, "I've been coming here to this truck stop for 18 years and giving church services. There are a lot of Christian truckers and we're everywhere throughout this entire country. The Lord is working in a powerful way."

"Wow, you're right," I responded. "Chaplain Paul, here's my card, let's keep in touch."

"Thank you. I will stay in touch," he said "Thank you for these books. They're just the kind of books I like to read."

As I walked back to my car, I was floating on air. What an amazing, unexpected, surprising time given by the Lord! And then, the realization struck me like a bolt of lightning.. I stopped in my tracks and looked heavenward, "That was You Lord, wasn't it?" A serendipity time planned by the Sovereign God who is in control of everything. These times are the Aha! God moments when He reaches through the sky, grabs your heart, wrestles you to the ground, and imprints your mind with His Spirit. It becomes crystal clear to you that this moment is etched in time, important for your life story, and an obvious place in your history where God is connecting the dots in His plan for your life.

My best friend at work, where I was the Director of Women's Ministries, was an internationally known author, speaker, and life coach. Pastor Jim Smoke and I used to sit and talk for hours at a time about theology, spiritual formation, and the ways of God. We would come to these profound conclusions in the sharing of Scripture and events in our lives. And then, Jim would look at me with his great smile and say, "God connects the dots." I've never forgotten that phrase. That was Jim's way of saying, "God is sovereign and God is telling the story."

God is calling us to realize that though we cannot see Him; God expects us to *trust* that He is working out His plan and purpose in our lives. He is sovereign and perfectly in control. We are created for a destiny designed by Him. David, the man after God's own heart, discovered this promise. He wrote, "The Lord directs the steps of the godly. He delights in every detail of their lives" (Psalm 37:23 NLT). The details here are important, and the more we notice God in all the details, the more we will trust Him moment by moment. We will begin to notice His hand in everything in our lives. He is the Master Artist and Author, always painting in the fine color and detail of God-ordained moments where He connects all the dots and writes new chapters in the story of our life.

I believe one of the greatest ways God moves in a sovereign way is in the friends He gives us all along the way. This was definitely true for a youthful David, long before He became Israel's King. One of David's very best friends was Jonathan, the son of King Saul. That King Saul became jealous of David, ultimately his enemy, and chased after David to trying to kill him, is rich in irony. God used Jonathan, David's friend, and King Saul's own son as an important instrument in saving David's life.

There came a pivotal point in time when David suspected his very life was in danger, "But truly as the Lord lives and as your soul lives, there is hardly a step between me and death." (1 Samuel 20:3 NLT), David confessed his panic to Jonathan. But Jonathan fiercely sought to protect his friend. He basically told David, "I will let you know what my father has in mind for you." God-inspired, Jonathan came up with a plan, "because he loved him [David] as he loved his own life." (I Samuel 20:17) Here was Jonathan's plan. He would go out to a field where David could wait and watch. Jonathan would shoot three arrows. He would bring a boy along with him to go pick up the arrows. If he told the boy to keep going because the arrows were well beyond David, then that would be the message telling David his life was in danger and he would need to quickly escape. "Behold, the Lord is between you and me forever," Jonathan said, comforting David.

Imagine this moment from David's standpoint. It was a defining moment that would determine the course of David's life. Those arrows would be arrows from heaven because God was the One in charge of David's life. David knew that God was ordering his steps, "the steps of the godly." (Psalm 37:23 NLT) And so, an obedient and trustful David watched and waited. And when the arrows were sent flying by Jonathan, the arrows flew well beyond the boy, confirming David's worst fears. David must escape!

Alan Redpath, brilliant author of *The Making of a Man of God*, describes this moment with the arrows as a metaphor for our own lives: "It was a symbol of the will of God, and behind its flight was the loving purpose of God for His harassed child." *What, then, must we do? Why has God place this obstacle in our path? How can we handle the times when God's will takes us where we do not want to go and tells us what we do not want to hear?* Redpath explains, "You have to be still and wait, if God has shot His arrows beyond you. You have leaned upon Christian friends, seeking their counsel in prayer. You have agonized and wept and prayed. You have tried to hold on to the immediate circumstances, for your heart clings to the familiar, to the beloved, to the things around you with their promise of shelter and security." *How can I let go of all that I desired? I must believe that God has something better planned even though I find it difficult to accept.* "But the arrow has landed on target beyond you—perhaps because God has called you to some far distant surroundings, or it may be because He will leave you where you are. The message of the arrow beyond you is not primarily geographical, it is spiritual."[1]

Every day, arrows from heaven are sent flying, as *God connects the dots* and writes the story of our lives. Some of the greatest results of *the calling* from God are divine appointments with people and defining moments in our lives. It really comes down to *what story does the Lord want to tell with you and your life?* The things that happen, those *Aha!* moments, are unexplainable in the temporal realm. They are inexplicable without the light of God's Word and the voice of the Holy Spirit. Only God can paint the picture and write the message that is meant to come forth. He is the Master Designer.

You may have watched your life unravel before your very eyes and you are so undone that you literally sat down in surrender to say, "I just give up. There's no way out of this catastrophe! It's over. Why even go on? All I had hoped for will never happen." And in one sense, you are right. The picture you had in mind, the story you wanted to tell, the life you thought you would have will never exist. But there is more—more than you designed, more than you told, and more than you thought. God does more than you can imagine according to His power that is at work in you. You will see it in His time and way through divine appointments God creates and defining moments that He arranges, and you will say, "That was You Lord, wasn't it!"

If your life—the life you had imagined—has not come to pass—and in fact, it has unraveled completely, then here is what you can know to be true. God is doing something greater and miraculous as the Master Designer (Ephesians 3:20). God is lovingly preparing the canvas of your life as a masterpiece. God is getting His colors and ink and paints at the ready. And God will paint rainbows of color on the landscape of your life in ways you have never seen before, ways you could never have imagined. God will write a page, a chapter, an entire treatise for each event that was never what you had in mind. The best yet, God will create and design something of His infinite power and wisdom. And as you see *the calling* unfold in your life, you will stand in awe and bow in humble worship at what He has done. You will exclaim, "That was You, Lord, wasn't it!"

So draw near to Him. Open His Word. "Be still and know that He is God" (Psalm 46:10). Let your thoughts stand still. And allow Him to pour in His comfort and encouragement. Watch your faith grow strong. Have confidence in Him. Believe God. Be assured that He is with you. Do not be afraid. He will help you. He loves you with an everlasting love. Love Him. Look to Him.

I think about the importance of friends in my own life over the years. Pay attention to all the people that God brings into your life, but especially your friends. They are in your life for a reason. God's reason. They are an integral part of the calling in your life.

I have had heart friends who have been like Jonathan was for David. I think of Joyce, the girl I met at my very first church Bible study, who became my dear friend after I surrendered my life to Christ. Nancy, the first person I called after I became a Christian, helped me find a church. Karen, Denora, Sherry, and Peggy have been friends since high school. My friend Helen traveled together with me for retreats with the Lord in Sedona, Arizona. I'm so thankful for Leann in my life to show me how to live for the Lord. Then, Dottie McDowell, a most important friend who loved me and helped me serve the Lord with my whole heart while with the Josh McDowell Ministry. Andy is a lifelong friend who introduced me to my husband and brings such joy when we are together. When God gave me the idea for Quiet Time Ministries, my friend, Shirley, prayed together with me and helped me dream big. Jane is my dear friend and we have spent many mornings sharing the Lord over breakfast and steaming hot coffee. Conni, an inspiring warm heart I first met in my new desert home, is my dear friend who encouraged me to write my first book, *Pilgrimage of the Heart*. Beverly, so dear to me, is a loving mentor and encourager, and has been the one to show me God's unfailing love as I have served Him over the years. Cindy, faithful and brilliant, has been one to help make my dreams in Quiet Time Ministries become a reality. Stefanie, who writes and sings amazing music is a joy to serve with in ministry. I will never forget the day Johnny Mann wrote the song "Glorify His Name in Quiet Time" for Quiet Time Ministries. Julie, a wise mentor and lover of the Word, prayed for me in Quiet Time Ministries. Kelly has continued to pray with me through the darkest times of my life even to today. Kayla, who served with me in Quiet Time Ministries, showed me what it means to be a humble servant of the Lord. In recent years, Barb has been my blessed heart friend to encourage and support me in Quiet Time Ministries. Vonette Bright was such an amazing mentor for me. And Ney Bailey has been such an example for me over the years. And I think of Paula, Sandy, Karen, Betty, Judy and so many others.

I could go on and on about all the friends brought into my life by my Sovereign Lord—all of them whom I dearly love and often say, "That was You Lord, wasn't it." Without them, my story written by the Lord—my calling—would never have been what it is today.

And then, my family has been integral to the story of my life. I thank the Lord for my incredible mother, dear father, my wonderful brother Robert who is always there for me, my precious niece Kayla who lights up my life, Andy, Keegan, James, Eloise, and my beloved husband David. "That was You Lord, wasn't it!"

What about you? What will help you notice the hand of God at work in your life?

I have four *resolves*—The Calling Resolves—that have helped me.

Linger excessively—spend more and more time with the Lord every day. Make it your resolve to linger long with your Lord.

Listen eagerly—pay attention to what the Lord says to you. Develop a listening ear when you open the Bible. Listen for the voice of the Lord, His message, His calling. When certain words and verses in God's Word seem especially significant, you can know that's the Lord.

Look expectantly—watch for God's overtures, those times when He reaches out of the sky to touch your life and work a detail into your story. Write what you see in your journal.

Love extravagantly—find ways every day to tell the Lord you love Him. Keep the fire of love burning for the Lord. Sometimes I just say, "Lord, I love You so much. Thank You for how You are working in my life." Sometimes I will grab my Bible and go have breakfast with the Lord, just to be with Him.

The story is told of a time in the 1920s when Stalin, revolutionary and politician, ordered a purge of all Bibles and believers. In one city, Stavropol, this order was completely carried out with thousands of Bibles taken from believers. Many years later, a commission team of Christians was sent to Stavropol. They had no knowledge of the history of that city. They needed Bibles for their work and were having difficulty with getting the Bibles. Someone mentioned that they knew of a warehouse where there were Bibles being stored since the time of Stalin. They prayed and one member courageously went to the warehouse to see if the officials would let them have the Bibles. Surprisingly, they said, "Yes."

So the next day, the commission team arrived with a truck and some helpers to load the Bibles. One of the helpers was a young agnostic skeptic, a university student who just wanted the wages for the work. As they loaded the Bibles, they noticed the student had disappeared. After a search, they found him in a corner of the warehouse weeping. He had slipped into the back hoping to get a Bible for himself. When he opened the Bible, he discovered something that deeply touched him to the depths of his heart. The inside page of the Bible he picked up had the handwritten signature of his own grandmother. It was her personal Bible. Out of thousands of Bibles that he could have picked up, he took the one that belonged to his own grandmother. His grandmother had prayed for him and her city her whole life. Only God in the whole world could have chosen to answer that woman's prayers, orchestrate events, connect the dots, and have her grandson find her Bible.

It is a powerful affirmation to experience the calling of saying yes to God's sovereignty and allowing Him to connect the dots of our life. Keep your eyes open for the hand of the Lord at work in your life. And when you see Him work, be the first to stop everything and say, "That was You, Lord, wasn't it!"

The LORD directs the steps of the godly. He delights in every detail of their lives.

PSALM 37:23

CHAPTER 24

HERE AM I LORD, SEND ME

Then I heard the voice of the Lord, saying, "Whom shall I send, and who will go for Us?" Then I said, "Here am I. Send me!"

ISAIAH 6:8

It was my last year of college. Amen. First, at the University of Arizona, majoring in Archaeology, changing to English Literature, and on to Education. Then, to Arizona State University, majoring in Radio and Television, and, yes, finally, a Bachelor of Science degree in Business Advertising. I had a roller coaster undergraduate career deciding what to do with my life. It was, as my mother always said, " Catherine, you really majored in Campus Crusade for Christ." Yes, that was instantly my first love, consuming all my time. So I had this wonderful opportunity to attend a Christmas conference sponsored by Campus Crusade for Christ at Arrowhead Springs, nestled in the mountains of southern California. The main speaker for this conference was Elmer Lappen, the director of Campus Crusade for Christ at Arizona State University. I knew him well. And this man had become dear to me because he had challenged me to be a radical disciple for Jesus Christ.

You must understand that Elmer Lappen suffered from crippling arthritis and was confined to a wheelchair. But he had such an on-fire faith in Jesus Christ that anyone who knew him thought him a superman and was inspired to live passionately for the Lord. He was a leader. And now, here I was, sitting in a room with a thousand other Campus Crusade students from colleges and universities all over the United States, listening to Elmer give his characteristic final challenge on the last day of his series on discipleship.

At the end of his message, Elmer Lappen issued the call that God gave to Isaiah in Isaiah 6:8: "Then I heard the voice of the LORD, saying, 'Whom shall I send, and who will go for Us?'" Elmer Lappen's voice seemed to hang in the air reverberating in the large auditorium. How does *any* man or woman of God respond when they hear the voice of the Lord asking them to do something? Isaiah had come forth five simple words, words that were to alter the course of his life. Isaiah responded, "Here am I. Send me!"

As Elmer explained Isaiah's heart response, my mind blurred and my heart raced, Elmer's voice receding into the far distance, all sounds muffled into the background. No one was in this auditorium but me and the Lord. *This is the moment God had been building up to in my own life for two years. This is it! My dedication to Campus Crusade for Christ, my growing relationship with the Lord my sharing of faith in Christ with others.*

Leann Pruitt, dear friend, Campus Crusade leader, would take me out on the campus once a week and show me how to explain the gospel to someone and give them an opportunity to make a decision for the Lord.

I remember the day when Leann stared me down and said, "Now it's your turn." I backed off, uncertain. I said to her, "I'm afraid. I don't know if I can do it." She encouraged me that my job was to share my faith in the power of the Holy Spirit and leave the results to God. "Okay," I responded timidly, "I'm going to go for it." I'll never forget the first time I shared my faith on my own with a young woman on campus. I had rambled on in a slightly haphazard fashion with the four spiritual laws written by Dr. Bill Bright. Breathless, I finally wound down. *What would happen next? What should I do, now?* Knock me over with a feather! I just couldn't believe it. The young woman said, "Yes, I want to receive Jesus into my life." Oh, how exciting it was to see God at work when I stepped out in faith and shared the gospel with others.

After this mind-blowing experience, Leann challenged me to take what she was teaching me and share it with others. And so, as is my talent, I leaped right in and began a discipleship ministry with a group of girls from Arizona State University. With what I was learning in leaps and bounds from the Word, I showed them how to have a quiet time, share their faith, and disciple others. It was such an exciting time. All I wanted to do was to live for Jesus Christ with a passionate and wholehearted devotion to Him. I could have stayed in my comfort zone forever, but God had other ideas.

And now, here I was in Arrowhead Springs at the last Christmas conference before college graduation. *Had Elmer Lappen stopped speaking?* The abrupt silence slammed me back into reality. Elmer Lappen voice once again filled my ears. "If you want to be sold out to Jesus Christ, go where He leads and do what He asks, stand, state your name, and say, 'Here am I, Lord. Send me.'" It was a moment etched in time for me. Elmer had issued his call. *No, wait, it was God who was issuing His call! Personally to me!* Young people all around the room began to stand, state their names, and respond to God. My heart was beating fast. Now was the time for me. I stood and said, "My name is Catherine. Here am I, Lord. Send me!" By the time the dust had settled, there were a thousand young men and women standing tall for Jesus Christ. That group included me. I'll never forget it.

That was many years ago. Between then and now, I have had a full life. I was on staff with Campus Crusade for Christ for four years working directly with Josh McDowell and The Josh

McDowell Ministry. I married my husband David in 1982. I graduated from Bethel Theological Seminary in 1993 with a Masters in Theological Studies. I founded and am President of Quiet Time Ministries, a worldwide ministry teaching devotion to God and His Word since 1994. And I've also had the privilege to lead amazing women at a number of churches in southern California, as Director and Pastor of Women's Ministries. He has led me through traumatic bends in the road, deep dark valleys, and high mountaintop experiences. That's my curriculum vitae, but what, really, has all this "life" taught me?

That response to God in Arrowhead Springs was a defining moment and it altered the course of my life. It became the determining factor in everything I have done over the years. Saying "Here am I Lord. Send me!" was not just about going somewhere. It was answering the call of God to be His servant and His disciple, to daily open His Word, to answer His continuous calling and to live and walk with Him all the days of my life. In essence, God has been in the business of making me a surrendered, sold-out servant and radical disciple of Jesus Christ. He is still doing His work in me.

There have been times when I have been tempted to give up, throw it all away, and run in the opposite direction because the fiery trial has been so unbearably hot. There have been times when I have given in to despair and discouragement, and would rather cry into my hands than live in The Word And there have been high times of triumph and victory when I have seen God do what only He can do in my life and the lives of others. Ultimately, I have discovered that following Jesus Christ and surrendering to Him, moment-by-moment, is not just another way to live. It is the *only* way to live. And it is a life of faith—F.A.I.T.H.—as Holocaust survivor Corrie ten Boom has penned—*a fantastic adventure in trusting Him*. What is your fantastic adventure? What is your calling for the rest of your life?

Jesus said that in the last days "many will turn away from the faith" and "the love of most will grow cold" (Matthew 24:10,12, NIV). I believe we are living in a time when what Jesus described is now happening in our world. I believe that we are living in a world that is in trouble. When is a world in trouble? When it is no longer outraged over immorality. When it is more afraid of governments than of God. When the computer consumes more time than Christ. When the most popular book on knowing God contains very little mention of Jesus Christ. When prayer becomes optional in the church. When worship of God is considered intolerant and narrow. When the church is no longer different from the world. When pursuit of the good life takes precedence over the pursuit of God. When its greatest heroes are people whose personal lives are in disarray. That is when a world is in trouble.

And many in the church are also in trouble these days. In *The God of All Comfort*, Hannah Whitall Smith described a conversation she had with an intelligent agnostic she very much wanted to influence. He listened to her for a while and then said, "Well madam, all I have to say is this. If you Christians want to make us agnostics inclined to look into your religion, you must try to be more comfortable in the possession of it yourselves. The Christians I meet seem to me to be the very most uncomfortable people anywhere around. They seem to carry their religion as a man carries a headache. He does not want to get rid of his head, but at the same time it is very uncomfortable to have it. And I for one do not care to have that sort of religion."

Why are Christians so uncomfortable these days? I believe that it is because they are desperately in need of personal spiritual revival. So many have barren hearts that can be traced back to a neglect of God and His Word. The busyness of life has simply crowded God out of most lives. Look around at what has grabbed the attention of most people—their cell phones. Everyone sits for hours looking into the screen of a cell phone. What would happen if people spent that much time in God's Word? One thing you can count on: If you are superficial with God and His Word, you will be a superficial Christian who is easily swayed and compromised. If you will plumb the depths of God through consistent study of His Word and through prayer, then you will have spiritual depth that draws upon your heavenly Father's resources in times of trouble (see Jeremiah 17:5-8).

I see so many believers falling by the wayside these days. The fiery trials have come upon them, and in their own strength they have been unable to bear the pain. Life can be unbearable and uncertain at times, perhaps most of the time. How can anyone experience the victorious, abundant life that Jesus promised? It is possible in only one way: personal, spiritual revival. I believe God is issuing a call to you and me for such a time as this. What will your answer be?

One of God's greatest callings to you is to personal, spiritual revival. You cannot say, "Here am I. Send me!" without experiencing personal, spiritual revival every day. What does it mean to be revived? Personal revival is a quickening of heart and soul by God, imparting whatever is necessary to sustain one's spiritual life and enable a return to the experience of one's true purpose as ordained by God. God wants you to know Him and make Him known. He desires an intimate relationship with you. Then, He desires that you live for Him in this world. As you live in His power and strength, you will make an incredible difference in the world as Christ lives His life in and through you.

Personal spiritual revival daily brings you to the place where you say along with Isaiah: "Here am I. Send me!" And then, you go where Jesus leads, do what Jesus asks, and glorify the Lord in everything. It has been said that the world has yet to see what God can do in and through the lives of those whose hearts are wholly yielded to Him. According to 2 Chronicles 16:9, "The eyes of the LORD search the whole earth in order to strengthen those whose hearts are fully committed to him." This is what I believe is on the heart of God. He repeats this message throughout His Word. I believe personal spiritual revival, where you are continually being restored to your purpose in life, has always been on God's heart. Then, God can write His story on the tablets of your heart and share it with the world.

The psalmist in Psalm 119, is not named, but could have possibly been Ezra. We know the author of this psalm was a servant of God who had a heart in trouble. He wanted the Lord and loved His Word. But he was so broken that he called himself "a wineskin in the smoke" (Psalm 119:83). Again and again, he prayed an important prayer: "Revive me O LORD" (Psalm 119:25, 37, 40, 50, 88, 93, 107, 149, 154, 156, 159). The big discovery in Psalm 119 is that the answer to his revival was the Word of God. And that is your answer as well. If you want to be the one who says, "Here am I Lord, send me," then grab your Bible and experience personal, spiritual revival where you are led continually by God into His plans and purposes as He calls out to you in His Word, day by day.

Oh, that you might grow into a deeper, more intimate knowledge of Jesus Christ and become His radical disciple, recklessly abandoned to the will of God, and willing to sacrifice all to follow Him. What is the secret to such a life? To draw near to Him, day by day, listening to what He says in His Word, talking to Him, and being consistently and powerfully transformed into the person He wants you to be. This is your calling.

One day a friend of mine gave me a beautifully wrapped package. I opened it to discover an incredible print of a painting of a woman by Randall Hasson with these words in elegant calligraphy: "Here am I. Send me." My friend knew how important those words were to me and thought I would love it. She was right. But what was even more profound was the story behind the painting. The woman in the painting is Marie, the mother of David Green, the founder of Hobby Lobby Stores, Inc., a successful chain of American arts and crafts stores. She was a woman of faith and her response to God of "Here am I. Send me!" represented her heart for the Lord. The painting is so amazing and seems to represent my life as well. The background is a faint map of the world highlighting the Great Commission of Matthew 28:18-20. I smile at this remembrance because for years we have had a map of the world at Quiet Time Ministries and inserted pins to represent everywhere my books and ministry have travelled thanks to the power and leading of the Lord. The woman in the picture seems excited and willing to take on the task God asks of her.

This "Here am I. Send me" painting reminds me of my Arrowhead Springs-Campus Crusade response to God's call asking whom He could send and who would go for Him. Every day His calling comes to you and me in new ways and sometimes with great challenges. And every day God is listening for our response. May we always say, "Here am I Lord, send me."

CHAPTER 25

ON OUR WAY HOME

Things which eye has not seen and ear has not heard, and which have not entered
the heart of man, all that God has prepared for those who love Him.

1 CORINTHIANS 2:9

The calling of God—the irresistible voice of God—providentially leads us to our heavenly home.

One of the treasured books in my spiritual library is *The Letters of Samuel Rutherford*, written in flowery poetic prose by a Scottish Presbyterian pastor, theologian, and author who lived in the 1600s. The atmosphere of heaven is all throughout this book. I have had emotional times in reading this work when I just had to set it down to drink in the overwhelming presence of God.

"Oh what a sight to be up in heaven, in that fair orchard of the new paradise, and to see and smell and touch and kiss that fair field flower, that ever-green Tree of Life! His bare shadow was enough for me. A sight of Him would be the earnest of heaven to me," opines Samuel Rutherford, Scottish Presbyterian pastor, theologian, author with the assurance that he is looking at God and knows Him intimately. He valued his salvation! He yearns for the heavenly experience, saved by grace, washed in the blood of the Lamb, "Since He looked upon me, my heart is not mine own." Samuel Rutherford's home, surrendered in his own mind and heart and spirit, was in heaven.

As we hear God's words to us, day by day in His Word, we have to always remember that we are on our way home. There is the hope of a real, true destination for any who know the Lord. Jesus said, "Don't let your hearts be troubled. Trust in God, and trust also in me. There is more than enough room in my Father's home. If this were not so, would I have told you that I am going to prepare a place for you? When everything is ready, I will come and get you, so that you will always be with me where I am" (John 14:1-3). My friend, Jim Smoke, a pastor I served with for many years, often visited people in the hospital, and he would always share these John 14:1-3 verses for hope and encouragement. Pastor Jim Smoke was not afraid to be in the presence of the sick and dying, for he knew the real truth—we are all on our way home to heaven.

Paul wrote of his own journey home. "So we are always confident, even though we know that as long as we live in these bodies we are not at home with the Lord. For we live by believing and not by seeing. Yes, we are fully confident, and we would rather be away from these earthly bodies, for then we will be at home with the Lord" (2 Corinthians 5:6-8). I have another pastor friend, the great H.B. London, Pastor of Pastors at Focus on the Family and author of *The Heart of a Great Pastor*, who used to say these 2 Corinthians 5:6-8 verses were his "go-to" verses about what happens when we die. Whenever he would say that to me, I would always smile, pretend it was the first time, and say, "I know, H.B. They're my 'go-to' verses, too." At home with the Lord. There's a sweet aroma about the phrase that delights my heart. When we die, we absolutely change our address instantly, from earth to heaven, and we are present with the Lord. Turn your mind to the land of the blessed.

My favorite place to read about my heavenly home is in Revelation 21-22, a short treatise on the place of heaven and the activities of heaven. In these profound chapters, we see that heaven is a brilliant place made of precious materials where everything is new—and there are no more tears or death. Christ lights up heaven and there is never any darkness. We will see His face, we will serve Him, and we will reign forever and ever with Him. The realm of heaven will be so spectacular that we can't even begin to come close to comprehending it in our minds. My niece Kayla believes there will be chocolate drinking fountains and chocolate chip cookie rain. Those words make me smile. Heaven will truly be more than we can imagine. Paul summarized heaven succinctly this way: "Things which eye has not seen and ear has not heard, and which have not entered into the heart of man, all that God has prepared for those who love Him" (1 Corinthians 2:9).

Charles Haddon Spurgeon has written one of my favorite meditations in his classic devotional book, *Morning and Evening*, about those who are in heaven. He observes that when we are in heaven we will no longer weep or be distressed for some very good reasons.

> The glorified weep no more, for *all outward causes of grief are gone*. There are no broken friendships, nor blighted prospects in heaven. Poverty, famine, peril, persecution, and slander, are unknown there. No pain distresses, no thought of death or bereavement saddens.

> [The glorified] weep no more, for *they are perfectly sanctified*. No 'evil heart of unbelief' prompts them to depart from the living God; they are without fault before his throne, and are fully conformed to his image. Well may they cease to mourn who have ceased to sin.

> [The glorified] weep no more, because *all fear of change is past*. They know that they are eternally secure. Sin is shut out, and they are shut in. They dwell within

a city which shall never be stormed; they bask in a sun which shall never set; they drink of a river which shall never dry; they pluck fruit from a tree which shall never wither. They are forever with the Lord.

[The glorified] weep no more, because *every desire is fulfilled*. They cannot wish for anything which they have not in possession. The joy of Christ, which is an infinite fulness of delight, is in them. They bathe themselves in the bottomless, shoreless sea of infinite beatitude. That same joyful rest remains for us.

Spurgeon believed that the more difficult life becomes on earth, the more we are drawn to the joys of heaven. We no longer hold on to the here and now; we look forward to our eternal destination. "It may not be far distant. Ere long the weeping willow shall be exchanged for the palm-branch of victory, and sorrow's dewdrops will be transformed into the pearls of everlasting bliss. 'Wherefore comfort one another with these words.'"

We are on our great journey home to the beautiful place of heaven. Our calling to a journey with a heavenly home means death is very different for us because we have a great future and hope.

I often think about Lilias Trotter at the end of her life. At her deathbed, her friends gathered around her, and they all sang together Wesley's *Jesus, Lover of My Soul*, Lilias' favorite song.

Jesus, lover of my soul,
let me to Thy bosom fly,
While the nearer waters roll,
while the tempest still is high.
Hide me, O my Savior, hide,
'til the storm is past;
safe into the haven guide,
O receive my soul at last!

After they sang those words, Lilias looked up, and then out toward the window—she said, "a chariot and six horses." And someone said, "Are you seeing beautiful things?" And she said, "Yes, many, many beautiful things."

I was in Orlando, Florida, for the Christian Booksellers Association convention where I had been invited to participate in a book signing event as the author of *A Heart that Dances, Pilgrimage of the Heart*, and *Revive My Heart* just released by NavPress. An envelope arrived, and I opened it with great excitement. "You are invited to a Women's Tea by Vonette Zachary Bright." I had known Vonette since my days with Campus Crusade, then the honor of the placement of my

"Radical Disciple" quote on a plaque at Campus Crusade For Christ International headquarters; Vonette had graciously written the Foreword to my first book with Harvest House, *Six Secrets to a Powerful Quiet Time*.

When the time came to go to the tea, I was overwhelmed with the thought of attending. I felt so humbled to have been invited. I rang the doorbell and the moment I walked through the door, Vonette ran up to me and gave me a big hug. "Catherine, I'm so glad you are here. Let me introduce you to some of my friends." I was blessed to meet so many wonderful women of God! After about an hour, Vonette walked up to me and spoke privately using a soft voice. She asked, "Catherine would you stay after this is over? I have something for you."

So after the tea ended, Vonette invited me to sit with her in their living room. We chatted about what God was teaching us, and she asked, "Tell me about the books you are writing." I shared, "I'm writing a very personal book on intimacy with God entitled, *A Woman's Heart That Dances*. In fact, Ney Bailey is going to write the Foreword." "Oh I'm thrilled," said Vonette, as we both knew Ney well, a Campus Crusade staff member and our beloved friend. I sensed some tension in Vonette's face, but we kept the interplay light and airy. After about a half hour, right in the middle of our conversation, Vonette stood abruptly and said, "Catherine, would you excuse me for a moment." She walked out of the living room and was gone for about five minutes, then returned and said, "Catherine, would you come with me?"

She led me into another room. I was afraid and excited at the same time. We walked through the doorway, and there was none other than her husband, Dr. Bill Bright, co-founder of Campus Crusade for Christ. He was in bed, and he smiled at me. I will never forget that smile on his face. He was holding my book, *Revive My Heart*. I knew that revival was a great passion for him, and I was so thrilled and privileged that he had written the Foreword. He looked over and said to Vonette, "I want to pray for Catherine." Vonette stood there with her arm around me, and they both prayed for me and for Quiet Time Ministries. Tears flowed down my face as I heard this beautiful, powerful prayer from one of my great heroes of the faith. I sensed the presence of God in the room that day, and I have never forgotten that moment. It was a very powerful time as though I had touched heaven. I found out sometime later, it was the last day Dr. Bill Bright was conscious. And he went home to be with the Lord soon after. So, when I had met with him, he was very close to the gates of heaven. A divine appointment designed by God specifically for me because He loves me.

Vonette gave me his book, *The Journey Home*, written by Dr. Bill Bright when he knew he didn't have much time left on earth. It is a special treasure to me. And in that book he writes about heaven, "The main joy of heaven will be the heavenly Father greeting us in a time and place of rejoicing, celebration, joy, and great reunion…we can expect expressions of love beyond measure; perhaps the intimacy of a hug from God the Father and our Lord Jesus Christ will be our first joy. Wrapped in His loving embrace, we will sense peace, delight, assurance, abundant love, warm fellowship, total security, and absolute calm."[1] Oh, how I love those words. They are such a comfort to me.

Vonette wrote some precious words to me in the flyleaf of that book: "To Catherine Martin, You were one of the last to have a visit with my beloved. He was so proud of you and we both so appreciate your ministry. We are so proud that you are a 'Crusade baby'. This is almost a text book on the subject of leaving for heaven—May you find it useful and an inspiration. Lovingly, Vonette Z. Bright, John 14:28."

I will never forget the special gift of both Bill and Vonette Bright in the story of my life.

The last day I was with my mother who had suffered a devastating stroke, I felt as though I was just on the other side of heaven. I walked out of mother's room and I took one look back at her, and I said quietly only in the audience of my Lord, "Mother I may not see you again here on earth, but I shall see you again someday in heaven where we shall all be face to face with our Lord." And from the hallway I waved goodbye to my precious dear mother.

Two days later she stepped into heaven. And she is now with my Lord, she has no more pain and she is walking and dancing—no longer bedridden or suffering from multiple sclerosis. I rejoice in that thought, and though I miss her greatly, I look forward to being together with her and all my friends who are in that better country, my heavenly home, the promised land where I will live someday.

Heaven is the place where your faith becomes sight. Earth is the place where you are called to faith and the eternal perspective. But dear friend, heaven is the place where you are called to open your eyes, enjoy your Lord, and never have to walk by faith again. Your faith will be sight. The veil will be pulled back and you will be face to face with your Lord. And when you see Him, I believe that you and He will have a very special moment where there is a familiar, loving, knowing of all you shared together while you were on earth. You lived by the calling you heard from Him, and now your story continues in heaven. Your joy will become complete, for you will be together with Him forever.

C.S. Lewis describes the reality of heaven in *The Last Battle*, a volume in *The Chronicles of Narnia* series: "The things that began to happen after that were so great and beautiful that I cannot write them…for them it was only the beginning of the real story. All their life in this world and all their adventures in Narnia had only been the cover and the title page: now at last they were beginning Chapter One of the Great Story which no one on earth has read: which goes on forever: in which every chapter is better than the one before."[2]

May we all say with Paul, "I have fought the good fight, I have finished the race, and I have remained faithful. And now the prize awaits me—the crown of righteousness, which the Lord, the righteous Judge, will give me on the day of his return. And the prize is not just for me but for all who eagerly look forward to his appearing" (2 Timothy 4:7-8 NLT).

I love the picture painted in the words in a song that is sung by the renowned Brooklyn Tabernacle Choir in New York. The song describes our first moments as we approach the city called "Glory." The angels meet us and take us from mansion to mansion. We see our friends, the streets of heaven, and even Abraham, Isaac, and Jacob. But even seeing sights too beautiful to describe, there is only one thought in our mind: *I want to see Jesus. He's the One who died for me.*

Oh, what a moment when we first see Jesus face to face. Just imagine looking into His eyes, wonderfully familiar and filled with love. May we all hear the words He has saved for those who have answered His calling and served Him, "Well done good and faithful servant" (Matthew 25:23).

Anne R. Cousin wrote a beautiful hymn, titled *Immanuel's Land,* about heaven in response to reading Samuel Rutherford's letters and Rutherford's words just prior to his death. "I shall shine," Rutherford whispered to his friends, "I shall see Him as He is, and all the fair company with Him, and shall have my large share—I have got the victory, and Christ is holding forth His arms to embrace me." His last words inspired the words of Cousin's hymn, "Glory, glory dwelleth in Immanuel's Land." This hymn was a favorite of D.L. Moody and was sung just prior to Spurgeon's death.

Oh, what a day it will be when your faith becomes sight and you enter "Immanuel's Land." Until that day, may we hear the voice of our beloved Lord calling to us every day in His Word. And may our response echo the words of Paul the apostle when he said, "I do not consider my life of any account as dear to myself, so that I may finish my course and the ministry which I received from the Lord Jesus, to testify solemnly of the gospel of the grace of God" (Acts 20:24). So dear friend, fix your eyes on Jesus who is always with you, run the race set before you, fight the good fight of faith, be steadfast and immovable, think about the things of heaven, and know always that the best is yet to come.

The sands of time are sinking, The dawn of Heaven breaks;
The summer morn I've sighed for, The fair, sweet morn awakes:
Dark, dark hath been the midnight, But dayspring is at hand,
And glory, glory dwelleth In Immanuel's land.

O Christ, He is the fountain, The deep, sweet well of love!
The streams on earth I've tasted, More deep I'll drink above:
There to an ocean fullness His mercy doth expand,
And glory, glory dwelleth In Immanuel's land.

The King there in His beauty Without a veil is seen;
It were a well-spent journey, Though sev'n deaths lay between:
The Lamb with His fair army, Doth on Mount Zion stand,
And glory, glory dwelleth In Immanuel's land.

With mercy and with judgment My web of time He wove,
And aye, the dews of sorrow Were lustered by His love;
I'll bless the hand that guided, I'll bless the heart that planned
When throned where glory dwelleth In Immanuel's land.

The Bride eyes not her garment, But her dear Bridegroom's face;
I will not gaze at glory But on my King of grace;
Not at the crown He giveth But on His pierced hand:
The Lamb is all the glory Of Immanuel's land.

ANNE R. COUSIN, IMMANUEL'S LAND, 1857

1. Leann's CCC action group ASU, 1977, p.119. 2. With Mother and Robert, 1960s, p.89. 3. First speaking retreat, 1994, p. 121. 4. Quiet Time Ministries team, p.100, 221. 5. With Andy Kotner, Josh & Dottie McDowell, p.137, 221. 6. The pineapple girl, Hawaii,1977, p.17. 7. A Woman's Heart that Dances dedication to my father, 2009, p.189. 8. Bethel Seminary graduation, 1993, p.99. 9. Always sharing my quiet time, 2014, p.100. 10. A special day with Bill & Vonette Bright, 2003, p. 234. 11. First booksigning CBA with David, 2003, p.100. 12. Six Secrets from Harvest House Publishers at Walmart, 2006, p.100.

APPENDIX

❦ THE CALLING DEVOTIONAL GUIDE ❦

Preparing For The Calling Journey

Welcome to the journey and adventure of *The Calling*. This Devotional Guide is designed to enhance your experience and help you grow deeper in your walk with the Lord. I invite you to get a journal to write your thoughts and responses as you read the chapters in *The Calling*. Your journal can be in many forms. You may want to get *The Quiet Time Journal* or *The Quiet Time Notebook* available through Quiet Time Ministries. Then, I encourage you to get a sketchbook or watercolor/mixed media journal with 140 lb. paper from an art supply or craft store. So you may choose to have two journals for *The Calling* Journey—one to write your thoughts and one that will be your spiritual art journal.

I will include questions for you think about and write your own insights and observations in *The Quiet Time Journal* or *The Quiet Time Notebook* (or other writing journal). These journal prompts will also include various ideas to encourage you in a creative direction including photography, collage, drawing, and painting—then you will use your spiritual art journal. These ideas may lead you in a new creative direction—I encourage you to allow yourself the creative freedom to follow your heart here and grow in artistic expression. I truly believe that when we express ourselves creatively through drawing, painting, photography and/or collage that our hearts and souls are touched, moved and changed in a new and deep way. So even if you don't consider yourself an artist in any way, I still encourage you to step out of your comfort zone. I promise that you will be amazed when you see and experience firsthand what happens as a result!

To that end, you may want to have an inkjet printer for photography printing and/or a small watercolor paint set with a brush for some of the creative ideas contained here. I use the Epson Photomate PM-400 for printing my photos to paste in my journal. You can use a glue stick, matte medium, modge podge, or even double-sided tape for adhering photographs or pictures from magazines or scrapbooking resources in your journal.

If you use the camera on your phone, you can get an App to print images or even have them printed locally at stores equipped with photo printing (like Costco or Walgreens). You may want to use scrapbook materials for collage. These are available at stores like Michaels, Hobby Lobby, or JoAnn's. Then, I have many different watercolor sets, but suggest you begin with any of the following: Winsor & Newton, Da Vinci, Daniel Smith, Sennelier, M. Graham, Jane Davenport Glitz-Sea, Daler & Rowney Aquafine, Koi, or Kuretake Watercolors. Some of these sets even come with a watercolor brush. You can get an inexpensive watercolor brush or a watercolor brush set at your local craft store or at Amazon. Also, feel free to use acrylics or pastels, or other desired materials in your art journal. Art supplies are available at your local art/hobby stores or online at Amazon, DickBlick, or CheapJoe's.

For the writing in your journal I like to use a Pentel mechanical pencil with eraser. Then, for the words and writing in your creative art journal, there are a number of choices and options you may want to consider. For the main titles you can use alphabet stamps and archival permanent ink. I like using TomBow Dual Brush pens for larger writing. If you do calligraphy or brush lettering, then use the appropriate tools that you already have. If you would like to learn calligraphy, faux calligraphy, or brush lettering, then I have a few recommendations – see creativelive.com, craftsy. com, kellycreates.ca or thepostmansknock.com. Then, to write out the verses, prayers, or quotes in your art journal, I recommend a fine point permanent ink black pen like Micron Pigma permanent ink pens. I'm excited about this expressive part of the journey in your creative art journal. I'm a firm believer that *artwork is heart-work.*

The photographic images from my SmugMug devotional photography portfolio included in *The Calling* are designed to enhance your journey. I will include some thoughts about these images here in this devotional guide and will ask you to write your own thoughts. As Fred Barnard has said, "A picture is worth a thousand words." These black and white images may also be seen in full color at my SmugMug myPhotoWalk Portfolio at catherinemartin.smugmug.com.

You will notice that *The Calling* chapters are divided into five themes and journeys: Called To A Life, Called To A Person, Called To A Passion, Called To A Cross, and Called To A Destiny. You may want to read through *The Calling* with a group of friends, and then come together to share what you have learned. You can use this Devotional Guide to lead your discussion, sharing your thoughts and observations and your spiritual art journals with each other. You also may want to join with me online as we share *The Calling* together at Quiet Time Ministries Online (www.quiettime.org), The Calling Community on Facebook (https://www.facebook.com/groups/thecallingcommunity/)and also on Instagram (QuietTimeMinistries).

I have also filmed six video messages to enhance your experience and learning in *The Calling*. You may watch these on your own or use as part of a group study as you read through *The Calling*. The first message in this series serves as the Introduction week where you can hand out the books in preparation for your journey in *The Calling*. Viewer Guides for each of these messages may be found here in the Appendix of *The Calling*.

As You Begin The Calling Journey

Introduction To *The Calling* – As you begin your journey in *The Calling*, I encourage you to open your journal and add a date to the first page. Read prayerfully through the Introduction of

The Calling. Then, write a letter to the Lord asking Him to speak to you and transform as you take this journey. Pour out your heart to the Lord as you write this letter in the form of a prayer to the Lord

At the top of the next page in your journal or your creative art journal (with heavier weight paper of 140 lbs), write the words *My Calling*. If you want to get a bit more artistic, you might want to paint these words with a brush marker. Or you can even get alphabet stamps from a craft store to form the words, "My Calling." Allow at least two pages or more in your journal for "My Calling" because you will be writing out all the verses and different aspects of your calling discovered through the many chapters in *The Calling*. For example, you will write such things as I am called to salvation — John 3:16, I am called to have an eternal perspective – 2 Corinthians 4:18, and I am called to be an ambassador for Christ — 2 Corinthians 5:20. You will have a long list of the high and magnificent calling from the Lord by the time you have finished reading this book. If you have chosen to add the video messages and experience my personal insights, and encouragements from God's Word, then watch the Introduction Message, "The Irresistible Voice Of God," and take notes using the Introduction Viewer Guide here in the Appendix.

Guide For Groups: Welcome your group and open in prayer. Have each person share their name and what brought them to the group. Pass out the books then explain that you will be reading together for five weeks. Show the group the table of contents and the five different themes and journeys in the book. The assignment for the first week is to read the Introduction and Chapters 1-5. You can also ask those in your group to get a journal and a creative art journal and answer the questions and journal prompts in this study guide for the first journey, Called To A Life.

The Calling Journey One: Called To A Life — Introduction and Chapters 1-5

This journey in *The Calling* is personal and is designed for you to experience firsthand with the Lord Himself. Draw near to Him now and ask Him to speak to you in His Word as you learn more about His calling in your life and the story He wants to tell in and through you. Read through My Story and the Introduction in *The Calling*. Then, read Chapters 1-5.

Optional: After you have read Chapters 1-5, watch *The Calling* Message One—The One Life. You may take notes using the Message One Viewer Guide here in the Appendix.

Guide For Groups: Share together, chapter by chapter, your insights and observations you have written in The Quiet Time Journal or The Quiet Time Notebook (or other journal) and your creative responses in your spiritual art journal. Watch *The Calling* Message One—The One Life together. You may take notes using the Message One Viewer Guide here in the Appendix.

INTRODUCTION: The Calling

1. As you begin, take some time to look at the details of the full image entitled "The Strong Tower Of God" of Heavy Runner Mountain in Glacier National Park on pages 12-13. Imagine that you are walking with the Lord out there in that beautiful place. What would you like to talk about with Him as He leads you on a journey up the mountain? Write your thoughts in your journal.

2. Describe a time when you became aware that the Lord was real and working in your life.

3. What do you desire to have happen in your life as you engage in this journey of The Calling? Write a letter to the Lord expressing all that is on your heart.

CHAPTER 1: A Voice From A Distant Land

1. Reflect on the Chapter 1 image on of Sedona, Arizona entitled "The Calling From God" on page 26. What is your favorite part of this image? Imagine walking out in that beautiful red rock country and hearing God out your name and inviting you to open His Word and hear Him speak. What is your response? Write your thoughts in your journal.

2. Have you heard the voice of God calling you to enter into a relationship with Him? If so, when? How have you responded?

3. What is the calling?

4. How can you hear the voice of God calling to you each and every day?

5. Write out one verse from the Bible that you read in this chapter – how is God calling to you in that verse?

6. Take your camera and go outside and make some images of God's creation. Print them out and paste them in your journal. Or you can find a beautiful landscape image in a magazine, cut it out and paste it in your journal. What do you see about God in His creation? You might take your pencil or paints and create an image of something beautiful from God's creation like a flower or a tree. Write out what this image tells you about your God. How is He calling to you from His creation? Note: If you are using watercolors for the first time, just dip your brush in water

and a favorite color in the palette, then brush it across the page in your spiritual art journal. As you paint, remember how the Lord can paint color in all of your days.

7. Write out the verse(s) from this chapter and what God is calling you to from that verse on the page that you have titled "My Calling." Example—John 3:16—I am called to salvation and believing in Jesus.

CHAPTER 2: When Fairy Tales Become Real

1. Meditate on the Chapter 2 image of a beautiful butterfly on page 38 entitled "A New Creation." How does this image help you see that the fairy tale is real? In the same way a caterpillar becomes a butterfly, so too, we become a new creation in Christ (2 Corinthians 5:17).

2. What does the plan of God and invitation to salvation in John 3:16 mean to you?

3. In what way does God's plan for you to be in a relationship with Him make sense and how is it different than what you see in the world?

4. Take your camera and make an image of a view of your city or town with people walking around. Then, print it out and paste it in your journal. Or you can find a beautiful image of a cityscape or street scene in a magazine, cut it out and paste it in your journal. Write the words of John 3:16 next to that image to remind you how God so loves the world that He gave His only begotten Son…You might want to paint a cityscape or even a round circle representing the world. Then paint or write the words of John 3:16 on the page.

5. Write out the verse(s) from this chapter and what God is calling you to from that verse on the page that you have titled "My Calling."

CHAPTER 3: Answering The Calling

1. Focus on the Chapter 3 image of the open gate on page 44 entitled "Opening The Door." Imagine what it is like for you and Jesus to sit together in the beautiful garden beyond this gate. What would you like to talk about with Him?

2. What did you learn from D.L. Moody about how to answer the calling from God?

3. Describe a defining moment in your life when you have responded to God.

4. Take a photograph of a door—it could be a beautiful door at a church, a bright and interesting door, or any door that is significant to you. Print it out and paste it into your journal. Or you can find an image of a door in a magazine, cut it out and paste it in your journal. Then, write the words of Revelation 3:20 next to it to remind you of the Lord's invitation to open the door so you can fellowship with Him every day. You might take your pencil or paints and draw an image of a door, then write out or paint the words of Revelation 3:20.

5. Write out the verse(s) from this chapter and what God is calling you to from that verse on the page that you have titled "My Calling."

CHAPTER 4: The Life Of Christ In You

1. Look at the Chapter 4 image on page 53 of the vineyards just below San Gimignano nestled in the Tuscan countryside in Italy. How does this image entitled "Life In The Vine" help you think about your union with Christ and your dependence on Him as your life source for everything?

2. Describe in your own words what it means to have Christ living in you.

3. How does knowing that your life belongs to Christ—that it's His life—help you in your current life situations?

4. What is your favorite quote in this chapter?

5. Capture an image of a cross with your camera, then paste it in your journal. Or you can find a beautiful image of a cross in a magazine, cut it out and paste it in your journal. Write Galatians 2:20 somewhere on the page near the cross. Or you might take your pencil or paints and draw an image of the cross, then write or paint the words of Galatians 2:20. You can get creative by adding any beauty around the cross that you'd like, such as flowers, greenery etc.

6. Write out the verse(s) from this chapter and what God is calling you to from that verse on the page that you have titled "My Calling."

CHAPTER 5: Christ Is Your Life

1. Take some time to reflect on the Chapter 5 image on page 62 entitled "Jesus Touches Lives Through You." Do you see what is happening in this special moment of drama

captured on Santa Monica Pier in Santa Monica, California? A seemingly homeless man is dropping some money into the collection bucket of a street musician playing the guitar. How does this speak to you about the way Jesus can touch the lives of others through you?

2. Describe in your own words what it means to have Christ as your life. How does this truth make a difference in how you live?

3. How has this chapter impacted you and encouraged your own relationship with the Lord?

4. Write out your favorite and most significant quote.

5. Take a photograph of something that stands alone—it could be anything—a flower, a fountain, a tree – just about anything that is solitary and singular. It could even be a picture you have of yourself. Or you can find a beautiful image of something solitary that stands alone in a magazine, cut it out and paste it in your journal. Then, write out C.T. Studd's quote – *Only one life twill soon be past, only what's done for Christ will last.* Draw or paint something that stands alone like a flower, tree or anything that comes to your mind. Then, write out C.T. Studd's quote to remind you that Christ is your life.

6. Write out the verse(s) from this chapter and what God is calling you to from that verse on the page that you have titled "My Calling."

7. Optional: After you have read Chapters 1-5, watch *The Calling* Message One—The One Life. You may take notes using the Message One Viewer Guide here in the Appendix.

The Calling Journey Two: Called To A Person — Chapters 6-10

As you read Chapters 6-10 in *The Calling*, ask the Lord to grow your intimate relationship with Him and show you more and more about Himself.

Optional: After you have read Chapters 6-10, watch *The Calling* Message Two—The Magnificent Obsession. You may take notes using the Message Two Viewer Guide here in the Appendix.

Guide For Groups: Share together, chapter by chapter, your insights and observations you have written in The Quiet Time Journal or The Quiet Time Notebook (or other journal) and your creative responses in your spiritual art journal. Watch *The Calling* Message Two—The

Magnificent Obsession together. You may take notes using the Message Two Viewer Guide here in the Appendix.

CHAPTER 6: A Passion To Know Jesus

1. Look at the Chapter 6 image on page 70 entitled "Keeping Company With Jesus" taken along Oak Creek in Sedona, Arizona. This is one of my favorite places in the whole world. Just imagine sitting there with the Lord, reading your Bible, writing in your journal, listening to the rushing water, hearing the wind rustle through the tree, and watching the many birds and other wildlife. How does this inspire you to more quiet time with the Lord?

2. What stood out to you the most about Gladys Aylward and what did you learn from her life?

3. What does it mean to know Jesus and how well do you know and love Him?

4. Take an image with your camera or find an image in a magazine of something that reminds you of love. It could be something in the shape of a heart or a certain flower. Go for a walk with your camera until you see what you want to capture as an image. Then print it out and paste in your journal. Write a prayer to the Lord, telling Him how much you want to know Him and love Him more. You might take your pencil or paints and draw a heart on a journal page. Then, write a prayer next to the heart, telling the Lord your desire to know Him. You may want to leave an extra page to create a list of everything you learn about the Lord as you read through The Calling.

5. Write out the verse(s) from this chapter and what God is calling you to from that verse on the page that you have titled "My Calling."

CHAPTER 7: The Wind In Your Sails

1. Look at the Chapter 7 image of the sailboat on page 78 entitled "The Wind In Your Sails" taken in the San Diego harbor in San Diego, California. As you take in the details of this sailboat on the waters, how does it help you understand the work of the Holy Spirit in your own life?

2. Why is the Holy Spirit important in your life? What will it take for you to "run before the wind?"

3. How have you experienced the power of the Holy Spirit?

4. How do you need the power of the Holy Spirit today?

5. Capture an image of something that represents wind and power that you can print out or look for an image in a magazine that you can cut out – it could be a sailboat, a windmill, the movement of leaves in a tree, etc. Then, paste it in your journal. Write out your favorite verse about the Holy Spirit from this chapter, reminding you of His power in your life. Draw or paint an image that represents wind and power to you. Then write your favorite verse about the Holy Spirit from this chapter.

6. Write out the verse(s) from this chapter and what God is calling you to from that verse on the page that you have titled "My Calling."

CHAPTER 8: The Magnificent Story Of You

1. Take some time with the Chapter 8 image of "The Italian Gentleman" on page 86 taken on the streets of Florence, Italy. What is your favorite part of this image? As you look more closely, think about how this gentleman has a story and imagine some of that story. Every life tells a story including yours and those around you. When you realize the significance of a life story, how does this change how you treat yourself and others?

2. How is God telling a story in your life right now?

3. What has been the most difficult part of your story so far? What is your favorite part of your story so far?

4. How is your story telling others about the Lord? How have you seen Him work in your life to glorify Himself?

5. Take an image of one of your favorite books with your camera. Print it out and paste in your journal. Or find an image of a book in a magazine and cut it out and paste it in your journal. Write your first name at the top of the page, and then the words, "The Story Of My Life." Then, find some of your favorite pictures of you throughout the years of your life including when you were very young. Make copies of them and put them in your journal to remind you of your story and the beauty of you. Write out five or more of the most important and defining moments in your life. This will remind you of how the Lord is telling a unique story in and

through you. If you choose to use your spiritual art journal, you might even draw or paint a picture of an open book. Then write your name at the top and title the page "The Story Of My Life." You can put the copies of the photos of you on that page. Then, list five or more defining moment in your life.

6. Write out the verse(s) from this chapter and what God is calling you to from that verse on the page that you have titled "My Calling."

CHAPTER 9: The Beautiful Masterpiece Of You

1. Look at the Chapter 9 image on page 94 entitled "Loved Forever" of a very special statue that sits in a rose garden along the coast of southern California. What is your favorite part of this image and how does it help you understand more the beautiful masterpiece of you?

2. What did you learn from the life of Lilias Trotter?

3. What does it mean to be God's masterpiece as described in Ephesians 2:10?

4. What was your favorite quote from this chapter?

5. What are the unique circumstances and life situations that are the tools God is using in your life to write the story He wants to tell the world?

6. Describe your most unique gifts and talents—those things that are true about you. What are some dreams and desires on your heart that you may want to pursue?

7. Take a picture of yourself, print it out and paste it in your journal. Then, write your first name at the top of the page. Now, list all the things that best describe who you are. Use a pencil or paints to draw an image of a face representing you—this doesn't have to be the Mona Lisa and you don't have to be Leonardo da Vinci. If you are an accomplished artist or would like to practice drawing and/or painting, then I encourage you to take time and do a more detailed self-portrait. Then, write your name at the top of the page and list all the things that describe who you are. Include your dreams and desires for your life.

8. Write out the verse(s) from this chapter and what God is calling you to from that verse on the page that you have titled "My Calling."

CHAPTER 10: Sitting At His Feet

1. Look at the Chapter 10 image on page 106 entitled "Born To Dance" of a dancing girl on a bridge over the River Arno in Florence, Italy. As you look at this girl dancing, how does it help you understand what it means to have a heart that dances with a desire to sit at the feet of Jesus and be intimate with Him?

2. How have you cultivated a quiet time alone with the Lord and what does this time mean to you?

3. What is your favorite thing to do in your quiet time?

4. Where in your quiet time do you want to grow deeper and draw closer to the Lord? How will you cultivate this aspect of your quiet time in the days to come?

5. Take a photograph of a quiet place that makes you think about quiet time. It could be your study, your back porch, a park, or a beautiful garden. Paste it in your journal and write "My Quiet Time" at the top of the page. Or find an image of a quiet place in a magazine, cut it out, and paste it as a collage piece in your journal. Then, write out one of your favorite verses about quiet time that you read in this chapter. You might draw or paint an image that reminds you of a quiet place. Write or stamp the words "My Quiet Time" somewhere on the page. Then, write out a favorite verse about quiet time.

6. Write out the verse(s) from this chapter and what God is calling you to from that verse on the page that you have titled "My Calling."

7. Optional: After you have read Chapters 6-10, watch *The Calling* Message Two—The Magnificent Obsession. You may take notes using the Message Two Viewer Guide here in the Appendix.

The Calling Journey Three: Called To A Passion — Chapters 11-15

And now, as you continue your journey in The Calling, you are going to go deeper into your relationship with the Lord and learn more about the difference knowing Him makes in you and the story of your life.

Optional: After you have read Chapters 11-15, watch *The Calling* Message Three—The Defining Moment. You may take notes using the Message Three Viewer Guide here in the Appendix.

Guide For Groups: Share together, chapter by chapter, your insights and observations you have written in The Quiet Time Journal or The Quiet Time Notebook (or other journal) and your creative responses in your spiritual art journal. Watch *The Calling* Message Three—The Defining Moment together. You may take notes using the Message Three Viewer Guide here in the Appendix.

CHAPTER 11: I Want To Follow Jesus

1. Look at the Chapter 11 image on page 114 entitled "I Will Follow Jesus" taken in a garden in Montepulciano, a quaint town in the Tuscan country side in Italy. Imagine that the Lord Jesus is inviting you to follow Him along that path. What will it take for you to say "Yes Lord" even though you cannot see what is around the corner?

2. When have you sensed the Lord inviting you to follow Him? How did you respond to His calling to follow Him? What happened as a result?

3. How is the Lord asking you to follow Him even now? In what ways are you passing on all that God is teaching you (2 Timothy 2:2).

4. Take a picture of a pair of your shoes. Print it out and paste it in your journal. Or you might find an image of shoes in a magazine, cut it out, and paste in your journal. Write "Follow Me" and Matthew 4:19 on the page. Then, write a prayer of response to the Lord. Draw or paint a pair of shoes or even footprints in sand along the ocean. Write "Follow Me" and Matthew 4:19, and a prayer of response to the Lord.

5. Write out the verse(s) from this chapter and what God is calling you to from that verse on the page that you have titled "My Calling."

CHAPTER 12: Embracing The Eternal Perspective

1. Look at the Chapter 12 image on page 124 entitled "The Eternal View" of a beautiful sunset in Palm Desert, California. What is your favorite part of this image and how does it help you think about the eternal perspective?

2. What does it mean to have an eternal perspective and why is the Lord calling you to have it?

3. What did you learn from the life of Amy Carmichael?

4. How does the Lord use difficult times to lead you to His eternal perspective?

5. Where in your life do you need the eternal perspective from the Lord and what verse helps you the most right now? Take time to make your Bible a dear friend.

6. Capture an image of beautiful clouds in the sky with your camera. You may even include a far-away view of mountains along with the clouds. Print it out and paste in your journal. Or find a beautiful cloud image in a magazine, cut it out, and paste in your journal. Write The Eternal Perspective at the top of the page. Write out the words of 2 Corinthians 4:18 on the page. Write a short prayer to the Lord as a response to the calling of 2 Corinthians 4:18. You might draw or paint an image of the sky, then write out the words The Eternal Perspective and 2 Corinthians 4:18, along with a responsive prayer.

7. Write out the verse(s) from this chapter and what God is calling you to from that verse on the page that you have titled "My Calling."

CHAPTER 13: Sharing God's Heart

1. Take some time with the Chapter 13 image on page 135 entitled "Your Heart's Desire" taken at a quiet place by Oak Creek in Sedona, Arizona. Look at all the details. What do you notice and what is your favorite part of the image. As you look at the reflections in the water, think about what it means to share God's heart.

2. What did you learn from the life of Helen Roseveare and how did she live out the calling from the Lord?

3. What have you learned about God's dreams for you so far and how has He surprised you with unexpected directions in your life?

4. Do you have a life verse? If not, ask the Lord to give you a life verse. When you know that one verse that simply will not leave your mind, and challenges and inspires you to know and love the Lord, then write it out in your journal.

5. Take a picture of something beautiful in God's creation. Print it out and paste in your journal. Or find an image from God's creation in a magazine, cut it out, and paste it as a collage piece in your journal. Then write "My Life Verse" at the top of the page. Write out your life verse. You might draw or paint something beautiful;

anything that is in your heart and mind. Then write "My Life Verse" and write out your life verse.

6. Write out the verse(s) from this chapter and what God is calling you to from that verse on the page that you have titled "My Calling."

CHAPTER 14: The Called-Out Ones

1. Look at the Chapter 14 image of a beautiful flower on page 145 entitled "Set Apart For God." This flower is flourishing and opened up fully facing the sun. How does our relationship with the Lord make a difference in how we live as one who is in the world, but not of the world?

2. Describe the church and why it is important in our lives.

3. As part of the church, how are we in the world, but not of the world? What does that mean?

4. Take a picture of your church or a church in your town. Paste it in your journal. Or find an image of a church in a magazine, cut it out, and paste in your journal. Then, write a prayer to the Lord for those in your church. Draw or paint a picture of a church. Then, write a prayer for the church.

5. Write out the verse(s) from this chapter and what God is calling you to from that verse on the page that you have titled "My Calling."

CHAPTER 15: The Power Of An Influential Life

1. Reflect on the Chapter 15 image on page 154 entitled "An Influential Life" taken at Corona Del Mar near Newport Beach, California. How does this image help you see how a person can greatly influence the life of another?

2. Who has the Lord called to be influences in your life? List them out in your journal. This list can include friends, mentors, authors, and speakers. Then, open your Bible to Hebrews 13:7 and write at least five names of people who have been influences in your life.

3. What are your favorite books and what books would you like to add to your reading list?

4. Who are you influencing in your life? This can include your children, friends, those in a Bible study, or another way your passing on all that the Lord is teaching you.

5. Write a prayer to the Lord asking Him to give you a faith that can be imitated.

6. Take a picture of a stack of your favorite books. Print it out, then paste in your journal. Or find an image of books in a magazine, cut it out, and paste in your journal. Write out Hebrews 13:7 on the page. Draw or paint a stack of books and write out Hebrews 13:7 on the page.

7. Write out the verse(s) from this chapter and what God is calling you to from that verse on the page that you have titled "My Calling."

8. Optional: Watch *The Calling* Message Three—The Defining Moment. You may take notes using the Message Three Viewer Guide here in the Appendix.

The Calling Journey Four: Called To A Cross — Chapters 16-20

As your journey of *The Calling* continues, your walk with the Lord takes you in unexpected directions as the Lord tells a unique and powerful story in and through your life.

Optional: After you have read Chapters 16-20, watch *The Calling* Message Four—The Passion For The Impossible. You may take notes using the Message Four Viewer Guide here in the Appendix.

Guide For Groups: Share together, chapter by chapter, your insights and observations you have written in The Quiet Time Journal or The Quiet Time Notebook (or other journal) and your creative responses in your spiritual art journal. Watch *The Calling* Message Four—The Passion For The Impossible together. You may take notes using the Message Four Viewer Guide here in the Appendix.

CHAPTER 16: The Fellowship Of His Sufferings

1. Look closely at the Chapter 16 image on page 162 entitled "Called To Suffer" taken in a garden in southern California. What stands out to you the most as you think about sharing in the sufferings of the Lord?

2. How has the Lord called you to share in His sufferings? Describe how this helps you become more intimate with the Lord.

3. How did Annie Johnson Flint's life story encourage you?

4. Take another image of a cross—it could be from a church or somewhere in your town. Or you could lay out a group of rocks in the shape of a cross and take a picture of it. Then, print it out and paste in your journal. Write a prayer to the Lord thanking Him for the privilege to share in the intimacy of His sufferings. You might draw or paint another image of a cross, then write out a prayer to the Lord.

5. Write out the verse(s) from this chapter and what God is calling you to from that verse on the page that you have titled "My Calling."

CHAPTER 17: The World, The Flesh, And The Devil

1. Look at the Chapter 17 image on page 172 entitled "Not Of This World" and taken in the heart of Hollywood and Beverly Hills, California. The lights of the city are always so beautiful, and also a reminder that we are very much in the world, but not of the world. Write your own thoughts about this image and what it's like to live in the world, but not be of the world. How do you need courage, bravery, and confidence right now in the face of spiritual warfare involving the world, the flesh, and the devil?

2. Where are you most fearful in your life and what verse encourages you the most today?

3. What lie or story are you tempted to believe and what promise in God's word gives you the truth instead?

4. Take a picture of your Bible, print it out, and then paste it in your journal. Write out Ephesians 6:17 "the sword of the Spirit, which is the Word of God" at the top of the page. Then, write out the most important promises from God's Word that give you courage today to counteract any lies or stories. You might draw or paint a Bible on a journal page. Then, follow the rest of the journal instructions above.

5. Write out the verse(s) from this chapter and what God is calling you to from that verse on the page that you have titled "My Calling."

CHAPTER 18: A Passion For The Impossible

1. Spend some time looking at the different aspects of the Chapter 18 image on page 180 entitled "A Bird In A Tree." What is your favorite part of this image and how does it encourage you?

2. What is your impossible right now and how do you hear God calling to you in the midst of that impossible?

3. What encouraged you the most in this chapter for any impossible situation or Red Sea place you are experiencing right now?

4. How can you develop a passion for the impossible and how do you see this as a call from God?

5. Take a picture of something that represents your impossible situation. Or find an image in a magazine that represents your impossible situation. Then after you have pasted it in your journal, write out a promise from God's Word that gives you hope in your impossible. You might draw or paint a picture that represents your impossible situation. Then, follow the rest of the journal instructions above.

6. Write out the verse(s) from this chapter and what God is calling you to from that verse on the page that you have titled "My Calling."

CHAPTER 19: Failure, Regret, And Imperfection

1. Look at the Chapter 19 image on page 189 entitled "Forgiven." This man is holding a Bible and walking on the streets of Rodeo Drive in Beverly Hills, California sharing the gospel. What stands out the most to you in this image and how does it impact you today?

2. How does our life *in Christ* give us hope in the face of failure, regret, and imperfection?

3. How do our failures, regrets, and imperfections become an advantage for us in our life with Christ?

4. What failures, regrets and imperfections do you need to lay at the foot of the cross?

5. Again, this day of reading is a time to think about the power of the cross and how we are "in Christ only." Take a new image of another cross and paste the printed picture in your journal. List all you've been given and all that is true because you

are "in Christ." You might draw or paint another cross in your journal, then follow the instructions written above.

6. Write out the verse(s) from this chapter and what God is calling you to from that verse on the page that you have titled "My Calling."

CHAPTER 20: When You Forget Your Calling

1. Take some time with the Chapter 20 image on page 195 of the great-horned owl entitled "Wisdom From God." Oh how I love my owl. I captured many images, but this was one of my favorites. What stands out to you the most and how does it impact you?

2. Has there ever been a time when you've forgotten your calling? If so when, and how did the Lord lead you out of that valley?

3. What did you learn from this chapter that will help when you need to remember your calling?

4. Take a picture of something that reminds you to never forget your calling. It could be a place in your town that is significant to you. It could be a book that has greatly helped you in difficult times. You might find the image from a magazine. Then, paste the picture in your journal. Write a prayer to the Lord, thanking Him for His faithfulness in your life. You might include an important verse from the Bible that has been your strength in your difficult time. You might draw or paint a picture of something that reminds you to never forget your calling. Then, follow the rest of the journal instructions above.

5. Write out the verse(s) from this chapter and what God is calling you to from that verse on the page that you have titled "My Calling."

6. Optional: Watch *The Calling* Message Four—The Passion For The Impossible. You may take notes using the Message Four Viewer Guide here in the Appendix.

The Calling Journey Five: Called To A Destiny — Chapters 21-25

In your journey of *The Calling*, the story of your life has a powerful plan, purpose and eternal perspective designed by God Himself.

Optional: After you have read Chapters 21-25, watch *The Calling* Message Five—The Story Heaven Will Tell. You may take notes using the Message Five Viewer Guide here in the Appendix.

Guide For Groups: Share together, chapter by chapter, your insights and observations you have written in The Quiet Time Journal or The Quiet Time Notebook (or other journal) and your creative responses in your spiritual art journal. Watch *The Calling* Message Five—The Story Heaven Will Tell together. You may take notes using the Message Five Viewer Guide here in the Appendix.

CHAPTER 21: A New Kingdom

1. Look at the Chapter 21 image on page 203 entitled "Called To A New Kingdom." This image of Bell Rock in Sedona, Arizona was captured on a cloudy day along the hiking trail in the area. Imagine that you are walking along the trail with Jesus. What would you like to ask Him about the kingdom of God?

2. What does it mean to you that you are called to be a citizen of the kingdom of God?

3. What does this teach you about your relationship with the world? How can you be a better citizen of God's kingdom and less influenced by the world?

4. Take a picture of fruit, print it out, then paste it in your journal. Or find a picture of fruit in a magazine, cut it out, and paste in your journal. Write "Growing In The Kingdom Of God." Then, list the fruit of the Spirit from Galatians 5:22-23 in your journal. Write a prayer asking the Lord to work in your life to enable you to shine for Him as a citizen of His kingdom. You might draw or paint a page of different fruit, then follow the instructions above to complete your journal page.

5. Write out the verse(s) from this chapter and what God is calling you to from that verse on the page that you have titled "My Calling."

CHAPTER 22: The Eternal Now Of Today

1. Look at the Chapter 22 image on page 209 entitled "Only One Life" and captured on the beach at sunset in La Jolla, California. How does this image encourage, impact, and inspire you today?

2. Why is time one of the most important truths about our calling?

3. How are you learning to make the most of your time?

4. Take a picture of a clock, print it out and paste it in your journal. Or you can find a clock in a magazine, cut it out and paste it in your journal. Then, write the words of Ephesians 5:15-16 on the same page. You might draw or paint a clock in your journal, then follow the other instructions above.

5. Write out the verse(s) from this chapter and what God is calling you to from that verse on the page that you have titled "My Calling."

CHAPTER 23: When God Connects The Dots

1. Take some time with the Chapter 23 image on page 217 entitled "More Than You Can Imagine" and taken on the coast of Kona, Hawaii at sunset. Imagine that you are there with the Lord and talking to Him about the story of your life. What events have been a mystery to you and how does God's ability to paint the sky and create such a beautiful sunset help you trust Him today?

2. Describe a time in your life where you saw God do something only He could do; a time when you can say, "That was You, Lord!"

3. Who are the friends that the Lord has brought into your life over the years and how have they been significant to you?

4. What was the most important truth you learned in this chapter?

5. Take a picture of the steps of a staircase. Print it out and paste in your journal. Or you find an image of stairs with steps in a magazine, cut it out, and paste in your journal. Write the words of Psalm 37:23, "The Lord directs the steps of the godly." Then, write a prayer of thanksgiving to the Lord for how He has led you in your life. You might paint or draw a picture of stairs with steps on a page in your journal. The, follow the other journal instructions above.

6. Write out the verse(s) from this chapter and what God is calling you to from that verse on the page that you have titled "My Calling."

CHAPTER 24: Here Am I Lord, Send Me

1. Look at the Chapter 24 image on page 24 entitled "Here Am I Send Me" and describe what you see with these widgeon ducks in Palm Desert, California. How

does this image impact you and show us the sense of passion and excitement we can have saying *yes* to the Lord and serving Him?

2. How has God called you to surrender to Him and follow His lead in life? Describe a defining moment of surrender and how that impacted you in life.

3. How are you encouraged to surrender to God in a new way today?

4. Take a picture of a fountain, the print it out, and paste it in your journal. Write at the top of the page, "Here Am I, Send Me." Then, write a prayer asking the Lord to continually revive your heart through the power of the Holy Spirit as you follow Him. Or you can find a fountain in a magazine, cut it out and paste it in your journal. You might draw or paint a fountain, then follow the journal instructions above.

5. Write out the verse(s) from this chapter and what God is calling you to from that verse on the page that you have titled "My Calling."

CHAPTER 25: On Our Way Home

1. Meditate on the Chapter 25 image on page 231 entitled "On Our Way Home." As you look at this sunrise through thick multi-colored clouds, think about how the journey home with Jesus is not an end, but a true beginning in your life. What are your thoughts as you look at this image?

2. Why is our calling to live in heaven forever the ultimate hope in our lives?

3. What do you have to look forward to in heaven?

4. Read your Letter to the Lord written at the beginning of your journey in *The Calling*. Reflect on all that the Lord has taught you, then talk with the Lord about your journey.

5. Take a picture of a beautiful sunrise or sunset out in God's creation. Print it out and paste it in your journal. Then, write a prayer thanking the Lord for all you've learned in *The Calling* and why you are looking forward to seeing Him in heaven. Or you can find a beautiful image of a sunset in a magazine, cut it out and paste it in your journal. You might draw or paint a sunrise or sunset in your journal, then follow the other journal instructions above.

6. Write out the verse(s) from this chapter and what God is calling you to from that verse on the page that you have titled "My Calling."

7. Optional: Watch *The Calling* Message Five—The Story Heaven Will Tell. You may take notes using the Message Five Viewer Guide here in the Appendix.

Viewer Guide

The Irresistible Voice Of God

Welcome to *The Calling - The Story of Who You Are and Why You Are Here*. These Viewer Guides are designed to give you a place to write notes from my *The Calling* messages available on DVDs, Digital M4V Video, and Digital MP3 Audio for your computer or mobile device. I like to think of these messages as conversations based on all that you are learning in the Devotional Journey, *The Calling*. In our time together today, we are going to look at some important truths about the Word of God in Isaiah 55:10-11.

"For as the rain and the snow come down from heaven, and do not return there without watering the earth and making it bear and sprout, and furnishing seed to the sower and bread to the eater; so will My word be which goes forth from My mouth; it will not return to Me empty without accomplishing what I desire, and without succeeding in the matter for which I sent it (Isaiah 55:10-11).

Some important surprises from God after I entered into a relationship with Him

1. He surprised me with His _____ in my life.

2. He surprised me with His _____.

3. He surprised me with His _____.

4. He surprised me with His _____ to me.

Important truths we learn from Isaiah 55:10

1. The Word of God comes from the very _____ of God.

2. God's Word is _____ for you.

3. God's Word has a _____ in your life.

---

4. God's Word is _____.

What is the calling?

The calling is the voice of God in His Word claiming you as His treasured possession. It is the communication of God's choice entreating you to an intimate vibrant relationship. He has set His love and affection on you. When you come to know Him, then He makes His home in you. He designs divine appointments for you. He entrusts responsibilities to be lived out by Christ in and through you in the power of the Holy Spirit. This is a beautiful story that declares and displays His glory forever.

You discover God calling out to you in every verse in His Word and in His calling you learn more and more who you are and why you are here. Every verse in God's Word is Him calling to you and He has something to say, something for you given with great purpose. You discover all that God is asking of you and all He promises you, day by day and moment by moment.

Romans 8:28, 1 Corinthians 1:9, 1 Corinthians 7:15, Galatians 5:15
Matthew 4:4, John 6:63

What is your response to God, as He calls out to you in His Word? Will you open the Word of God day by day in your quiet time alone with Him? Close by writing a prayer expressing all that is on your heart.

Video messages are available on DVDs or as Digital M4V Video. Audio messages are available as Digital MP3 Audio. Visit the Quiet Time Ministries Online Store at www.quiettime.org.

The One Life

You have just read the Introduction and Chapters 1-5 of *The Calling* in the first journey entitled *Called To A Life*. Today I want to talk with you about some important words from Paul in 1 Corinthians 9:23-26. Then, I am excited to share a bit of the life of C.T Studd and his challenging quote, "Only one life 'twill soon be past, only what's done for Christ will last." I love this quote so much and look forward to talking about it with you.

"I do all this for the sake of the gospel, that I may share in its blessings. Do you not know that in a race all the runners run, but only one gets the prize? Run in such a way as to get the prize. Everyone who competes in the games goes into strict training. They do it to get a crown that will not last; but we do it to get a crown that will last forever. Therefore I do not run like a man running aimlessly; I do not fight like a man beating the air" (1 Corinthians 9:23-26 NIV).

How to win the prize

1. We live our lives for _____thing. All things for one thing. We need to have a single-minded focus. 1 Corinthians 9:23

We need to become _____ thinkers.

2. We live for _____.
We must be clear about the destination, the goal, the finish line, and what this life is about.

Christ is your _____.

Colossians 3:1-4, Galatians 2:20

3. Live to _____.

Hebrews 12:1-3

---

4. To win, we live with _____ that controls us in everything we do.

It's the power of the _____.

Acts 1:8, Ephesians 5:18

5. To win, we live for something that lasts _____.

1 Corinthians 9:25 an imperishable wreath (crown)

6. To win, you live with purpose and _____.

2 Timothy 4:7-8

How can we respond to the one life? How do we respond to the quote: Only one life 'twill soon be past, only what's done for Christ will last.

Surrender—laying it all down to have the Lord take it up—to have the Lord take up this one life and use it as His own—to take us where He pleases, do what He pleases, and How He pleases. It will involve sacrifice, challenge, and saying "no" to many things to say "yes" to the best thing.

How do you respond to all you have learned? Write a prayer expressing all that is on your heart.

⚜ *Video messages are available on DVDs or as Digital M4V Video. Audio messages are available as Digital MP3 Audio. Visit the Quiet Time Ministries Online Store at www.quiettime.org.*

Viewer Guide
❧ THE CALLING MESSAGE TWO ❧

The Magnificent Obsession

You have just read the Chapters 6-10 of *The Calling* in the second journey entitled *Called To A Person*. In our conversation together in this message, we are going to talk about the most magnificent obsession that eclipses all other passions in life—knowing and loving Jesus Christ. We are going to spend some time living in Paul's letter to the Ephesians where we learn important truths about the calling.

"I pray that from his glorious, unlimited resources he will empower you with inner strength through his Spirit. Then Christ will make his home in your hearts as you trust in him. Your roots will grow down into God's love and keep you strong. And may you have the power to understand, as all God's people should, how wide, how long, how high, and how deep his love is. May you experience the love of Christ, though it is too great to understand fully. Then you will be made complete with all the fullness of life and power that comes from God" (Ephesians 3:16-19 NLT).

Jesus Christ living in us and telling a unique and powerful story to the world through us is our calling.

What we learn about the calling in the book of Ephesians

1. You are called to a great _____by Jesus Christ. Ephesians 1:18

2. You are called to be a new _____in Christ Jesus with a high purpose — to do good works. Ephesians 2:10

We are God's _____.
The word for "masterpiece" is *poiema* and means that you are the Lord's work of art, His poetry, His masterpiece.

3. You are called to be a _____ for Christ. Ephesians 3:14-19

4. You are called to a _____ as part of the body of Christ. Ephesians 4:3-5, 12-16

5. You are called to a special _____ in life. Ephesians 4:1, 5:2-18

6. You are called to be Christ's _____. Ephesians 5:27

7. You are called to _____ in the Lord. Ephesians 6

How God works His calling in your life so you can understand who you are and why you are here

1. Out of His glorious, unlimited resources, you have inner _____ through the Spirit of God.

2. Out of His glorious, unlimited resources, He gives you a _____ in Jesus Christ.

3. Another result of the glorious, unlimited resources of God is that Jesus Christ makes His _____ in my heart as I trust in Him.

4. From His glorious, unlimited resources, your roots will grow down into God's _____ and keep you strong.

5. Another result of the glorious, unlimited resources of God is that you will experience the width, length, height, and depth of the _____ of Christ.

6. Out of God's glorious, unlimited resources, He makes you _____ with all the fulness of life and power that comes from God.

Write a prayer to the Lord expressing all that is on your heart.

≫ *Video messages are available on DVDs or as Digital M4V Video. Audio messages are available as Digital MP3 Audio. Visit the Quiet Time Ministries Online Store at www.quiettime.org.*

Viewer Guide
❧ THE CALLING MESSAGE THREE ❧

The Defining Moment

You have just read the Chapters 11-15 of *The Calling* in the third journey entitled *Called To A Passion*. In our conversation together in this message, we are going to talk about those defining moments that alter the course of your life. These are the times when you make a move in a direction and experience moments of surrender to God and His Word and give in to His will and His ways. We will look at Hebrews 12:1-3 and learn all about surrender to God.

"Therefore, since we are surrounded by such a huge crowd of witnesses to the life of faith, let us strip off every weight that slows us down, especially the sin that so easily trips us up. And let us run with endurance the race God has set before us. We do this by keeping our eyes on Jesus, the champion who initiates and perfects our faith. Because of the joy awaiting him, he endured the cross, disregarding its shame. Now he is seated in the place of honor beside God's throne. Think of all the hostility he endured from sinful people; then you won't become weary and give up" (Hebrews 12:1-3 NLT).

Defining moments of decision, resolve, conviction, and surrender from Hebrews 12:1-3

1. The defining moment where we make a decision about the life of _____. 2 Corinthians 5:7, Hebrews 11

2. The defining moment of saying "no" to anything that _____ us down in our race. Hebrews 12:1

3. The defining moment when we say "no" to the _____ that so easily trips us up. 1 John 1:7-10, Hebrews 12:1

4. The defining moment of the decision and resolve of _____. Hebrews 12:1

5. The defining moment of _____you choose to fix your eyes,

day by day and moment by moment. It is the defining moment of fixing your eyes on Jesus. Hebrews 12:2

6. The defining moment of the dark night of the _____. Hebrews 12:3

What defining moment is the Lord placing before you right now in your life? How will you respond to Him? Write a prayer expressing all that is on your heart.

Video messages are available on DVDs or as Digital M4V Video. Audio messages are available as Digital MP3 Audio. Visit the Quiet Time Ministries Online Store at www.quiettime.org.

Viewer Guide

The Passion For The Impossible

You have just read the Chapters 16-20 of *The Calling* in the fourth journey entitled *Called To A Cross.* In our conversation together in this message, we are going to talk about our life with Christ and the fellowship of His sufferings as described by Paul in Philippians 3:10-11. Then I want to share with you secrets from the promises of God in impossible situations and all that will help you to develop a passion for the impossible.

"That I may know Him and the power of His resurrection and the fellowship of His sufferings, being conformed to His death; in order that I may attain to the resurrection from the dead" (Philippians 3:10-11).

Truths about our life with Christ on our way to heaven

1. We will experience _____. Acts 14:22, John 16:33

2. Suffering is not considered *our* suffering, but _____ sufferings. Philippians 3:10

3. You are not _____ in suffering. Jesus is with you. Hebrews 13:5

Promises from God for impossible situations

1. The Lord has a _____ in the impossible you am experiencing, and He is working out that plan. Jeremiah 29:11

2. God can cause even the worst, impossible thing in your life to work together for _____. Romans 8:28

3. The impossible is only impossible to you, _____ to God. Matthew 19:26, Jeremiah 32:27, Genesis 18:13-14

---

4. The Lord loves you with an everlasting _____. Jeremiah 31:3

5. You have the _____ of Christ for you in your weakness. Hebrews 4:15

6. Another promise for you in the impossible are God's words in Hebrews 13:5 "I will never fail you. I will never abandon you." And then the promises of Hebrews 13:6 "The Lord is my helper. I will not be afraid."

7. In every situation, you can _____ to the throne of grace. Hebrews 4:16

What will help you through the impossible and actually develop a passion for the impossible?

1. Pay attention to the _____ of God.

2. _____ your plans, your self, your control to the Lord in exchange for His plan, His story, His life and desires, and His control.

3. Step out of your feelings into _____ in what God says.

4. _____ with the Lord about all that is in your heart. Pour out your heart to God every day.

5. Eagerly _____ for God every day. Pay attention to the things of God and for all that God does in your life.

What is your impossible situation right now? What promise encourages you today? Write a prayer to the Lord expressing all that is on your heart.

Video messages are available on DVDs or as Digital M4V Video. Audio messages are available as Digital MP3 Audio. Visit the Quiet Time Ministries Online Store at www.quiettime.org.

Viewer Guide
✧ THE CALLING MESSAGE FIVE ✧

The Story Heaven Will Tell

You have just read the Chapters 21-25 of *The Calling* in the fifth journey entitled *Called To A Legacy*. In our conversation together in this message, we are going to talk about the rest of the story, and all we have to look forward to as outlined in the book of Revelation. It's the story that heaven tells and help you to stand strong in the midst of difficult hours.

"So we don't look at the troubles we can see now; rather, we fix our gaze on things that cannot be seen. For the things we see now will soon be gone, but the things we cannot see will last forever" (2 Corinthians 4:18 NLT).

"He will wipe every tear from their eyes, and there will be no more death or sorrow or crying or pain. All these things are gone forever" (Revelation 21:4 NLT).

What can we know about the rest of the story in Revelation?

1. God will wipe every _____ from your eyes. Revelation 21:4

2. There will no longer be any _____, mourning, crying, or pain. Revelation 21:4

3. God will make all things _____. Revelation 21:5

4. You will _____ from the spring of the water of life without cost. Revelation 21:6

5. The Lord will be your God and you will be His child. He will live with you and make His _____ with you forever. Revelation 21:3

6. Heaven is beautiful and the streets are pure _____, as clear as glass. Revelation 21:21

7. The glory of God shines through the city, and the Lamb is its _____.
There is no night in heaven. Revelation 21:23

8. The _____ of God and the Lamb, the Lord Jesus is there.
Revelation 22:3

9. You will see His _____ and His name will be written on your
forehead. Revelation 22:4

10. The Lord God will shine on you and you will reign _____.
Revelation 22:5

"For now we see only a reflection as in a mirror; then we shall see face to face. Now I know in part; then
I shall know fully, even as I am fully known" (1 Corinthians 13:12 NIV).

*How does the rest of the story in Revelation encourage you today? What is your favorite promise and
what do you look forward to. Write a prayer to the Lord expressing all that is on your heart.*

*Video messages are available on DVDs or as Digital M4V Video. Audio messages are available as
Digital MP3 Audio. Visit the Quiet Time Ministries Online Store at www.quiettime.org.*

☙ THE LOVE STORY ☙

Suppose with me that there is a God who is Creator. One who created the heavens, the earth, and also created you and me? And just suppose that He created human beings, you and me, for a purpose. And that purpose was simple: He wanted a love relationship with us. It would be a love relationship so beautiful that it would shine with God's glory and show off His majesty. And suppose that, in the beginning, the love relationship flourished. When God created the first human beings, the relationship was idyllic, and the fellowship – the exchange of love between God and His creation – was perfect.

Within that idyllic existence boundaries existed, set up by God Himself, to allow for this love relationship to thrive. The boundaries were basic: God's creation was not to exist independently of Him, but was to be dependent upon Him as the source of everything. And then one day, God's human beings crossed those boundaries. They decided on their own, with the help of one whose purpose was to destroy their relationship with God, to make a choice that was independent and directly against what God had commanded. Once the human beings had crossed that boundary, sin entered the world.

Now suppose with me, that when sin entered the world, the love relationship with God was affected: sin separated the human beings from a holy God, and they could no longer enjoy this intimate fellowship with Him for which they were designed. This sin created a great, uncrossable chasm between man and God that affected all of mankind. The Bible says that all have sinned and fall short of the glory of God, and that the sentence or penalty for sin is death (Roman 3:23, 6:23). Now let us suppose again that God saw the inability of man to reach Him because of sin. He knew that it was impossible for man to reach Him, and so He reached down to man, and determined to pay the penalty for sin Himself. Man needed a Redeemer who could accomplish redemption for him. That Redeemer was God Himself.

Jesus claimed to be God. It is a fact of history that the Jesus was arrested at night, secretly tried, and publicly crucified on a cross. While Jesus was on the cross, His followers mourned and His disciples fled, fearing for their own lives. His death devastated those who knew and loved Him. And while He was on the cross, Jesus cried out three words, "It is finished." What was finished? Your redemption was made complete. He paid the penalty for our sin – all our sins – so that we can be forgiven and live with God forever. Three days later, something happened – something that Jesus had said would happen. Josephus, the Jewish historian, once again tells us that after three days, Jesus rose from the dead. He appeared to his disciples and more than five hundred other people. Jesus is who He claimed to be.

Lord Jesus, I need You. Thank You for dying on the cross for my sins. I ask You to come into my life, forgive my sins, and make me the person You want me to be. Amen.

❧ FAVORITE BIOGRAPHIES ❧

A Chance To Die by Elisabeth Elliot — the biography of Amy Carmichael

A Man Of The Word by Jill M. Morgan — the biography of G. Campbell Morgan

A Passion For The Impossible by Miriam Rockness — the biography of Lilias Trotter

Bush Aglow by Richard Ellsworth Day — the biography of D.L. Moody

Rees Howells: Intercessor by Norman Grubb — the biography of Rees Howells

The Hiding Place by Corrie ten Boom — the autobiography of Corrie ten Boom

The Life of A.W. Tozer: In Pursuit of God by James L. Snyder — the biography of A.W. Tozer

The Shadow of the Almighty by Elisabeth Elliot — the biography of Jim Elliot

The Shadow of the Broad Brim by Richard Ellsworth Day — the biography of Charles Haddon Spurgeon

Some of my favorite compendiums with good biographical sketches of heroes of the faith are *Walking with the Giants* by Warren Wiersbe (now titled *50 People Every Christian Should Know*), *Faithful Women and Their Extraordinary God* by Noel Piper about Sarah Edwards, Gladys Aylward, Lilias Trotter, Esther Ahn Kim, and Helen Roseveare, *They Found the Secret* by V. Raymond Edman, *Deeper Experiences of Famous Christians* by J. Gilchrest Lawson, *Heroes of the Holy Life* by Wesley L. Duewel, and *Found Faithful* by Elizabeth Skoglund.

❧ FAVORITE AUTHORS AND BOOKS ❧

There is a powerful influence from great men and women of God by reading the books they have written. There are many books that have changed my life forever and have become an integral part of the story of my life including:

Knowing God by J.I. Packer

Morning and Evening by Charles Spurgeon

My Utmost For His Highest by Oswald Chambers

The Making of a Man of God by Alan Redpath

The Pursuit of God by A.W. Tower

Thou Givest, They Gather by Amy Carmichael

With Christ in the School of Prayer by Andrew Murray

Women of God who have a faith that can be imitated and have greatly influenced me include Corrie ten Boom, Amy Carmichael, Elisabeth Elliot, Lilias Trotter, Hannah Whitall Smith, Henrietta Mears, and Vonette Bright. I will read any book written by these amazing women.

THE CALLING KEY VERSES

I pray that the eyes of your heart may be enlightened, so that you will know what is the hope of His calling, what are the riches of the glory of His inheritance in the saints.

EPHESIANS 1:18

Therefore I, the prisoner of the Lord, implore you to walk in a manner worthy of the calling with which you have been called.

EPHESIANS 4:1

Jesus answered, "It is written: 'Man shall not live on bread alone, but on every word that comes from the mouth of God.'"

MATTHEW 4:4

For we are God's masterpiece. He has created us anew in Christ Jesus, so we can do the good things he planned for us long ago.

EPHESIANS 2:10 NLT

Therefore, brethren, be all the more diligent to make certain about His calling and choosing you...

2 PETER 1:10

So will My word be which goes forth from My mouth; It will not return to Me empty, Without accomplishing what I desire, and without succeeding in the matter for which I sent it.

ISAIAH 55:11

I have been crucified with Christ; and it is no longer I who live, but Christ lives in me; and the life which I now live in the flesh I live by faith in the Son of God, who loved me and gave Himself up for me.

GALATIANS 2:20

Therefore if you have been raised up with Christ, keep seeking the things above, where Christ is, seated at the right hand of God. Set your mind on the things above, not on the things that are on earth. For you have died and your life is hidden with Christ in God. When Christ, who is our life, is revealed, then you also will be revealed with Him in glory.

COLOSSIANS 3:1-4 NLT

And this is the secret: Christ lives in you. This gives you assurance of sharing his glory.

COLOSSIANS 1:27

Do not fear, for I have redeemed you; I have called you by name; you are Mine!

ISAIAH 43:1

And we know that God causes all things to work together for good to those who love God, to those who are called according to His purpose.

ROMANS 8:28

God is faithful, through whom you were called into fellowship with His Son, Jesus Christ our Lord.

1 CORINTHIANS 1:9

For consider your calling, brethren, that there were not many wise according to the flesh, not many mighty, not many noble.

1 CORINTHIANS 1:26

For you were called to freedom.

GALATIANS 5:13

Look! I stand at the door and knock. If you hear my voice and open the door, I will come in, and we will share a meal together as friends.

REVELATION 3:20

NOTES

INTRODUCTION

1. J.I. Packer, *Knowing God* (London: InterVarsity Press, 1973), p. 16.

CHAPTER 1

1. Mark Batterson, *Whisper-How To Hear The Voice Of God* (Colorado Springs: Multnomah Press, 2017), pp. 21-22.

2. A.W. Tozer, *The Pursuit Of God* (Camp Hill: Christian Publications, 1982, 1993), pp. 73-83.

3. Dallas Willard, *The Divine Conspiracy* (New York: Harper Collins Publishers, 1997), p. 11.

4. Os Guinness, *The Call* (Nashville: W. Publishing Group, a Division of Thomas Nelson Publishers, 1998, 2003), p. 6.

5. Dallas Willard, *Hearing God* (Downers Grove: InterVarsity Press, 1993) p. 159.

6. Richard Foster, *Life With God* (New York: Harper Collins Publishers, 2008) p. 57.

7. Geoffrey W. Bromiley ed., *International Standard Bible Encyclopedia* (Chicago: William B. Eerdmans Publishing, 1988), pp. 580-582.

CHAPTER 3

1. Sheldon VanAuken, *A Severe Mercy* (New York: HarperCollins Publishers 1977, 1980), December 23, 1950 letter, p. 93.

2. Annie Johnson Flint, *Best Loved Poems* (Toronto: Evangelical Publishers), p. 7.

CHAPTER 4

1. Dr. and Mrs. Howard Taylor, *Hudson Taylor's Spiritual Secret*, (Chicago: Moody Publishers, 1989, 2009), pp. 146-147.

2. Dr. and Mrs. Howard Taylor, *Hudson Taylor's Spiritual Secret*, p. 149.

3. Dr. and Mrs. Howard Taylor, *Hudson Taylor's Spiritual Secret*, pp. 149-150.

4. Miles J. Stanford, *Principles Of Spiritual Growth*, (Lincoln: Back To The Bible, 1982) p. 77.

5. W. O. Carver, *Ephesians: The Glory Of God In The Christian Calling* (Nashville: Broadman Press, 1949) p. 51.

6. C.S. Lewis, *Mere Christianity*, (New York: HarperCollins Publishers, 1952) pp. 109-110.

7. G.D. Watson, *Soul Food* (Cincinnati: Knapp, 1896) p. 63.

8. A.B. Simpson, *Walking In The Spirit* (Harrisburg: Christian Publications n.d.) pp. 53-57.

9. A.W. Tozer, *The Crucified Life* (Minneapolis: Bethany House, 2011), p. 171.

10. From A.W. Tozer, *The Crucified Life*, p. 177.

11. G.D. Watson, Poem by Frederick Faber in *Soul Food*, p. 64

CHAPTER 5

1. Dallas Willard, *Hearing God*, (Downers Grove: InterVarsity Press, 1993) p. 288.

2. Dallas Willard, *Hearing God*, p. 288.

3. Alan Redpath, *Victorious Christian Faith* (Old Tappen: Fleming H. Revell Company, 1960), p. 30.

4. Brennan Manning, *The Signature Of Jesus*, (Sisters: Multnomah Press, 1988) p. 159.

CHAPTER 6

1. Noel Piper, *Faithful Women and Their Extraordinary God* (Wheaton: Crossway Books, 2005), p. 72.

2. Noel Piper, *Faithful Women and Their Extraordinary God*, pp. 87-88.

3. Noel Piper, *Faithful Women and Their Extraordinary God*, p. 93.

4. Alistair Begg, *Preaching For God's Glory* (Wheaton: Crossway Books, 1999) p. 36.

5. Taken from In The Footsteps of Jesus. Copyright © 1997 by Bruce Marchiano. Published by Harvest House Publishers, Eugene, Oregon 97402 and Visual Entertainment, Dallas, Texas 75248, p. xi.

6. Basilea Schlink, *My All For Him,* (Bloomington: Bethany House Publishers, 1999) p. 21.

7. Dwight Hervey Small, *No Rival Love*, (Fort Washington: Christian Literature Crusade, 1983) p. 193.

CHAPTER 7

1. Herbert F. Stevenson ed., *Keswick's Authentic Voice* (London: Marshall, Morgan & Scott 1959) p. 445.

2. For an in-depth study of Acts and the power of the Holy Spirit, see *Run Before The Wind* by Catherine Martin (Palm Desert: Quiet Time Ministries, 2008) www.quiettime.org.

3. Andrew Murray, The Spirit of Christ (Fort Washington: Christian Literature Crusade 1963) p. 72.

4. Brian Edwards, *Revival-A People Saturated With God* (Darlington UK: Evangelical Press, 2004) p. 26.

5. Catherine Martin, *Revive My Heart* (Palm Desert: Quiet Time Ministries Press 2013), p. 111.

6. Annie Johnson Flint, Best-Loved Poems, (Toronto: Evangelical Publishers) pp. 18-19.

CHAPTER 8

1. John Bunyan, *Grace Abounding To The Chief Of Sinners, Vol. 1* (Bellingham: Logo

2. s Bible Software, 2006) p. 10.

3. John Bunyan, *Grace Abounding To The Chief Of Sinners, Vol. 1*, p. 36.

4. F.B. Meyer, *Devotional Commentary* (Wheaton: Tyndale House Publishers 1989) p. 532.

CHAPTER 9

1. Noel Piper, *Faithful Women and Their Extraordinary God* (Wheaton: Crossway Books, 2005), p. 46.

2. Noel Piper, *Faithful Women and Their Extraordinary God*, p. 46.

3. Miriam Rockness, *A Passion For The Impossible: The Life Of Lilias Trotter*, (Grand Rapids: Discovery House Publishers, 2003), pp. 332-333.

4. From Precept Austin at https://www.preceptaustin.org/index.php/gods_masterpiece-poiema_greek_word_study.

5. From Precept Austin at https://www.preceptaustin.org/index.php/gods_masterpiece-poiema_greek_word_study.

6. Chuck Swindoll, *Saying It Well,* (New York: FaithWords 2012), p. x.

7. From Precept Austin at https://www.preceptaustin.org/index.php/gods_masterpiece-poiema_greek_word_study.

8. Chuck Swindoll, *Saying It Well*, p. xi.

9. Selwyn Hughes, *Every Day With Jesus One Year Bible*, (Surrey: Waverley Abbey House, 2013), pp. 1058-1059.

10. Ann Kiemel, *I Love The Word Impossible* (Carol Stream: Tyndale House Publishers, 1977) pp. 119-120.

11. S.D. Gordon, *The Quiet Time including The Finnish Story* (Grand Rapids: Fleming H. Revell Company 1912) p. 52.

12. Lilias Trotter, *Parables Of The Cross* (London: Marshall Bros. ND) pp. 35-36.

13. Lilias Trotter, *Parables Of The Cross,* p. 36.

CHAPTER 10

1. Charles Spurgeon, *Beside Still Waters* (Nashville: Thomas Nelson 1999), p. 327.

2. Catherine Martin, *A Woman's Heart That Dances* (Eugene: Harvest House Publishers, 2009).

3. Catherine Martin, *Six Secrets To A Powerful Quiet Time, 2nd Edition* (Palm Desert: Quiet Time Ministries Press 2013). For more on quiet time, see Quiet Time Ministries Online at www.quiettime.org.

4. Richard J. Foster, *Prayer: Finding The Heart's True Home* (New York: HarperCollins Publisher, 1992) pp. 1-2.

5. Elisabeth Elliot ed., *The Journals Of Jim Elliot* (Grand Rapids: Fleming H. Revell, 1978) pp. 18-21.

CHAPTER 11

1. Bill Bright, *Come Help Change The World* (Wayne: New Life Publications, 1999), Locations 209-210 Kindle Edition.

2. Bill Bright, *Come Help Change The World*, Locations 209-210 Kindle Edition.

3. Bill Bright, *Come Help Change The World*, Locations 238-239 Kindle Edition.

4. Bill Bright, *Come Help Change The World*, Locations 315-322 Kindle Edition.

CHAPTER 12

1. Catherine Martin, *A Heart To See Forever-Embracing The Promise Of The Eternal Perspective* (Palm Desert: Quiet Time Ministries Press 2011, 2013).

2. Catherine Martin, *Walk On Water Faith-Discovering Power In The Promises Of God* (Palm Desert: Quiet Time Ministries Press 2014).

3. Elisabeth Elliot, *A Chance To Die* (Grand Rapids: Fleming H. Revell 2005) pp. 114-115.

4. Elisabeth Elliot, *A Chance To Die,* pp. 114-115.

5. Elisabeth Elliot, *A Chance To Die,* p. 168.

6. Elisabeth Elliot, *A Chance To Die,* p. 55.

7. Elisabeth Elliot, *A Chance To Die,* p. 84.

8. Elisabeth Elliot, *A Chance To Die,* p. 223.

9. Amy Carmichael, David Hazard, *I Come Quietly To Meet You* (Bloomington: Bethany House Publishers 2011) p. 66.

10. G.D.Watson, *Soul Food* (Cincinnati: Knapp, 1896) p. 35.

11. Mrs. Charles Cowman, S.D. Gordon in *Streams in the Desert* (Los Angeles: The Oriental Missionary Society, 1925) September 6 reading.

12. Amy Carmichael, David Hazard, *I Come Quietly To Meet You,* p. 34.

13. Amy Carmichael, *Toward Jerusalem,* (Great Britain: Society For Promoting Christian Knowledge, A Dohnavur Book, 1936) p. 94.

CHAPTER 13

1. Noel Piper, *Faithful Women and Their Extraordinary God* (Wheaton: Crossway Books, 2005), pp. 144-145.

2. Noel Piper, *Faithful Women and Their Extraordinary God*, p. 148.

3. See Wikipedia - Belgian Congo. (https://en.wikipedia.org/wiki/Belgian_Congo).

4. Noel Piper, *Faithful Women and Their Extraordinary God*, p. 152.

5. W. O. Carver, *Ephesians: The Glory Of God In The Christian Calling* (Nashville: Broadman Press, 1949) p. 121.

6. For more on spiritual gifts, see *Set My Heart On Fire* by Catherine Martin (Palm Desert: Quiet Time Ministries Press, 2018).

7. J.I. Packer, *God's Plans For You* (Wheaton: Crossway Books 2001), p. 102.

CHAPTER 14

1. Charles Spurgeon, *Lectures To My Students,* Lecture 2, The Call To Ministry.

2. Randy Alcorn, *We Shall See God*, (Wheaton: Tyndale House Publishers, 2011) p. xxii.

3. A.W. Tozer. *The Knowledge Of The Holy* (San Francisco: HarperCollins, 1992), pp. v2-v2i.

4. Anne Graham Lotz, *Wounded By God's People*, (Grand Rapids: Zondervan Publishing, 2013) p. 32.

5. Anne Graham Lotz, *Wounded By God's People*, p. 70.

6. Anne Graham Lotz, *Wounded By God's People*, p. 18.

CHAPTER 15

1. John Piper, *Brothers, We Are Not Professionals,* (Nashville: B & H Publishing Group, 2013) p. 89.

2. This story is found many places on the internet including http://www.sosmin.com/?p=2606.

CHAPTER 16

1. Andrew Murray, *The Secret Of Spiritual Strength,* (New Kensington: Whitaker House, 1997) p. 34.

2. Catherine Martin, *Walking With The God Who Cares,* (Palm Desert: Quiet Time Ministries Press, 2016, Second Edition) p. 81.

3. See *Trusting In The Names Of God - A 30 Day Journey* (Eugene: Harvest House Publishers, 2008) and *Trusting In The Names Of God - A Quiet Time Experience* (Palm Desert: Quiet Time Ministries Press 2015, Second Edition) for more on knowing and trusting God.

4. Catherine Martin, *Walking With The God Who Cares*, p. 91.

5. Rowland V. Bingham, *The Making Of The Beautiful,* (Grand Rapids: Zondervan Publishing House 1932) pp. 20-21.

6. Rowland V. Bingham, *The Making Of The Beautiful*, p. 17.

7. See *Trusting In The Names Of God - A 30 Day Journey* and *Trusting In The Names Of God - A Quiet Time Experience.*

CHAPTER 17

1. William Gurnall, *The Christian In Complete Armour, Volume 1,* (Carlisle: The Banner Of Truth Trust, 1993), p. 23.

2. Brene Brown, *Rising Strong*, (New York: Random House, 2015) p. 16.

3. Brene Brown. *Rising Strong*, p. 17.

4. Brene Brown. *Rising Strong*, pp. 20-21.

5. Jesse Penn Lewis, *War On The Saints,* (New York: Thomas E. Lowe, Ltd., 1973, original unabridged 1912 edition written with Evan Roberts) p. 144.

6. Jesse Penn Lewis, *War On The Saints*, p. 251.

7. William Gurnall, *The Christian In Complete Armour, Volume 1*, p. 307.

CHAPTER 18

1. Catherine Martin, *One Holy Passion,* (Palm Desert: Quiet Time Ministries Press, 2017).

2. Charles Spurgeon, *Beside Still Waters,* (Nashville: Thomas Nelson Publishers, 1997) p. 357.

3. Mrs. Charles Cowman, "Life Of Praise" in *Streams in the Desert* (Los Angeles: The Oriental Missionary Society, 1925) February 7 reading.

4. Mrs. Charles Cowman, *Streams in the Desert,* p. 21, pp. 354-355.

CHAPTER 20

1. Roy Hession, *The Calvary Road,* (Fort Washington: Christian Literature Crusade, 1980) p. 21.

2. This material is taken from My Utmost for His Highest by Oswald Chambers. Copyright © 1935 by Dodd Mead & Co., renewed © 1963 by the Oswald Chambers Publications Assn. Ltd., and is used by permission of Discovery House Publishers, Box 3566, Grand Rapids, MI 49501. All rights reserved. November 1 reading.

3. Bertha Chambers. *Oswald Chambers: His Life and Work* (London: Marshall, Morgan and Scott, 1941), p. 414.

4. Bertha Chambers. *Oswald Chambers: His Life and Work,* p. 415.

5. Bertha Chambers. *Oswald Chambers: His Life and Work,* p. 422.

CHAPTER 21

1. Warren Wiersbe, *50 People Every Christian Should Know,* (Grand Rapids: Baker Book House, 2009), pp. 281-286.

2. Warren Wiersbe, *50 People Every Christian Should Know,* pp. 281-286.

3. John Henry Jowett. *The Silver Lining: Messages of Hope and Cheer* (New York: Fleming H. Revell, 1907), p. 220.

4. John Bright. *The Kingdom Of God,* (Nashville: Abingdon Press, 1953, 1981) p. 218.

5. John Bright. *The Kingdom Of God,* p. 223.

6. John Bright. *The Kingdom Of God,* p. 273.

CHAPTER 22

1. Catherine Martin, *Six Secrets To A Powerful Quiet Time - Discovering Radical Intimacy With God,* (Palm Desert, Quiet Time Ministries Press, 2013, Second Edition).

2. Catherine Martin, *A Heart That Dances - Satisfy Your Desire For Intimacy With God,* (Colorado Springs: NavPress, 2003).

CHAPTER 23

1. Alan Redpath, *The Making Of A Man Of God,* (Grand Rapids: Baker Book House, 1962), pp. 64-65.

CHAPTER 25

1. Bill Bright, *The Journey Home: Finishing With Joy* (Nashville:: Thomas Nelson 2003), pp. 146-147.

2. C.S. Lewis, *The Last Battle,* (New York: Macmillan Publishing Co., Inc. 1956, 1970). pp. 183-184.

PHOTOGRAPHY

COVER

Cover and Interior Photography by Catherine Martin, myPhotoWalk—SmugMug, catherinemartin.smugmug.com, Custom Prints and Inspirational Gifts.

The Strong Tower Of God, 2013, Logan Pass, Glacier National Park, Montana, USA, Nikon D7000, Nikkor 12-24mm, FL 12mm, ISO 100, f/11, AEB.

EXPERIENCE THE DEEPER LIFE AS A MASTERPIECE CREATED BY GOD

THE CALLING MYPHOTOWALK SMUGMUG GALLERIES — Catherine Martin's very favorite images expressing themes from The Calling chosen from among photoshoots at Glacier, Zion, & Bryce National Parks, Monument Valley, Antelope Canyon, Hawaii, Tuscany, Sedona, Klamath Falls, Newport Beach, San Francisco, and Santa Fe, as well as the Mojave-Sonoran Desert. Enjoy.

Preface, Pages 12-13: THE STRONG TOWER OF GOD, 2013, Logan Pass, Glacier National Park, Montana, USA, Nikon D7000, Nikkor 12-24mm, FL 12mm, ISO 100, f/11, AEB.

Chapter 1, Page 26, The Calling From God, 2013, Upper Red Rock Loop, Sedona, Arizona, USA, Nikon D7000, Nikkor 12-24mm, FL 24mm, ISO 100, f/16, AEB.

Chapter 2, Page 38, A New Creation, 2017, Golden Pebble Habitat, Palm Desert, California, USA, Nikon D7000, Nikkor 70-300mm, FL 270mm, ISO 100, f/5.6, 1/200sec.

Chapter 3, Page 44, Opening The Door, 2017, Garden Gate, Newport Beach, California, USA, Nikon D810, Lensbaby Velvet 56, FL 56mm, ISO 200, f/8, 1/500sec.

Chapter 4, Page 52, Life In The Vine, 2011, San Gimignano, Siena, Tuscany, Italy, Nikon D7000, Nikkor 18-105mm, FL 28mm, ISO 110, f/8, 1/250sec.

Chapter 5, Page 62, Jesus Touches Lives Through You, 2017, Santa Monica Pier, Santa Monica, California, USA, Nikon D810, Nikkor 24-120mm, FL 120mm, ISO 250, f/8, 1/640sec.

Chapter 6, Page 70, Keeping Company With Jesus, 2013, Oak Creek Canyon, Sedona, Arizona, USA, Nikon D7000, Nikkor 12-24mm, FL 24mm, ISO 100, f/22, AEB.

Chapter 7, Page 78, The Wind In Your Sails, 2017, San Diego Bay, San Diego, California, USA, Sony A6000, Zeiss 16-70mm, FL 64mm, ISO 200, f/4, 1/4000sec.

Chapter 8, Page 86, The Italian Gentleman, 2011, Lungarno Amerigo Vespucci, Florence, Tuscany, Italy, Nikon D7000, Nikkor 18-105mm, FL 105mm, ISO 560, f/5.6, 1/60sec.

Chapter 9, Page 94, Loved Forever, 2017, Sculpture Garden, Newport Beach, California, USA, Nikon D810, Lensbaby Velvet 56, FL 56mm, ISO 3200, f/2.8, 1/250sec.

Chapter 10, Page 106, Born To Dance, 2011, Ponte Alla Carraia, Arno River, Florence, Tuscany, Italy, Nikon D7000, Nikkor 18-105mm, FL 85mm, ISO 250, f/14, 1/200sec.

Chapter 11, Page 114, I Will Follow Jesus, 2011, Montepulciano, Siena, Tuscany, Italy, Nikon D7000, Nikkor 18-105mm, FL 45mm, ISO 400, f/4.8, 1/100sec.

Chapter 12, Page 124, The Eternal View, 2014, Santa Rosa Mountains, Palm Desert, California, USA, Nikon D800E, Nikkor 24-120mm, FL 105mm, ISO 200, f/4, 1/3200sec.

Chapter 13, Page 134, Your Heart's Desire, 2013, Dixie National Forest, West Fork Trail, Sedona, Arizona, USA, Nikon D7000, Nikkor 18-105mm, FL 45mm, ISO 100, f/11, 1/60sec.

Chapter 14, Page 144, Set Apart For God, 2016, The Rose Garden, Newport Beach, California, USA, Nikon D810, Micro-Nikkor 200mm, FL 200mm, ISO 1250, f/5, 1/4000sec.

Chapter 15, Page 154, An Influential Life, 2017, Crystal Cove State Park, Newport Beach, California, USA, Nikon D810, Nikkor 24-120mm, FL 98mm, ISO 500, f/8, 1/3200sec.

Chapter 16, Page 162, Called To Suffer, 2017, Sculpture Garden, Newport Beach, California, USA, Nikon D810, Lensbaby Velvet 56, FL 56mm, ISO 200, f/8, 1/640sec.

Chapter 17, Page 172, Not Of This World, 2016, Santa Monica Boulevard, Beverly Hills, California, USA, Sony A6000, Zeiss 16-70mm, FL 35mm, ISO 3200, f/4, 1/5 sec.

Chapter 18, Page 180, A Bird In A Tree, 2014, Indian Wells, California, USA, Nikon D800E, Nikkor 50.0mm, FL 50mm, ISO 125, f/4.5, 1/250sec.

Chapter 19, Page 188, Forgiven, 2017, Rodeo Drive, Beverly Hills, California, USA, Nikon D810, Nikkor 24-120mm, FL 120mm, ISO 500, f/8, 1/400sec.

Chapter 20, Page 194, Wisdom From God, 2017, Golden Pebble Habitat, Palm Desert, California, USA, Nikon D810, Nikkor 80-400mm, FL 400mm, ISO 500, f/11, 1/40sec.

Chapter 21, Page 202, Called To A New Kingdom, 2015, Bell Rock—Courthouse Butte, Sedona, Arizona, USA, Nikon D800E, Nikkor 24-120mm, FL 32mm, ISO 100, f/16, 1/15 sec.

Chapter 22, Page 208, Only One Life, 2015, La Jolla Shores, La Jolla, California, USA, Nikon D810, Nikkor 24-120mm, FL 52mm, ISO 64, f/22, 1/50sec.

Chapter 23, Page 216, More Than You Can Imagine, 2012, Pauoa Bay, Waimea, Island Of Hawaii, Hawaii, USA, Nikon D7000, Nikkor 18-105mm, FL 75mm, ISO 200, f/5.6, 1/125sec.

Chapter 24, Page 224, Here Am I Send Me, 2018, Mountain Vista Lake, Palm Desert, California, USA, Nikon D810, Nikkor 80-400mm, FL 400mm, ISO 200, f/5.6, 1/500sec.

Chapter 25, Page 230, On Our Way Home, 2018, Coachella Valley Preserve, Palm Desert, California, USA, Sony A6000, Zeiss 16-70mm, FL 60mm, ISO 100, f/9, 1/160sec.

❧ ACKNOWLEDGMENTS ❧

My heart is greatly humbled to have the privilege to write *The Calling*. How does such a work come to life? It takes years of God etching these principles from the Word of God on the heart in such a way that it is lived out in life. *The Calling* has been quite a journey and first, I want to say a big thank You to the Lord for leading the way each day as I wrote.

Then, I especially want to thank my husband, David. This book would never have made it to print without you. Thank you, beloved husband, for serving together with me in Quiet Time Ministries, for your brilliant wisdom, planning, scheduling, editing, web design, and social media direction. Thank you for the beautiful cover of *The Calling*. You are truly amazing and I thank the Lord for thirty-seven years together.

Thank you to my precious family; David, Mother and Dad (both now with the Lord), Robert, Kayla, Linda, Christopher, Andy, Keegan, and James. Thank you especially for your unconditional love and encouragement as I write books and share the message that God has laid on my heart in my quiet times alone with Him.

I am so very thankful over these many years for the Quiet Time Ministries team for serving the Lord together with me—Kayla Branscum, Shirley Peters, Conni Hudson, Cindy Clark, Sandy Fallon, Paula Zillmer, Karen Darras Hawley, Kelly Wysard, Maurine Cromwell, and Cay Hough.

And then, thank you for dear friends who have offered such words of truth, encouragement, and hope that I have needed all along the way: Beverly Trupp, Conni Hudson, Cindy Clark, Andy Kotner Graybill, Jane Lyons, Julie Airis, Stefanie Kelly, Joe and Judy Patti, John and Betty Mann, Kelly Wysard, Jan Lupia, Barbara Waddell, Kathleen Rousar, and Vonette Bright.

Thank you to the Board of Directors of Quiet Time Ministries: David Martin, Conni Hudson, Andy Kotner Graybill, and Jane Lyons, for your faithfulness in this ministry. And thank you to all who have partnered with me both financially and prayerfully in Quiet Time Ministries. You have helped make possible this idea the Lord gave me so many years ago called Quiet Time Ministries and have allowed us to continue to spread God's Word to men and women throughout the world. I also want to thank those who have partnered financially with Quiet Time Ministries to sponsor myPhotoWalk photo shoots and purchase photographic equipment including my Nikon cameras, my Fuji camera, lenses, tripods, and filters.

Thank you to my Bethel Seminary professors who gave me such a love for God's Word and helped me learn to study with excellence, especially Dr. Ronald Youngblood, Dr. Walt Wessel, Dr. James Smith, and Dr. Al Glenn.

Thank you to those who have been such a huge help to me in the writing and publishing of books: Jim Smoke whose advice and help have, by God's grace, completely altered the course of my life and Greg Johnson, my agent, who has come alongside me and Quiet Time Ministries to help in the goals that the Lord has laid on my heart. I am also so very grateful to Bob Hawkins and Harvest House Publishers for publishing so many of my books.

I am especially grateful to Leann Pruitt McGee who discipled me early on in my relationship with the Lord. Thank you to Ney Bailey for teaching me about faith. Thank you to Elmer Lappen who taught me about being filled with the Holy Spirit. Thank you to Josh and Dottie McDowell and Bob Tiede for teaching me about ministry. Thank you to Nancy Martin for taking me to Bethany Bible Church and helping me grow as a new Christian. Thank you to Helen Peck for sharing wonderful retreats with the Lord in Sedona, Arizona and for your friendship. Thank you to Joyce Kinkead Anderson, who was such a good friend in the early days.

Thank you Marilyn Meberg for your friendship, for being such an example of the faith for thousands including me, and for writing the Foreword to *The Calling*. I am forever grateful.

Thank you to those who have encouraged me in devotional photography through workshops, conferences, books, videos, examples, portfolios, and personal training — I am so very thankful for you — Bill Fortney, Dr. Charles Stanley, Laurie Rubin, Kevin Toohey, Kathleen Reeder, Kathleen Clemons, Trey Ratcliff, Scott Kelby, Matt Kloskowski, Sebastian Michaels, R.C. Concepcion, Karen Hutton, His Light Friends, Jim Begley, Ben Long, Harold Davis, Art Wolfe, Tom Mangelsen, Chris Orwig, David DuChemin, Bryan Peterson, April Milani, and Diane Varner.

A special thanks to all those leaders who answer God's call to lead others and challenge them to draw near to God, study His Word, and live for His glory. Thank you to all the women I've been privileged to serve with in leadership over the years. Thank you to the Women's Ministries Directors and leaders in churches who encourage their amazing women to live in God's Word and love Him with all their hearts. And a special thanks to all the groups worldwide who are drawing near to God in quiet time using the different quiet time studies from Quiet Time Ministries. I am so very grateful to those women of God who love His Word and teach it every day of their lives, especially Anne Graham Lotz and Kay Arthur.

Finally, thank you to all those saints who have lived our their life with a passion for God and have encouraged me to love the Lord with all my heart: especially Corrie ten Boom, Charles Haddon Spurgeon, Oswald Chambers, F.B. Meyer, Octavius Winslow, Amy Carmichael, Lilias Trotter, Annie Johnson Flint, A.W. Tozer, Andrew Murray, and Mrs. Charles Cowman.

Thank You, Lord, for *the calling* — Your calling — for calling me to Yourself, for making me Your masterpiece, for being my life, for giving me Your Word, for leading and guiding me each day, for delightful times each morning in quiet time, and for that moment when I will see Your face and live forever with You in glory. I can't wait to see You and live with You in the place You have prepared just for me. Until that day, I look forward to every moment of *the calling* in Your Word.

ABOUT THE AUTHOR

Catherine Martin is a summa cum laude graduate of Bethel Theological Seminary with a Master of Arts degree in Theological Studies. She is founder and president of Quiet Time Ministries, a director of women's ministries for many years, and an adjunct faculty member of Biola University. She is the author of *Six Secrets to a Powerful Quiet Time, Knowing and Loving the Bible, Walking with the God Who Cares, Set my Heart on Fire, Trusting in the Names of God, Passionate Prayer, Quiet Time Moments for Women,* and *Drawing Strength from the Names of God* published by Harvest House Publishers, and *Pilgrimage of the Heart, Revive My Heart* and *A Heart That Dances,* published by NavPress. She has also written *The Quiet Time Notebooks, A Heart on Fire, A Heart to See Forever, Run Before the Wind, A Heart That Hopes in God, Walk on Water Faith,* and *One Holy Passion* published by Quiet Time Ministries Press. She is founder of myPhotoWalk. com dedicated to the art of devotional photography, publishing *myPhotoWalk—Quiet Time Moments, Savoring God's Promises of Hope,* and *The Story of Your Life.* As a popular keynote speaker at retreats and conferences, Catherine challenges others to seek God and love Him with all of their heart, soul, mind, and strength. For more information about Catherine, visit www.quiettime.org and www.myphotowalk.com.

ABOUT QUIET TIME MINISTRIES

Quiet Time Ministries is a nonprofit religious organization under Section 501(c)(3) of the Internal Revenue Code. Cash donations are tax deductible as charitable contributions. We count on prayerful donors like you, partners with Quiet Time Ministries pursuing our goals of the furtherance of the Gospel of Jesus Christ and teaching devotion to God and His Word. Visit us online at www.quiettime.org to view special funding opportunities and current ministry projects. Your prayerful donations bring countless project to life!

*Quiet Time Ministries | P.O. Box 14007 | Palm Desert, California 92255
1.800.925.6458 | catherine@quiettime.org | www.quiettime.org | www.myphotowalk.com*

ABOUT myPHOTOWALK

myPhotoWalk is first and foremost about photography — for people of all faiths, no faith, or just searching — that they may rejoice in the goodness of God. Whether you are an avid photographer seeking technical motivation and encouragement — or a spiritual disciple yearning for life inspiration and worship of the God of all creation — you will feel right at home at myPhotoWalk Devotional Photography.

Learn how you can support myPhotoWalk, a special Quiet Time Ministries outreach project. We have ongoing expenses for development and marketing of myPhotoWalk.com, the photography of God's great creation as a devotional and evangelical vehicle. Devotional Photography eBooks. Custom Devotional Photography Prints. All photography by Catherine Martin. Photo Shoot equipment, travel expenses, and production. Our goal is to see revival in the hearts of millions throughout the world by capturing God's creation in devotional photography. May the Lord multiply your gifts to this ministry and reach hundreds of thousands in His name!

Support a myPhotoWalk photo shoot!
—quiettime.org/myphotowalk/photoshoots

Visit myPhotoWalk — SmugMug.com
—catherinemartin.smugmug.com

MYPHOTOWALK

NOW THAT YOU HAVE COMPLETED THE CALLING

You have spent eight weeks consistently drawing near to God in quiet time with Him. That time alone with Him does not need to come to an end. What is the next step? To continue your pursuit of God, you might consider other books from the A Quiet Time Experience series, including *One Holy Passion, Walk On Water Faith, A Heart that Hopes in God, Run Before the Wind, Trusting in the Names of God,* and *Passionate Prayer.* The Quiet Times For The Heart series are also books of quiet times with titles such as *Pilgrimage of the Heart, Revive My Heart, A Heart that Dances, A Heart on Fire,* and *A Heart to See Forever..* To learn more about quiet time, read signature books from the A 30-Day Journey series such as *Six Secrets to a Powerful Quiet Time* and *Knowing and Loving the Bible.* Leader's Kits with DVD or downloadable HD Digital messages and Leader's Guides are available for each book. Learn more about quiet time from Catherine's many books, *Enriching Your Quiet Time* quarterly magazine, and *The Quiet Time Notebooks.* Quiet Time Ministries Online has many resources to encourage you in your quiet time with God. Find daily encouragement from Cath's Blog and view A Walk In Grace™, the devotional photojournal featuring Catherine's myPhotoWalk photography at www.quiettime.org. Join hundreds of other women online to study God's Word and grow in God's grace at Ministry For Women (www. ministryforwomen.com). Resources may be ordered online from Quiet Time Ministries at www. quiettime.org or by calling Quiet Time Ministries. For more information, you may contact:

Quiet Time Ministries
P.O. Box 14007
Palm Desert, California 92255
(800) 925-6458, (760) 772-2357
E-mail: catherine@quiettime.org
Website: www.quiettime.org

A Quiet Time
EXPERIENCE

ONE
HOLY
PASSION

A Sacred Journey in *Exodus* to *God's Amazing Love*

CATHERINE MARTIN
Author of *Walk on Water Faith*

A Quiet Time
EXPERIENCE

Walk on Water Faith

Discovering *Power*
in the *Promises* of God

Catherine Martin

Author of *Run Before the Wind*

MYPHOTOWALK
DEVOTIONAL PHOTOGRAPHY

THE STORY OF YOUR LIFE

Discovering a Heart to Follow the Master

CATHERINE MARTIN

Author of *Savoring God's Promises of Hope*

www.ingramcontent.com/pod-product-compliance
Lightning Source LLC
Chambersburg PA
CBHW062037090426
42740CB00016B/2933